Why Children Follow Rules

Why Children Follow Rules

*Legal Socialization and the
Development of Legitimacy*

Tom R. Tyler
and
Rick Trinkner

OXFORD
UNIVERSITY PRESS

OXFORD
UNIVERSITY PRESS

Oxford University Press is a department of the University of Oxford. It furthers
the University's objective of excellence in research, scholarship, and education
by publishing worldwide. Oxford is a registered trade mark of Oxford University
Press in the UK and certain other countries.

Published in the United States of America by Oxford University Press
198 Madison Avenue, New York, NY 10016, United States of America.

© Oxford University Press 2018

First issued as an Oxford University Press paperback, 2020

CIP data is on file at the Library of Congress
ISBN 978-0-19-064414-7 (hardcover) | ISBN 978-0-19-752069-7 (paperback)

CONTENTS

ACKNOWLEDGMENTS

Tom Tyler would like to thank his advisor David O. Sears for helping him to recognize the importance of legal socialization during his graduate studies at UCLA. Rick Trinkner was inspired by his graduate advisor Ellen Cohn's efforts to demonstrate the centrality of legal socialization to everyday life through her ongoing and programmatic research at the University of New Hampshire. This book owes a great deal to their pioneering work and to June Tapp, whose early writing served to define the field for future scholars. We would also like to thank our spouses—Doris Lambertz and Sarah Dudek—for putting up with us while we were engaged in writing this book.

Why Children Follow Rules

PART I

—————∽∾—————

Introduction

Legal scholars and social scientists studying the law recognize that a central issue in law is understanding why adults obey the law (Tyler, 2006a, 2011). Evidence suggests that law-related attitudes and values are central to motivating adult law-related behavior, and hence that it is important to understand how they develop during the process of legal socialization. Although this is true, legal scholarship has widely ignored the process of childhood and adolescent socialization. The lack of research on legal socialization is ironic in that by the time people become adults, their law-related attitudes and values are already well formed and they have often had formative personal experiences with legal authorities. This important development begins during childhood and adolescence as part of the overall process of socialization.

What distinguishes legal socialization from socialization in general? Legal socialization is a subset of larger socialization pressures in that it is specifically focused on the process whereby people come to develop and understand their relationship with the law. At its core, legal socialization assumes the law is an essential institution within the fabric of the social environment, one that is just as important in terms of ordering society, guiding human behavior, and facilitating interpersonal interactions as the home, the school, and other social institutions (Ewick & Silbey, 1998; Tapp & Levine, 1974). And, as with social institutions more generally, learning about law and how to relate to it is an important part of growing up.

Societies have legal institutions that are distinct from sources of moral authority and reflect the role of the state in regulating society, resolving conflicts, and managing social order. Legal institutions are tasked with regulating the behavior of citizens through codified rules of conduct (i.e., laws). To do this, legal authorities are given power by the state to enforce normative behavioral standards among the public and to resolve conflicts and disagreements among people. This represents control through state action and the application of public authority, rather than personal control via individualized standards of behavior.

The field of legal socialization is focused on how people develop their understanding and beliefs about the formal regulation of behavior via legal institutions. When should the law have the power to curtail people's behavior? What kinds of things should it be able to regulate? Why should it regulate some behaviors in some situations but not in others? Just as important, *how* should it regulate behavior? Should it enact control through punishment and retribution? What does the appropriate application of legal power look like in practice? When should people conform to laws? Is it all right to defy laws in some cases, but not others? The answers to these questions underlie how people experience and interpret their interactions with the law, which give rise to their attitudes about and support for legal authority.

There is also a large developmental literature on moral socialization (see Killen & Smetana, 2015), and it is important at the outset to distinguish moral development from legal development. Research on moral development focuses on the acquisition of personal values about what is right and what is wrong. In essence, moral socialization is the process where people develop their notions about what kinds of behaviors they ought to do, regardless of formal codified rules (i.e., laws). Once internalized, these values are used by people to guide their own behavior (e.g., I want to do what I believe is moral) and their judgments about others (e.g., You are immoral because you did something I believe is wrong). The key idea here is the development of an individual set of principles that act as personal standards of conduct and add meaning to the social world.

Although legal socialization has similarities to moral development, the two are not interchangeable. Moral development examines the acquisition of societal norms concerning appropriate personal conduct; legal development explores the acquisition of norms concerning how societal standards should be imposed on human beings. Whether or not a person agrees or disagrees with consuming drugs, getting an abortion, cheating on a spouse, or soliciting sex from a consenting adult are questions of moral values and moral development. Whether or not a person thinks the legal system should use its power to inhibit people's ability to do these things, how that power should be used once regulation is enacted, and whether people believe they should follow those regulations irrespective of their morals are questions of legal values and legal development.

The distinction between law and morality can be clearly seen through the consideration of the popular topic of decision dilemmas. Made famous by

Kohlberg (1963), an example of a moral dilemma involves the question of whether someone can justly steal a drug to save their spouse. The dilemma involves balancing two moral values: obeying laws and helping someone in need. Viewed differently, this is an issue of law. What obligations does a person owe to law and the directives of legal authorities? How can the legitimacy of a law be determined? What are the limits of legitimate legal authority? These issues are not focused upon the right thing to do to be true to moral principles, but rather on obligations to obey external state authorities (in spite of one's moral principles). Legal socialization concerns the formation of such perceptions of obligation.

The goal of legal socialization is to instill in people a felt obligation or responsibility to follow laws and accept legal authority. The goal of moral socialization is to instill in people a duty to follow societal standards of proper behavior independent of rules and codes. Given that in normal everyday life those behaviors that society considers immoral are frequently prohibited by law, the two usually work toward the same goal. However, that is not always the case. Criminalizing a behavior does not make it immoral, nor is all immoral behavior necessarily criminalized. Most people can think of an instance where they believe a behavior is immoral, but would not support criminalizing it or using the full force of the law to stop people from doing it. At the same time, even if people do abstractly support legal regulation of immoral behavior, they vary in how and the extent to which they want the legal system to intervene. Such views are strongly shaped by the way in which people understand the position and function of the law within society.

Central to discussions of legal socialization is the emergence of popular legitimacy of the law among the public. This focus on legitimacy represents another area in which the content of moral and legal socialization differs. Moral values develop during general socialization as an individual set of principles of right and wrong. They are then used by adults to guide their conduct by judging each issue against individual standards of right and wrong. Perceptions of legitimacy, in contrast, lead individuals to feel that it is their obligation to obey rules irrespective of their content. Hence people authorize legal authorities to decide what is correct and then people feel an obligation to adhere to the law. Of course, as we will outline, this only occurs within a sphere of appropriate issues, but nonetheless within that arena people suspend their own values and rely upon the values of the authorities. Hence, there is a fundamental difference between legitimacy and morality in terms of their influence on the operation of the legal system.

Consistent with this distinction, the history of law is one of sometimes cooperating with and sometimes struggling against moral values.

Throughout history the state and the church have existed as alternative sources of normative authority. In the United States there are many instances of moral values conflicting with law. One example is abortion. Appeals to those who think abortion is morally wrong take the form of deference to legitimate authority. Hence, we regard legal socialization as distinct from moral socialization and more fundamentally related to the ability of the state to function in a society with diverse moral values.

On the other hand, it is equally important to acknowledge that moral values play a role in law-related behavior. Studies typically find that the morality of a behavior is the strongest predictor of whether people engage in it (Tyler, 2006a). Morality is stronger than either legitimacy or sanction threat. Consequently, an additionally important question to address in an effort to understand how to promote compliance with the law is the relationship of morality to legitimacy. We acknowledge both that this is an important question and that it is one that makes the literature on moral socialization immediately relevant to a discussion about the functioning of the legal system (see Killen & Smetana, 2015 for a review of the moral development literature). However, it is not the question we are concerned with here for the reasons noted above.

To study legal socialization is to study the relationship between law and society by examining the role that the legal system plays within our social world. It requires addressing a series of questions about the law. How do individuals come to understand their relationship with the legal system? What responsibilities and obligations—both on the part of the law and citizens—are associated with that understanding? What role does the legal system play in creating or undermining solidarity and cohesion among members of the community? How do people come to be motivated to participate and engage with the legal system in ways that shape such cohesion and influence their compliance with the law and their cooperation with legal authorities? All of these questions are pertinent to legal socialization scholars.

Our goal in this volume is to encourage scholars to pay greater attention to the issue of legal socialization. We do this by identifying the fundamental processes associated with such socialization. These are (1) the internalization of values about how legal authorities are supposed to act toward citizens and how people are supposed to behave toward authorities in their role as citizens; (2) the formation of attitudes about the tangible representations of the law, including courts, laws, police, judges, and other legal authorities; and (3) the development of the cognitive and biological capacity to reason and think about the appropriate role for the law as a social institution in society.

Additionally, we also examine how these processes both occur at any given point in the developmental process and evolve over time through the life course of that process. Particular emphasis is placed on childhood and adolescence since legal socialization has its greatest influence in the early years of people's lives (Tapp, 1991; Tapp & Levine, 1974). For most people, the first personal contact with legal authorities, particularly with the police, occurs during this time (Snyder, 2012). In fact, the primary period during which the majority of people commit crimes is in adolescence and young adulthood (Steffensmeier & Ulmer, 2002), and the majority of the personal contact that most people will ever have with the criminal justice system occurs before they become adults.[1]

While criminal law and criminal justice are a highly visible manifestation of people's experience with law, it is important to recognize that the argument being made here has broader implications. People's orientation toward law impacts many areas of their lives (Ewick & Silbey, 1998), ranging from whether they believe they should follow contracts, obey the laws regarding corruption and fraud at work, pay taxes, and generally obey the rules and decisions of legal authorities. As we will elaborate, the functioning of society is heavily influenced by the extent to which most people do or do not obey laws in their daily lives.

The initial views developed as a result of legal socialization during a person's early years predisposes them toward a particular set of later attitudes, values, and behaviors. These constitute a residue of legal socialization that frames and shapes later life. Consequently, in order to fully understand adult attitudes about and interactions with the legal system, it is crucial to study the processes through which children and adolescents develop their conceptions about law and their views about the police, the courts, and other legal authorities

Further, although adults continue to deal with legal authorities, their contacts with the system come about primarily in the context of service delivery (e.g., calls for help) and over minor offenses, such as breaking traffic laws.[2] Adolescents are also likely to be engaged in minor offenses, but these include crimes for which they may be arrested and even incarcerated—for example, vandalism, drinking, and marijuana use. These types of behaviors bring them into contact with the juvenile justice system. As a consequence of this pattern, legal development begins long before an adult calls the system for help in resolving a conflict.

What happens in response to early contact with the legal system has the potential to shape a person's entire life course and influence the type of experiences people have as adults. Adolescents' lives can go in very different directions based upon the type of actions that are taken by juvenile justice authorities in response to their mostly minor criminal conduct before they are eighteen, and so the impact of personal contact with the legal system on the trajectory of many peoples' lives has largely happened before they become adults. Well-established predispositions are brought into adulthood, and prior actions have already created a potential future path toward or away from law-abidingness (Sampson & Laub, 1993).

This lifelong trajectory highlights the important point that an orientation toward law that is learned early in life has broad implications for behavior later in life. A parent whose style intensifies their child's alienation promotes bullying in school and later delinquency. The way a teacher *enforces* rules—which is different from what the actual rules are—alters law-related values and attitudes going forward. And the behavior of a police officer is an educational experience that shapes future interactions. In an important way, these early actors shape adult actions. The actions of authorities encountered early in life and the system's responses to minor crimes echo into adulthood. Whether a business executive commits corrupt acts as CEO can be traced back to legal socialization roots, as can whether someone becomes a lifelong violent offender.

A key application of these ideas is to institutional design. Legal scholars have long puzzled over how to induce greater compliance with the law. To advance this goal they often redesign institutions to alter the likelihood or severity of punishment in response to crime; more recently the use of incentives rather than punishment has been suggested (Brezina, 2002; Collins, 2007; Pratt, Cullen, Blevins, Daigle, & Madensen, 2006). In addition, we argue that compliance among adults is determined by other institutions that influence adults by changing their experience as children with regards to their orientation toward authority. This recognition changes the way they think about how to address adult behavior. We argue that three earlier phases of children's lives have a great influence on their interactions with authorities as adults: family, school, and juvenile justice. The policy implication is that interventions in designing these institutions are the key to addressing the issue of how to shape adult compliance with the law.

UNDERSTANDING THE IMPACT OF LEGAL SOCIALIZATION

In a post-Ferguson era, ongoing tension and deep-seated mistrust characterize the relationship between many communities in the United States and the legal system that serves them.[3] In this climate concerned citizens, community leaders, law enforcement personnel, and legal scholars are committing significant resources to understanding and ultimately finding ways to reshape that relationship (President's Task Force on 21st Century

Policing, 2015). In particular, there is concern that the public increasingly views legal authorities negatively and that new strategies must be developed that are specifically focused on rebuilding trust and confidence.

Studies assessing the factors that drive interactions and dissatisfaction with legal authorities have extensively examined adult experiences with and attitudes toward police and the courts. However, despite the importance of the early period in life to developing these attitudes, there has been little focus in recent legal scholarship on how young people learn about the nature of the law and form their initial opinions about legal authorities.

Here we address this missing component—preadult socialization—specifically examining issues relevant to legal socialization and its potential impact on the problems we face. We ask a series of questions. Why is it important to study legal socialization? Which psychological model of legal socialization offers the best opportunity to influence law-related adult behaviors? How does this process transpire as young people move through a sequence of phases in life marked by distinct yet overlapping domains of authority: family, school, and the juvenile justice system? How can an understanding of legal socialization be used to foster the popular legitimacy of the law and help re-establish trust? What are the implications for current efforts to reshape the relationship between community members and legal authorities?

In our own view of law and legal authority, the focus should be on understanding when children, adolescents, or adults reason in ways that lead them to judge the law as right, proper, or just and therefore accept it. We will argue that a key part of legal socialization is developing a sense of what the appropriate exercise of legal authority looks like. It is developing this sense that will ultimately provide the framework to make judgments concerning the legitimacy of the various authorities that individuals engage with during their everyday lives. These judgments are vital to authorities, as they will influence whether children, adolescents, and adults respond to them by both deferring to authority when it is deemed appropriate and questioning authority that is not appropriate either because of who the authority is or how that person is exercising power.

In other words, we emphasize the idea that people choose whether to defer to authorities, rather than being socialized into unquestioning (blind) obedience. While such blind obedience can and does occur, our own focus is on the development of a framework within which children, adolescents, and adults differentiate among authorities and institutions both in terms of the values they promulgate and the procedures they enact, and through that process decide when and where to accept their dictates. The ideal product of legal socialization, in other words, is a critical stance toward rules and authorities; accepting the responsibility to follow laws and obey authorities, but retaining a perspective that enables people to hold authorities accountable for how they act and exercise their power.

LEGITIMACY AND CONSENSUAL AUTHORITY

This volume presents two broad styles of legal socialization: coercive and consensual. Our argument is that there are models of socialization policies and practices that lead to the development of the types of legal attitudes and values that enable consensual models of legal authority based upon peoples' socialized values. There are also policies and practices that are coercive and lead to a relationship with the legal system based upon personal risk assessments (If I steal from a store how likely is it that I will be caught and punished?) as well as more general considerations of reward and punishment.

The distinction between these two models is rooted in alternative arguments about why people follow or break rules. A coercive model is rooted in rational choices based upon instrumental judgments of reward and punishment (Becker, 1976; Gibbs, 1968, 1975; Nagin, 1998). People balance the anticipated gains of rule-breaking against the possible risks of punishment. Consensual models emphasize willing rule-following based upon the belief that authorities ought to be deferred to when they exercise their authority appropriately (Beetham, 1991; French & Raven, 1959; Jackson, Bradford, Stanko, & Hohl, 2013; Tyler, 2006a). Instead of focusing on instrumental issues, people focus on normative judgments; that is, they evaluate whether or not they believe that the authorities are legitimate and thereby entitled to be obeyed.

People consent when they decide to willingly follow rules because they believe it is the right thing to do. This can be based upon personal reasoning and deliberation and/or dialogue and discussions with authorities about rules, their purposes and their implications for behavior in a given situation.

The degree to which these styles develop during the legal socialization process depends on the nature of the parental, educational, and legal authority that young people experience during childhood and adolescence. The development of attitudes and values is not automatic, and not all socialization practices lead to the formation of favorable attitudes and the development of values.

The key point is that early experiences have a major influence on the trajectory of most peoples' lives. Their orientation toward law has been largely formed before people are studied as adults. Adolescents' lives can go in very different directions in terms of the way they relate to law, as well as the nature of their subsequent involvement with law, based upon the type of actions that their parents and teachers engage in and that are taken in response to their mostly minor criminal conduct before they are eighteen. Hence a focus upon adults misses much of what is important in understanding the origin of adult attitudes, values, and behaviors. Important and already formed predispositions are brought into adulthood, and prior actions have already created a potential future path toward or away from law-abidingness.

Our argument is that these varying trajectories do not only have implications for the future life and well-being of individuals. Society benefits when it is largely managed consensually and the law, in particular, has a more desirable impact upon democratic society when it is consensually rooted and not coercive. This is true in terms of the everyday relationship of people to the law and also of the impact of law on society and democratic politics. The values underlying consensual law also underlie vibrant democratic processes that serve to invigorate community viability and personal well-being (Tyler & Jackson, 2014).

Despite the importance of this early period in life to the person and to democratic society, recent legal scholarship has generally underemphasized the study of how young people learn about the nature of law and legal authority and form their initial predispositions concerning legal authorities (Fagan & Tyler, 2005). Because of their focus on adults and their values, attitudes, and experiences, most contemporary studies of the police and courts are missing the importance of this early period of life.

KEY PHASES OF LEGAL SOCIALIZATION

We consider the interplay of these two models of legal socialization during three key phases of the process: in the family, in schools, and through interactions with the juvenile justice system. We argue that at each of these three phases young people can experience variations among different styles of authority practiced by their parents, teachers, school resource officers, police officers, and judges. At each stage authority can be exercised in different ways that can either support or undermine the formation of attitudes and legal values, as well as communicate either positive or negative views about authorities and institutions.

Within each of these three domains, research shows a style of exercising authority that does not build favorable law-related values or lead to the development of supportive attitudes (Fagan & Tyler, 2005; Gregory & Ripski, 2008; Trinkner, Cohn, Rebellon, & Van Gundy, 2012; Tyler, 1997). This style is characterized by the threat or use of physical force to compel obedience. In addition, it is associated with styles of making decisions that are experienced as unfair (Larzelere, Klein, Schumm, & Alibrando, 1989; Weisz, Wingrove, & Faith-Slaker, 2007/2008). Those styles include inconsistent rule application, lack of transparency and explanation, failure to allow participation and voice, exhibiting prejudice and bias, and over-reliance on the use of force and coercion. These styles are also associated with a lack of respect for, courtesy toward, and concern about those subject to authority, as reflected in cold or hostile demeanor, humiliation or harassment, and actions that are viewed as reflected indifference or even a motivation to exploit subordinates (Arum, 2003; Straus & Donnelly, 2001; Tyler, 2011). Finally, authorities of this type fail to recognize and acknowledge spheres of individual autonomy and choice (Huq, Jackson, & Trinkner, 2016; Trinkner, Jackson, & Tyler, 2016). This coercive style is associated with the failure to develop supportive attitudes and values, and may even socialize antisocial attitudes and cynical values, producing distant and alienated individuals (Anderson, 1999; Delgado, 2008; Mukherjee, 2007; Trinkner & Cohn, 2014). It also leads to childhood bullying and interpersonal aggression, as well as juvenile delinquency and adult criminality (Aizer & Doyle, 2015; Fagan & Piquero, 2007; Farrington, 2005; Mayer & Leone, 1999; McCord, 1991; Trinkner et al., 2012; Way, 2011).

Of course, not all systems based upon rewards and punishments are the same. One difference is whether they have features like those that lead to consent. It is possible to explain why punishment is used and to emphasize the consistent and rule-based application of punishments. Research shows that when punishment systems are implemented in ways that people view as fair they can support the idea that the law is legitimate (van Prooijen, Gallucci & Toeset, 2008). In other words, while these two models are presented as distinct, their features can overlap.

An alternative style promotes the socialization of favorable attitudes and supportive values. That style is characterized by three important aspects of authority: decision-making, quality of treatment, and boundaries.

First, it involves making decisions in ways that people experience as being fair. This includes allowing input and participation, making the nature of the rules and the circumstances under which they are being applied transparent, explaining the reasons for decisions, showing how facts and not biases are the reason for decisions, and allowing opportunities for criticism and mechanisms for appeal and correction. These elements fit well with traditional legal concerns about fair procedures.

Second, it involves treating people fairly. Fair interpersonal treatment involves treating people, their status, and their needs and concerns respectfully; listening to and considering what people say; and acting in ways that show benevolence and sincerity. In addition to concerns about making legally appropriate and factually accurate decisions, legal authorities are societal authorities and the way that they treat people communicates messages that shape people's self-esteem and evaluations of their inclusion and standing in society. Humiliation, ridicule, or other behaviors that are associated with dismissing the value and worth of a person or casting doubts on their standing in society, at least in the eyes of societal authorities, are equally important. These are relational concerns because they are messages that have a social meaning (Tyler & Lind, 1992).

Finally, it involves recognizing the boundaries of authority and supporting the idea of individual autonomy. Autonomy involves understanding that individuals deem certain domains as outside of the jurisdiction of authorities, recognizing that there are limits on the degree to which authorities can encroach on these domains, and that authorities' directives can be rejected if they insist on trying to control behavior outside appropriate domains. For people to develop a set of personal values, moral or obligatory, they must first conceive of a distinct sense of self, a self that makes decisions about what is or is not appropriate in terms of deferring to authority. Central to such decisions is the continuing effort to distinguish when authorities' orders ought to be obeyed.

When parents, teachers, or legal authorities act in these ways they create a framework for understanding legitimacy, which is the foundation of consensual authority (Beetham, 1991; Tyler, 2009). Children come to believe that they ought to obey authority *when* it acts in ways that give it legitimacy (Trinkner & Cohn, 2014). The fair exercise of authority communicates legitimacy and leads to deference. When socialized to hold such values and when viewing existing authority as worthy of trust children, adolescents, and adults are more likely to generally abide by rules and law, and are less likely to be interpersonally aggressive, to be delinquent as an adolescent, or engage in adult criminal behavior (Sunshine & Tyler, 2003a; Trinkner et al., 2012; Tyler, 2006a).

A large empirical literature on adults supports two core aspects of this argument (see Tyler, Goff, & MacCoun, 2015; Tyler & Jackson, 2013 for a review). First, it has been repeatedly demonstrated that adults who believe legal authorities are legitimate and who evaluate existing authorities favorably both obey laws and cooperate with legal authorities without focusing primarily upon what they have to gain or lose instrumentally. People support the law in their everyday lives in a wide variety of ways, ranging from obeying the law to serving on a jury or acting as a witness.

Second, studies show that legitimacy flows from the judgment that legal authorities are creating and implementing the law via fair procedures. This includes making decisions fairly, treating people fairly, and recognizing appropriate limits for the exercise of authority. A wide variety of studies of adults make it clear that these elements define legitimacy to a much greater extent than judgments about community problems, police effectiveness, or even the legality of police behavior (Jackson, Bradford, et al., 2013; Kochel, Parks, & Mastrofski, 2013; Meares, Tyler, & Gardener, 2016; Tyler, 2006a; Tyler & Huo, 2002).

It is important to contrast these two models from a societal perspective. Coercive models can work. However, they are an inefficient use of collective resources. Because it is the probability of swift and certain punishment that deters, it is necessary to create and maintain a surveillance system, backed up with resources for adjudication and incarceration (Garland, 2001; Meares, 2000). Further, even when deterrence works, its effects are small in magnitude (MacCoun, 1993; Paternoster, 2006), so effective resource levels are often so high that their societal costs are prohibitive, and society defaults to detecting and punishing a limited set of crimes. A consensual system is more efficient because it seeks to maximize the degree to which people are internally motivated to comply because of their felt responsibilities and duties as members of society. Hence, optimality suggests investing resources early on to facilitate value socialization and attitude development with the goal of minimizing enforcement costs later.

LEGAL SOCIALIZATION FROM A DEVELOPMENTAL PERSPECTIVE

We will examine legal socialization from a classical and historical perspective, through an overview of strategies for value socialization, and for the development of political and legal attitudes. The relevant literatures address four points. The first is the development of a framework within which to understand authority. Part of the developmental process is the increasing cognitive capacity to think abstractly, allowing conceptions of rules and authority to develop (Tapp & Levine, 1974). A key literature underlying legal socialization is the study of reasoning ability.

Second, at the same time that reasoning ability is developing, the legal socialization process involves the incorporation of values into one's identity. These values are a reflection of social and individual norms concerning the legal system, its role in society as a source of formal social control, and how it should wield its authority (Jackson, Bradford, et al., 2013; Tyler, 2006a). Ultimately, they form the basis upon which people decide if the legal system is a legitimate institution, with the result that people will feel obligated to defer to authorities that exemplify those values.

Third, legal socialization involves the development of attitudes toward existing political and legal authorities. Using their cognitive abilities and values, people evaluate the actions of authorities, leading to favorable or unfavorable attitudes toward them (Cohn & White, 1990). On one level this includes the degree to which people trust or distrust legal actors such as police officers or judges (Tyler & Huo, 2002). More fundamentally, it involves support for or cynicism about the institutions of law and the idea of law itself (Sampson & Bartusch, 1998; Trinkner & Cohn, 2014).

Fourth, underlying these processes is biological development. It has long been recognized that biology undergirds the developmental process, as people acquire increasing skills in reasoning, emotional regulation, and self-control as they age. Any attempt to understand socialization, legal or otherwise, must address the underlying biological changes that are part and parcel of the socialization process (Grusec & Hastings, 2015). The study of biology is especially important in the case of legal socialization because the course of neurological development is toward people who are better able to handle a consensual relationship with the law as they become older. This aging process is not complete until after adolescence, so youth have greater difficulty with self-regulation than do adults (Steinberg, 2009).

As noted previously, for most people their primary experiences with criminal law occur in response to minor crimes committed during the preadult period: crimes that are motivated by faulty judgment (Steinberg & Cauffman, 1996), poor impulse control (Gottfredson & Hirschi, 1990), and overinfluence by peer pressure (Gifford-Smith, Dodge, Dishion, & McCord, 2005). Research suggests that if these activities do not draw adolescents into contact with criminal justice authorities, they "age out" of delinquency as their increasing capacities for reason and control become ascendant and almost all become normal law-abiding adults (Moffitt, 2007; Steffensmeier & Ulmer, 2002).

However, to the degree that adolescents are drawn into the juvenile justice system through these activities, their trajectory veers more toward adult criminality (Aizer & Doyle, 2015; Petrosino, Turpin-Petrosino, & Guckenburg, 2010). As noted by Bartollas and Schmalleger (2011, p. 310): "The earlier youths come to the attention of the juvenile justice system, the more likely they are to continue with juvenile crime; the more time they spent in the juvenile justice system, the more likely they are to go on to adult crime; and the deeper they go into the system, the higher the rates of recidivism when they leave and the more serious crimes they tend to commit as adults." While contact with the juvenile justice system does not necessarily lead to these negative outcomes, the punitive and harsh nature of the system tends to exacerbate the problem rather than fix it (Slobogin & Fondacaro, 2011).

INSTITUTIONAL DESIGN

Why care about the socialization of views about the law, legal authority, and law-related behavior? Our argument has clear implications for the design of legal institutions. Developing a consensual orientation toward law among most people in society has clear advantages, and our societal institutions ought to be designed to do that. However, at this time a paradox exists within American perspectives on legal socialization. The studies we will review suggest that consensual approaches to law produce societal benefits. And studies indicate both that value socialization is possible and suggest mechanisms for its success.

These facts notwithstanding, the appropriateness of using coercive or consensual approaches in legal socialization is heavily contested and there is considerable support for coercive approaches in families (Regalado, Sareen, Inkelas, Wissow, & Halfon, 2004) and schools (Arum, 2003), as well within both the juvenile (Rios, 2011) and adult (Garland, 2001) justice system. Irrespective of whether the issue is corporal punishment, strict classroom rules and discipline, adolescent boot camps, or harsh prison conditions, many people—including criminal justice authorities and political leaders—favor instrumental approaches to managing social order. Research on legal socialization provides and important counterweight to such views by demonstrating that the socialization of values and fostering of supportive attitudes is clearly linked to motivating not only compliance with the law, but voluntary deference and willing cooperation with legal authorities.

As we will detail in the third part of this book, two messages consistently emerge from the research on legal and nonlegal authority. First, it is not inevitable that the legal socialization process will promote a consensual orientation toward the law. Depending on their experiences with people who hold power and use it to regulate behavior, people can develop a relationship with the law that is based on dominance, fear, and instrumental motivation. Second, a consensual orientation toward the law is promoted when people experience authorities who treat them respectfully, make fair decisions, and recognize personal autonomy. This encourages the acceptance of the law as a value based motivational factor and the belief that society works best when people follow the rule of law.

Across legal and nonlegal contexts, authorities can act in ways that will hinder the acquisition of legal values. In fact, many widely used practices have been shown to undermine the socialization of law-related values. This observation begins with parenting, with many parents engaging in inconsistent and nontransparent rule enforcement, being cold or rejecting parents, and using physical punishment to enforce rules (Regalado et al., 2004; Straus, 1991; Straus & Donnelly, 2001). The widespread use of corporal punishment reflects the reality that many parents raise their children through mechanisms of coercion. They do not explain their decisions, do not discuss and explain rules and rule application, and they do not treat their children with dignity and respect. Not only do these practices fail to create supportive attitudes and values, they are also directly linked to a higher likelihood of later delinquency and adult criminality (Earls, 1994; Gershoff & Bitensky, 2007; Straus & Donnelly, 2001; Trinkner & Cohn, 2014; Trinkner et al., 2012).

In schools overly strict rule systems and punitive responses to rule-breaking, as well as punitive and indifferent teaching strategies, similarly lead to a greater likelihood of breaking school rules (Gendron, Williams, & Guerra, 2011), membership in gangs (Rios, 2011), and later delinquency (Jenkins, 1997). On the other hand, those teachers who exercise their authority in ways that are experienced as fair build trust, are viewed as legitimate, and are associated with greater rule-adherence behavior in class and in other domains of the school environment (Arum, 2003; Gregory & Ripski, 2008; Trinkner & Cohn, 2014).

Finally, police officers, courts, and other juvenile justice authorities are commonly found to be unfair, disrespectful, and overly punitive in their interactions with young people (Carr, Napolitano, & Keating, 2003; Gau & Brunson, 2010; Humes, 1997). Unsurprisingly, the general result of such contact is the undermining of supportive legal values and attitudes and the encouragement of delinquency (Fagan & Tyler, 2005). In fact, unfair and punitive behavior on the part of legal authorities tends to promote cynicism about the law and its ability to maintain social order (Trinkner & Cohn, 2014), a belief that has been linked to adult criminality and resignation toward the violence in high-crime neighborhoods (Kirk & Matsuda, 2011; Kirk & Papachristos, 2011).

A CLASH OF CULTURES

Within each sphere of development there are actions that authorities can take that have positive consequences. Within these spheres parents, teachers, and legal authorities can each promote value acquisition by exercising authority fairly and by acting in ways that facilitate trust and create social bonds.

Despite the robustness of these findings, it is equally important to note the general popularity of coercive styles of authority that have been shown to not promote positive development and value acquisition

(Arum, 2003; Kupchik, 2010; Petrosino et al., 2004, 2010; Straus & Donnely, 2001). This suggests that a key aspect of any efforts to understand how society can generally create supportive values needs to involve addressing the romance of instrumentalism: the exaggerated belief in the ability of sanctions and strict, physical discipline to promote law-abiding behavior.

This model is itself open to question on its own merits (Tyler & Rankin, 2012). It is further important because as law has moved from a compliance model to a model focused upon deference and cooperation (President's Task Force on 21st Century Policing, 2015; Rahr & Rice, 2015; Schulhofer, Tyler, & Huq, 2011), behavior has become more strongly shaped by values and attitudes and largely unrelated to instrumental judgments (Tyler, 2006a, 2009, 2011).

The potential advantages of consensual models aside, there is an ongoing clash about the desirability of these two styles of legal authority. The popularity of instrumental approaches continues despite evidence that they do not build legitimacy or promote long-term rule-following. Corporal punishment in the home is associated with a higher likelihood of future criminality (Straus, 1991; Straus & Donnely, 2001); strict rules in schools do not lessen disciplinary problems (Arum, 2003); school resource officers do not change the rate of disorder in schools (Kupchik, 2010); and punitive juvenile justice programs (e.g., boot camps) do not reduce future criminal behavior (Petrosino, Turpin-Petrosino, & Buehler, 2004). In all of these arenas the desirability of engaging in the styles of child-rearing that promote value acquisition and the development of favorable attitudes toward legal authorities is widely contested, even when research suggests that instrumental approaches are ineffective or that socializing supportive values and favorable attitudes promotes law-abiding behavior among adolescents and adults.

The institutional design implications of our approach speak to an appropriate and productive way to exert authority and regulate behavior with the families, schools, and the juvenile justice system. In each sphere, authority should be exercised in ways that promote legitimacy and facilitate the consensual exercise of legal authority. This suggests strategies for positive parenting, it supports deliberative approaches to education, and it argues against punitive and punishment-based ways of addressing juvenile misconduct.

At its core, our argument asks what type of society people want to live in. Democratic societies do not simply focus on efficiency. They are concerned with people's feelings about themselves and others in their community. They want to live in a society in which people freely choose to engage (Tyler, 2011). The studies reviewed here argue that such a society is not only possible, it is superior and more desirable. Hence, it is striking how hotly contested issues of authority are in America today. This volume argues for the virtues of designing our social institutions to achieve legitimacy and through it, to enable consensual models of law.

Of course, this contrast between the two perspectives outlined should not be overstated. While we argue for the virtues of consensual authority we recognize that both models of authority will have a role in any legal system. As will be shown in later chapters it seems likely that there will always be some people who lack values and who must be managed via the threat of sanctions. Similarly, there are some situations that are best responded to via sanction threats. One example is a setting in which immediate compliance is essential. In the presence of the threat of force people generally change their behavior quickly and in some cases it is important for authorities to have the capacity of achieving rapid compliance. It is not always possible to take the time needed to build legitimacy and motivate consent.

An example of an effort to balance these two perspectives is the work of Ayres and Braithwaite (1992). They argue for a pyramid of regulation through which people are initially approached in value-based appeals. This is effective with most people but identifies a smaller group who do not or cannot respond to such appeals. That group is then managed via sanctions. A gain from this approach is that the resources needed to maintain credible sanctions are only required when dealing with a small group of the population.

SUMMARY

Our goal for this book is to present an argument for the possibility—as well as the desirability—of a legal system that operates largely through consent. Consent-based models of legal authority require that (1) most people in a society have supportive law-related values and attitudes, and (2) that legal institutions behave in ways that foster consent through the fair exercise of legal authority. In order for this to happen, children must develop an understanding of what it means for an authority to be legitimate. This understanding is driven by their internalization of legal values, formation of law-related attitudes, and the acquisition of reasoning capacities.

Our goal in this volume is to review prior literature on legal socialization to demonstrate that it is possible to encourage children to develop a consensual relationship with the legal authority that is built on their understanding of the proper role of the law and their responsibilities as law-abiding citizens. Further, we present a broader and expanded perspective on legal development by tracing the formation of such a relationship to experiences with authority in families, schools, and the juvenile justice system. Throughout, we highlight the ongoing argument in America today about the desirability of instilling a consensual relationship versus one that is based on coercion and strict obedience. It is our hope that this book will stimulate interest in the legal socialization process, a discussion about the most desirable form of legal authority, and an effort to consider the impact of different styles of socialization upon the nature of peoples' adult relationship with the law.

It is also important to emphasize that while many of our examples involve criminal processes, the orientation outlined has broader implications. People in a democratic society have widespread engagements with law and legal authority. They deal with criminal law, but also with the civil justice system and with administrative agencies. Many of the obligations they confront are not about criminal laws. They are asked to pay taxes and fight in wars. While the failure to do so may ultimately be criminal, what society seeks and needs is for people to step forward and follow through on these obligations without coercion. In fact, in the face of widespread unwillingness to do so, society struggles to survive. Further, modern society emphasizes the desirability of active and creative engagement, and such voluntary and nonrequired behavior is linked to identification with society, something that flows from consenting to participate with others in an ordered world.

Of course underlying all of these arguments is the suggestion that legitimacy can be created and sustained by exposure to just institutions. At the core of the institutional change implications of our argument is the need for institutions to be experienced by those who deal with them as just. Legal socialization is not only about the acquisition of values, but also stresses the importance of legal institutions that embody those values. This requires institutions that operate from a framework of public concerns not only about crime and behavioral regulation, but also about their role within the broader social fabric.

From this perspective, the most important recent research development is the demonstration that legitimacy flows from procedural justice. Further studies have identified a clear model of procedural justice, ensuring that institutions have clear guidelines about how to build legitimacy (Jackson, Bradford, et al., 2013; Schulhofer et al., 2011; Tyler, 2004, 2009). Strikingly, these findings about what adults consider when evaluating authorities echo through the literature on families, schools, and juvenile justice authorities. This accords with research showing that even young children understand the principles of procedural justice and use them as a framework for evaluating the actions of themselves and others (Grocke, Rossano, & Tomasello, 2015; Shaw & Olson, 2014).

CHAPTER 1

༺ঌ

Legal Socialization and
the Elements of Legitimacy

Early pioneers of modern social science, including figures such as Emile Durkheim (1973), Max Weber (1968), and Sigmund Freud (1930), all emphasize both the centrality of civic attitudes and values to the viability of democratic societies and the importance of attitude and value acquisition during childhood and adolescence. In their view democracies require broad support for their legitimacy from citizens to remain viable, and must seek to create this support through the development of institutions such as public schools that socialize favorable attitudes and supportive values. This perspective continued through the work of later twentieth-century social theorists such as Parsons (1937) and Easton (1965), and led to the widespread study of the processes of moral development (Kohlberg, 1963, 1981) and legal socialization (Tapp & Levine, 1974, 1977). These authors generally assume that it is important both that people have attitudes and values relevant to law and legal authority and that those attitudes and values are supportive.

AN ERA OF DECLINING TRUST AND CONFIDENCE

We argue that today the United States is experiencing an era of heightened mistrust, and we cannot assume that the values and attitudes held by citizens will continue to support our democracy and its institutions, including the legal system. This decrease in public trust in the United States is not necessarily occurring because people no longer have values concerning what they think the law should be. Instead, it reflects their increasing judgment that the existing legal authorities no longer embody the same values that they hold. For example, to measure trust in national government in surveys of politicians, the public is asked whether politicians make decisions based upon what is good for the community they represent. Scholars continue to regard this issue as an important marker of legitimacy. The problem, however, is that people are less likely to believe that politicians do in fact make decisions based upon what is good for their communities. Rather they believe that political leaders have been captured by special or big money interests and work for corporations, not the public.

In recent studies the American public's trust and confidence in police, the courts, and the law—that is, their perception of the legitimacy of legal authority—has been found to be somewhat positive, although a substantial percentage of adults express a lack of trust (Gallup, 2015). In addition, there are striking and long-term racial gaps in legitimacy and trust that do not appear to be disappearing, given that they have largely stayed constant since at least the 1970s. An examination of available evidence from opinion poll data (Pew Research Center, 2014a) suggests moderately positive support for the police among the general adult population (e.g., 50 to 60% express confidence in the police), but strikingly lower support among African Americans (20 to 30% less). Further, general adult support for the courts—in particular the criminal courts—is even lower, and has a similar but smaller racial gap. Additionally, there are suggestions that while support for the police is steady, support for the courts has been declining (Jones, 2015a).

There is also evidence that the public's belief that the overall federal government embodies civic values of the type that would make it trustworthy and give it legitimacy has declined in recent decades. Public opinion polls, scholars, and pundits have all noted the declining trust Americans feel for their government (Nye, Zelikow, & King, 1997; Pharr, Putnam, & Dalton, 2000; Public Policy Polling, 2013; Smith & Son, 2013). In particular, this is seen in studies of public trust and confidence in government as measured in the National Election Studies (Hetherington, 2005). Polls conducted between the late 1950s and today indicate that public trust in government has declined precipitously. For example, in 1958, 73% of Americans trusted the government to do what is right "just about always" or "most of the time." By 2013, only 19% trusted government to this degree (Pew Research Center, 2013). Today, 30% of respondents express anger at government, up from 12% in 1997.

Further, confidence in social institutions, as measured by the General Social Survey conducted by the independent research organization NORC at the University of Chicago, declined between 1973 and 2006 (Smith & Son, 2013). This study focuses upon national-level institutions such as organized religion and government institutions (e.g., US Congress, Supreme Court, executive branch). In general, institutions declined in public confidence, with the exception of the military and, to some extent, the Supreme Court. More recent polls suggest that even the Supreme Court is losing the public's confidence (Jones, 2015a).

All of this evidence is consistent with the view that in recent decades, feelings of legitimacy and trust have broadly decreased in the United States, creating problems for communities and government (Rodgers, 2011). While it is widely argued that legitimacy and trust facilitate government by making it more consensual (Beetham, 1991; Weber, 1968), it is also important to acknowledge that research has not identified specific levels of distrust below which societies cannot function, nor has it demonstrated that societies cannot function unless they have legitimacy. Rather, it is argued that societies, particularly democracies, can better function when public reactions to law and government are consensually-based.

Also of note is a discrepancy between the support for the police and courts and support for the federal government. Trust in federal government is lower (Pew Research Center, 2013, 2014a). This discrepancy is due in part to trust in local institutions generally being higher than trust in national-level institutions. For example, the 1996 National Election Study asked respondents in which level of government they most had faith to "do the right thing." It was found that 37% chose state government, 33% chose local government, and 30% chose the federal government (Blendon et al., 1997). When asked in which level of government they had the least faith, 48% said the federal government, 34% local government, and 19% state government. So it appears that legal authorities benefit from being primarily located at the local or state level, and it is there that a focus on legal socialization might best begin. It remains to be seen how events such as the police–public conflict in cities such as Ferguson, Missouri will influence local trust. Although initial polling showed a substantial decrease in public trust in the police (Jones, 2015b), that has largely returned to the stable numbers presented earlier (Saad, 2015).

These discussions use a variety of terms to talk about public feeling. Most generally the popular legitimacy of laws and legal authorities is measured in three ways. First, trust and confidence. This involves statements such as "judges are honest" or "police officers try to do what is best for people in the community." Second, the perceived obligation to obey. Third, the belief that legal authorities and members of the community share moral or normative values; that is, that they want the same things for their community in value-based terms.

Since perceptions of legitimacy are dependent on the legal values imparted during legal socialization, this process needs to be a key focus of study when there is concern about developing and maintaining the set of values that underpins effective legal, political, and social institutions in liberal democratic societies. As a result, we argue that it is time for legal socialization to again be a major focus of study. In this climate, renewed attention to the formation of values, attitudes, and reasoning capacities becomes increasingly relevant.[1]

Of course it is also important to note that designing institutions with the goal of creating values and attitudes is not simply a mechanism for avoiding the issues that might be leading to distrust. It is inherent in our discussion that people evaluate their social environment through a lens of values, particularly with regard to how legal authorities and institutions are behaving. People have a framework for evaluating the appropriateness through which legal rules are created and implemented (Cohn & White, 1990; Tapp & Levine, 1974; Tyler, 2006a). In order to be trusted, authorities must act in a trustworthy manner. So a primary focus for any institution interested in building and maintaining trust has to be on how authority is exercised and whether it is being evaluated as fair.

CONCERNS WITH THE DETERRENCE FRAMEWORK

If trust and confidence in the local police and courts is stable and at least moderately positive, why is there a need to focus on building support among the public via the socialization of law-related attitudes and values? A key factor is the growing recognition of the limited effectiveness and high costs of current policies based on deterrence. Concerns include the high costs of incarceration and the high recidivism rates associated with the US prison system (Travis, Western, & Redburn, 2014), the difficulties posed by continuing public noncompliance and unwillingness to cooperate (Kirk & Papachristos, 2011), and the growing cost associated with the use of surveillance to deter crime (Garland, 2001). Finally, there is the long-term impact of this approach on public trust. Coercion undermines trust and confidence (Gau & Brunson, 2010; Geller, Fagan, & Tyler, 2014).

Deterrence policies are based on rational choice models (Becker, 1976; Gibbs, 1968, 1975; Nagin, 1998), which focus attention on material rewards and costs in the immediate situation, and away from the role of long-term values in shaping behavior. Rational choice models assume that people have pre-existing attitudes and values (i.e., preferences) and examine how those preferences are translated into choices. The rational choice model emphasizes the role of deliberative thinking, during which adults consciously weigh the material and physical benefits and costs of any particular behavior in a given setting before making a decision to act. From this perspective, the central factor motivating compliance with the law is the threat of punishment or the promise of reward, and people's relationship with legal authorities is rooted in the desire to avoid punishments and secure gains.

There are two distinctions to be made. The first is between instrumental and value-based motivations. The second is whether the focus is on the origin of preferences and values or on their consequences for decisions. Legal socialization focuses on origins, and our model in particular is concerned primarily with the origin of values.

While some research acknowledges a role for norms, attitudes, and values (Brezina, 2002), the dominant conceptual framework underlying deterrence approaches has been one of material gains and losses—especially losses—leading to a system largely managed through sanctions, with some attention to incentives (Collins, 2007; Pratt, Cullen, Blevins, Daigle, & Madensen, 2006). The reward–cost approach to law and law-related behavior has been central to the last several decades of legal scholarship and to the development of the current policies and practices of legal authorities.

Why has deterrence been successful in the past? The focus on decision-making based upon existing preferences presumes that the preferences that exist are ones that lead to personally desirable decisions. But does this model support socially desirable decisions? Economic models have been successful because they have examined the unfolding of individual preferences during an era when people have generally held the type of supportive social attitudes and values (e.g., trust in government; trust and confidence in social institutions; support for legal authorities, institutions, and law) that have also shaped their behavior and thereby enabled society to function effectively. These attitudes and values have existed as part of a broader framework within which the unfolding of personal preferences has occurred. In other words, people have been supporting the law because of their attitudes and values, even while those attitudes and values have been outside of the framework that has been the focus on legal scholarship.

However, deterrence-based approaches, which focus on punishment (particularly harsh or severe punishment) and the use of force as a means of social control have encouraged people to view their attitudes and values as not relevant to their relationship to law; that is, to undermine the role of attitudes and values in shaping law-related behavior (Tyler, 2004). This approach has communicated to people that their relationship with the legal system is instrumental, rather than value-based. Second, this force-based approach has increasingly undermined supportive attitudes and values and bred defiance and rejection of the law (Carr, Napolitano, & Keating, 2007; Gau & Brunson, 2010; Geller, Fagan, & Tyler, 2014; Kane, 2005; Reisig & Lloyd, 2009; Sunshine & Tyler, 2003a). The public reservoir of support for the law has eroded over time, particularly among those communities that are most likely to feel the effects of such an approach (Trinkner & Goff, 2016).

The widespread and often uncritical support of the post-World War II generation for societal institutions and authorities has been described and critiqued both in classic books such as *The Lonely Crowd* (Riesman, Glazer, & Denney, 2001, originally published in 1950), and in contemporary depictions of that era in American history. Yet this broad and perhaps uncritical era of support lent legitimacy to political and legal institutions and authorities that in recent years has been slowly undermined (Gallup, 2015; Pharr et al., 2000). Against the background of this broad popular legitimacy a deterrence-based system has been able to sustain government and law, because of the exogenous role played by supportive attitudes and values that have been outside the scope of the factors in the cost-benefit framework.

Declining levels of institutional trust are now causing serious and seemingly intractable social problems, including problems with the deterrence model, to become increasingly apparent. In part this is because the everyday operation of the deterrence approach has had the unintended consequence of undermining those attitudes and values, and also because the the focus upon deterrence has led people to pay inadequate attention to the issue of value and attitude development, particularly during legal socialization.

THE NEED FOR A BROADER FRAMEWORK

Recent research makes clear both that the deterrence approach can be effective in shaping behavior; however, it is resource intensive (Chalfin & McCrary, 2014; Kleiman, 2009). As a consequence, the limits of deterrence are linked to resource limits (Meares, 2000; Tyler, 2004). For example, hot-spot policing shows that the police can lower crime by concentrating police officers in particular settings (Braga, Papachristos, & Hureau, 2012). However, the ability to marshal that level of resources is limited, especially if it has to be maintained over time. In other words, the limits of deterrence are not theoretical, but pragmatic. Societies find it hard to create and maintain credible risks of sanctioning across a wide variety of situations and in response to many crimes.

This problem is intensified by the recognition that punishment is most effective when it is swift and certain (Kleiman, 2009). This approach, while shown by research to be the most effective of various deterrence approaches, is also the most resource intensive. It requires sufficient societal commitment to have authorities involved in surveillance and in swift apprehension and adjudication. Hence these findings both highlight the possibility of a deterrence approach and emphasize its limits as a general strategy of legal authority.[2]

Deterrence also has limits as a framework for shaping adult law-related behavior. One important limit is that it fails to account for the impact of attitudes and values on behavior. Comparisons of rewards and costs to values and attitudes show that among adults, values and attitudes make an important distinct contribution to explaining behavior, and are in fact often more important than reward–cost concerns (Tyler, 2006a, 2006b). A model that fails to account for attitude and value influences misses an important lever in the legal arsenal.

As the importance of values and attitudes has become increasingly apparent, attention has been directed to the issue of understanding people's supportive civic values, attitudes of trust and distrust, and the reasoning capacities that underlie them (Tyler, 2011). It is important to employ a broader conception of human motivation that includes values, attitudes, and other factors. The relationship between individuals and the legal system—much like all social relationships—is not solely determined by deterrence, rationality, and instrumental control. Rather, it is also driven and defined by noninstrumental concerns. This includes the values people hold, the attitudes they form, and the cognitive skills they possess.

A focus on attitudes and values does not necessarily suggest a need to focus on legal socialization. If adults have supportive values and attitudes, then those preferences should also provide support for the law and law-abiding behavior. In this respect, one issue for future scholarship is to ensure that models of decision-making are broadened to include attention to the role of supportive values and attitudes in shaping behavior among adults (Tyler, 2006a, 2006b).

A second issue is to leverage what we know about the processes underlying the formation and internalization of values to design legal institutions that approach citizens in ways that both create and then evoke supportive attitudes and values. It is first important that people have values. But it is not just enough to create values. We also need to have a legal system that understands what those values are, and can design an approach to policing and the courts that harnesses that understanding to secure willing cooperation and compliance by motivating value-based behavior. As we will show throughout this volume, strategies that rely on force and coercion are limited in their ability to do this. However, value-based strategies that rely on consent and mutual respect can.

As trust and confidence in law-related authorities and institutions declines, the ability to maintain a public connection to government increasingly depends upon having favorable civic values and attitudes about local authorities. The police and courts are key local authorities because they are organized at the state, county, and city level. It is these agencies, particularly the police, that are the face of government to most citizens (Tyler & Huo, 2002). Hence, local authority is a natural focus of efforts to revitalize the relationship between the community, the law, and the state. An important goal of legal policy should be for these agencies to facilitate public support for law and democracy. The local legal system needs to become a basis upon which to build support for local communities and government, as well as national-level political and legal institutions (Meares & Tyler, 2014).

The courts also have a critical role to play in revitalizing the relationship with the public. US Supreme Court Justice Stephen Breyer recently argued that the courts are central to creating a context in which communities can "respond to the universal need present in every society, that for some method for resolving disputes among individuals" (Breyer, 2010, p. 138). Further, Justice Breyer recognized the importance of public legitimacy for legal authorities, suggesting that "public acceptance is not automatic and cannot be taken for granted" (p. xiii). He also notes the need to motivate public political participation with local communities and government as a way of maintaining a viable democracy. Peoples' civic attitudes and values shape their behavior toward their local community, law, and government, thereby influencing the viability of local institutions and authorities (Tyler & Jackson, 2014). Those institutions in turn influence attitudes toward law and government in general, and impact on public orientations toward the national government.

THE ROLE OF LEGITIMACY

There is also evidence that some of the behavioral problems resulting from the approaches in use today could be addressed by promoting higher levels of legitimacy, such as more trust and confidence in the police and the courts. Perceptions of legitimacy play a role in problems obtaining compliance with the law (Tyler, 2006a), difficulties gaining the acceptance of judicial and police decisions (Gibson & Caldeira, 1995), low levels of cooperation with the police and courts (Tyler & Fagan, 2008), an unwillingness to cede legal authority to the government (Jackson, Huq, Bradford, & Tyler, 2013), and a growing propensity to engage in collective actions that go outside the boundaries of law to attack the social system (riots, terrorism) (Carrabine, 2005). Studies show that higher levels of legitimacy, and trust and confidence, both encourage supportive behavior and discourage undesirable behaviors (see Tyler, Goff & MacCoun, 2015 for review).

ADULT VIEWS OF LEGITIMACY

While our focus on legal socialization leads us to be concerned with the development of legitimacy in childhood and adolescence, we can look for clues about how legitimacy develops in the large literature on adults. This work indicates that subjective procedural justice judgments are a key influence on a wide variety of important group attitudes and behaviors (Cohen-Charash & Spector, 2001; Lind & Tyler, 1988; Mazerolle, Bennett, Davis, Sargeant, & Manning, 2013; Tyler, 2000). Procedural justice has been especially important in studies of attitudes about legitimacy and behaviors such as decision acceptance and rule-following. In the case of legitimacy, people care about the way in which authorities use their power (Tyler, 2011). They want authorities to make decisions in a fair way by giving people a voice, encouraging participation, and being a neutral or impartial observer; at the same time, they also want authorities to treat them fairly by showing respect, being honest, and otherwise behaving in ways that communicate trustworthy intentions (Blader & Tyler, 2003a, 2003b; Leventhal, 1980; Tyler, 2006a, 2011).

Perceptions of whether authorities are making decisions fairly depend on voice and participation during interactions, such as the opportunity for people to explain their situation or tell their side of the story. The opportunity to make arguments and present evidence should occur before the authorities make decisions about what to do. People value having their point of view heard both when policies are being developed, and when authorities implement them on the street or in a courtroom.

People also base their perceptions of legitimacy on evidence that the authorities are neutral in their dealings. Neutrality involves making decisions based upon consistently applied legal principles and the facts of an incident, not personal opinions or biases. Having transparency and openness about the rules and procedures and about how decisions are being made also facilitates the belief that decision-making procedures are neutral.

Additionally, people's judgments of legitimacy are sensitive to whether they are treated with dignity and politeness, and to whether their rights are respected. The issue of interpersonal treatment consistently emerges as a key factor in reactions to dealings with legal authorities. People believe that they are entitled to treatment with respect, and react very negatively to dismissive or demeaning interpersonal treatment.

Finally, people focus on cues that communicate information about the intentions and character of the legal authorities (their trustworthiness). People react favorably when they believe that the authorities are benevolent and caring, and are sincerely trying to do what is best for the people with whom they are dealing. Authorities communicate this type of concern when they listen to people's accounts, and explain or justify their actions in ways that show an awareness of and sensitivity to people's needs and concerns.

Early discussions of legitimacy focused particularly upon voice and neutrality as central factors in people's evaluations. This is consistent with a view of legitimacy being based on decision-making when creating or implementing laws or legal regulations (Thibaut & Walker, 1975). However, subsequent research has made clear that in encounters with authorities, issues involving people's identity and status are equally important (Bradford, 2014; Bradford, Murphy, & Jackson, 2014; Tyler & Blader, 2003). Such relational issues matter because people use their interactions with authority to understand and define their self-concept and self-worth (Tyler & Lind, 1992). Studies suggest that it is interpersonal treatment that is especially central to inferences about self-concept and self-worth (Lind & Tyler, 1988; Tyler & Blader, 2003).

An additional key issue in shaping people's judgments of authorities' legitimacy is boundaries (Huq, Jackson, & Trinkner, 2016; Trinkner, Jackson, & Tyler, 2016). This issue has not been a focus in past studies of procedural justice, but is a clear and important one in discussions of legal socialization. Almost all domains of authority are potentially contestable, particularly during childhood. While individuals will readily concede power to authorities in some domains, they will resist or outright reject all attempts by an authority to control and regulate their behavior in other domains (Darling, Cumsille, & Martìnez, 2008; Smetana, 2002; Smetana & Bitz, 1996; Tisak, Crane-Ross, Tisak, & Maynard, 2000). This becomes especially pertinent as children move out of the family and begin confronting a world of varying and potentially conflicting authorities. They need a framework to identify which authorities are legitimate under which conditions. Thus, an important issue for scholars of legal socialization is to gain a better understanding of the lines along which such boundaries are demarcated and how authority interactions vary within the different domains.

A core issue with any type of authority is what gives one person the right to tell someone else what to do. As developed within a legitimacy framework, legal socialization involves building a sense of personal autonomy from which a person derives the idea that there are decisions which are properly within their own personal space. People struggle with the appropriate boundaries of their own person autonomy all their lives, just as our society seems to balance rights and privileges against obligations in the formal law.

Boundary issues are also central to discussion about legal and political authority given the practical everyday realities of a working legal system. There are usually multiple authorities seeking to gain the legitimacy to make decisions within a particular arena. In law, Congress and the judiciary constantly contest the range of each institution's authority. Congress, for example, passes sentencing guidelines to restrict the authority of judges, while the Supreme Court determines whether congressional decrees are constitutional. Judges regularly make rulings that are overturned by appellate courts. Police make arrests that are negated by prosecutors. The list goes on and on. And at the same time, at every point there is contentious and continuous public debate about where the boundaries of legal authority lie and what is the best institution to handle the issue at hand. Knowing when an authority is entitled to exercise their authority is key to multiple decisions that people make every day when dealing with the law.

LEGAL SOCIALIZATION AND THE ELEMENTS OF LEGITIMACY

The initial adoption of legal attitudes and values which shape judgments of legitimacy is not inevitable. Young people may or may not adopt values, and those values may or may not be supportive. Successful legal socialization (from societies' point of view) requires both that people develop the capacity for consenting to authority, and that they evaluate existing authorities and institutions as being entitled to their deference.[3]

Children begin their lives without such dispositions, and the extent to which they acquire them depends upon a variety of factors including their biological maturity, their genetic dispositions, and their social experience (Augustyn, 2015; Cumsille, Darling, Flaherty, & Martìnez, 2006; Tapp,

1991; Trinkner & Cohn, 2014). Social experiences are of particular interest here because it is in shaping those experiences that society can influence individuals, helping to form their preferences and create supportive citizens.

In later chapters we will explore examples from the research literature which suggest that it is possible to socialize children in ways that lead to the willing acceptance of authority based upon having supportive civic attitudes and values. Whether that occurs depends on the degree to which a child's social experiences conform to one or more of several conditions that lead to the development of supportive attitudes and values. However, the opposite outcome is also possible; there are social conditions that can encourage the development of predispositions reflecting opposition to and cynicism about authority and rules. The attitudes and values that result from legal socialization are found to be related to rule-following, with those who develop more supportive attitudes and values also more likely to obey existing rules and authorities and those with less supportive attitudes and values more likely to break the law.

Legal socialization is complicated because the goal is not that children should simply learn to obey authority regardless of context (Hogan & Mills, 1976; Tapp & Levine, 1974). In fact, in many cases when authorities emphasize the need for pure obedience, children and adolescents reject that authority (e.g., Trinkner, Cohn, Rebellon, & Van Gundy, 2012). An important part of family socialization involves children learning that in some areas they should obey their parents, while in other areas they have the right to make their own decisions free of parental authority (Darling et al., 2007, 2008; Smetana, 2002; Smetana & Daddis, 2002). Similarly, within a legal context it is legitimate to reject rules and authority when they are viewed as fundamentally unjust and immoral. This is something that even young children recognize (Kohlberg, 1963; Tapp & Kohlberg, 1971). So instead of instilling simple obedience, legal socialization through early childhood experiences provides children with an understanding of their interrelationship with authority and rule-based social institutions, an understanding that is shaped by instilling values and developing attitudes.

These attitudes and values, when developed, serve as the framework through which individuals define and understand their relationship with the legal system and lead them to have certain expectations about the behavior of legal authorities. Moreover, this framework also includes reciprocal expectations about how individuals should behave in deference to authority figures, thereby producing a symbiosis between the legal system and the individuals it serves. So long as both sides are abiding by and meeting these expectations for appropriate behavior, then the system functions well. However, when legal authorities do not behave in accordance with these expectations, individuals may not feel compelled to behave in accordance with them either.

It is also important to note that just as the public has expectations for the behavior of authority figures like police officers or judges, those officials also have expectations about the appropriate ways in which the public should respond to their authority (Paoline, 2004). This involves respect for the person, as well as for the role they represent. If individuals do not respond the way legal authorities expect them to, then they may feel compelled to use coercion to gain control of the situation. The police, in particular, may be looking for signs of defiance of authority in young people, which often elicits increased efforts to force compliance (Sherman, 1993).

There are three important dimensions of legal values that define the relationship between individuals and the legal system. The first dimension reflects attitudes and values concerning how people expect authorities to treat them (i.e., treatment concerns). This includes expectations that authorities should treat people respectfully, be honest with them, and show care about their concerns.

The second dimension reflects attitudes and values concerning how people expect authorities to make decisions (i.e., decision-making concerns). This includes expectations that authorities should give people a chance to express their point of view, that they should listen to people, and that people are entitled to an explanation of authorities' decisions.

The third dimension reflects attitudes and values concerning what behaviors authorities are allowed to regulate, as well as when and where that regulation can occur (i.e., boundary concerns). People demarcate their lives into different domains, and recognize that authorities have the right to regulate behavior in some domains but not others (Smetana, 2002). Thus in some areas, people accord authorities the right to control their behavior; however, in other areas, people would not agree that authorities have that right (e.g., lifestyle decisions). There will likely be substantially greater variation between individuals in what they judge as appropriate in the boundary dimension than in the quality of treatment or decision-making dimensions. Boundary concerns underlie many of the most contentious debates about legal policy today (the war on drugs, gay marriage, gun control and gun rights, stop and frisk laws, etc.), with people strongly disagreeing about domains that the legal system can legitimately regulate.

Our point is not to emphasize the contents of these different categories, but rather to call attention to the fact that people readily make these boundary distinctions and that the source of this tendency has its roots in childhood (Smetana, 2002). Some things can be legitimately controlled by legal authority, while other things cannot. The development of this understanding is a central feature of the legal socialization process.

In addition, while specific values can be widely held within a society (e.g., the belief that legal authorities should treat everyone the same), this does not mean they are universal. Although the basic value structure can probably be found in most if not all societies, this does not mean that every society has the same specific attitudes and values concerning the appropriate relationship between the legal system and the citizenry. In other words, all societies have values concerning the way authorities should treat people, how authorities should make decisions, and what domains authorities can regulate; however, *what* those specific values are will not be universal. For example, studies of high-power distance cultures suggest that people in such cultures neither expect to be consulted before decisions are made nor to receive an explanation afterward (Tyler, Lind, & Huo, 2000).

These findings come from studies conducted in China, so it is unclear whether their results reflect high power distance values or the reality that China is not a democratic society. They demonstrate that people can and do learn different models of authority, but everyone does in fact learn *some* model of authority. That model, whatever it may be, is based on their experiences concerning how authorities treat them, make decisions, and respect boundaries.

SUMMARY

Concerns about the decline of institutional trust, especially in terms of the law, are increasingly commanding more attention. In large part this is the result of a legal climate that for the past thirty years has been rooted in deterrence-based policies that frame issues in terms of rational choice theory and instrumental motivation. As we have highlighted in this chapter, regulation based on rewards and punishments can and does work, but is severely limited not only in terms of effectiveness to control crime, but also in terms of economic costs to maintain and social costs to implement. Indeed, the social costs of these policies can readily be seen in the wide disparities in police trust between white and minority communities, the latter of which are much more likely to be on the receiving end of deterrence-based regulation (Trinkner & Goff, 2016).

In response, we suggest that what is needed is a broader framework that recognizes the importance of legal values and supportive attitudes toward producing an effective legal system based on mutual respect between those that govern and the governed. Legitimacy is an essential feature of such a framework. Simply put, the law needs legitimacy. It reflects the justification of the station and function of the legal system as an important social institution. When citizens see the law as legitimate, they recognize its responsibilities as a source of formal social control, acknowledge its right to hold power over individuals within society, and uphold their responsibilities as citizens. Thus, legitimacy motivates people to voluntarily defer to the law and legal authority, unlike deterrence-based approaches that motivate people through force and dominance.

Based on the increased recognition of the importance of legitimacy to good governance and an effective legal system, we suggest that understanding how to implement legitimacy-enhancing strategies is going to become a key issue in legal scholarship in the twenty-first century. Our argument in this volume is that such efforts must take into account the process of legal socialization. Legal socialization is a fundamental issue for understanding the dynamic relationship between the public and the law. It is the process by which people internalize the values and competencies that establish what it means for the law to be legitimate and entitled to obedience. As a result scholars, legal officers, and policy makers can gain valuable insight in how to develop strategies that promote civic virtue by understanding the ways in which people acquire such values and attitudes, and how that acquisition shapes the way they interface with legal authority.

CHAPTER 2

༺ঐ༻

General Approaches
to Legal Socialization

In the previous chapter, we noted the failure of deterrence-based models as a strategy for creating a trusting relationship between the law and the public. And we suggested that a legal system based upon such a trusting relationship was desirable, identifying a problem in need of solution. That problem is how to create legitimacy and a value-based legal system built upon it.

The problems associated with deterrence models have been widely articulated (Garland, 2001; Whitman, 2003; Tyler, 2009). They include the difficulty of creating and maintaining sufficiently salient surveillance systems to deter behavior, the declines of cooperation that occur when people view their relationship with legal authorities as adversarial, and the overall impact of force-based strategies on trust and confidence in the police, the courts and the law. Ultimately, deterrence models have had limited effectiveness in securing lasting compliance and cooperation from the public (MacCoun, 1993; Paternoster, 2006; Pratt, Cullen, Blevins, Daigle, & Madensen, 2006), especially when one accounts for the exponentially rising costs to maintain such a system (Pew Center on the States, 2008).[1]

We argue that a broader approach is needed in which a healthy relationship between the law and the public is based on the instillation of supportive legal values and civic attitudes rather than on instrumental concerns about rewarding law-abiding behavior and punishing law violating behavior. In particular, the law is more effective when it can instill a sense of legitimacy in the population by behaving in ways that activate supportive values and in doing so motivate people to trust, cooperate, and comply. Legitimacy ultimately is a function of the values that are instilled during the legal socialization process. These values provide expectations about how people expect legal authority to behave and delineate obligations that develop when authorities act in appropriate ways.

If the argument is that people internalize values that promote acceptance and deference toward the law, then the logical next question is, what are those values? Early in American history there was an unstated assumption that the United States was a Christian nation, leading to a blurring of legal and moral values. In recent years there has been greater recognition that there are a variety of cultures and religions in the United States leading to a reluctance by government to be seeming to impose one set of values. As Twenge (2006, p. 30) notes:

> The curriculum reflects this lack of a central authority as well. It is no longer enough to teach only the "classics"; these are now known as Dead White Males. Few academics still agree that there is a "canon" of Western literature that all students should learn. Instead, students must take classes teaching a variety of perspectives, in which the works of women and minorities are also covered. Whether you agree or disagree with this "multicultural" approach to education, it's clear that we no longer answer to one definite authority. There are many opinions, and each is considered valuable. Though this has many advantages, it does mean that people will be much less likely to conform to societal rules— after all, which rules would they follow? Which culture or society is "right"? We are taught that none of them is, or all of them are.

Uncertainty about what values should be taught has led to a focus on schools as agents of skill acquisition. Instead of socializing children about potentially controversial ideas involving moral values, the goal is to achieve a consensus that schools should teach math and reading skills.

However, we argue that there are a set of core values that are distinct from moral views about the rightness or wrongness of particular policies and practices. These core values focus on the relationship between the people and formal agents of control (i.e., the law) and how authority and power is distributed to and used by these agents to regulate society. These are procedural rules about how laws are created and used to manage order amid pluralism. They are central to effective and efficient governance in that they promote social harmony, coordination, and cooperation regardless of people's moral stances on particular behaviors. Imparting these "legal" values is the backbone of the legal socialization process.

These values and attitudes are based upon the recognition that society cannot function if people do not accept the role of authority. Similarly, legitimacy is not effective if that authority does not abide by the people's expectations about the appropriate use of power. It is the reciprocity of expectations and responsibilities between the agents of the state and the people that is central to democratic governance. Authorities view deference as a responsibility of the public; the public views acting in appropriate ways and within appropriate limits as a duty of all legal authority. Both authorities and the public have the possibility of disappointing the other and either type of disappointment can undermine the effectiveness of the law in maintaining social harmony.

A TALE OF TWO SYSTEMS

Broadening the framework within which issues of law-related behavior are addressed to include a greater focus upon civic attitudes and values, leads us to ask several important questions: When civic attitudes and values are favorable, how do we best engage them? When they are absent, how do we best create them? How do we encourage the acquisition of desirable attitudes during childhood and adolescent legal socialization? What approach leads to social and legal policies and behaviors that support the legitimacy of legal institutions and authorities by evoking favorable attitudes and supportive values in citizens?

Two contrasting systems are possible, each depending upon a particular model of legal authority. One form of authority that is very basic is the coercive form. In this type of system authorities have power and can use their power to enforce obedience through the manipulation of rewards and punishments, especially punishments. Such obedience is based upon self-interest tied to material gains and losses and, at least in the case of deterrence, requires the ability to monitor behavior. This is because this type of system is maintained by appropriately rewarding good behavior and punishing bad behavior. When the authority is absent or behavior is hidden people cannot be rewarded or punished. Hence, in this system, value-based authority does not carry weight and people do not obey unless there is the possibility of detection and sanctioning. A classic example of this system is the autocratic authority whose directives are immediately ignored the moment they leave the room (Lewin, Lippitt, & White, 1939).

Another form of authority gains the consent of the governed by reflecting the values that society has for defining when someone is entitled to hold power over others and how they are supposed to exercise that power. Basing one's relationship to legal authorities upon legitimacy reflects an ability to deal with authority in a sophisticated way that leads to a more desirable form of legal system. This style ideally leads the public to see an authority as legitimate, and entitled to obedience and deference. Our central argument is that democratic societies depend upon their ability to create this second, more desirable, type of relationship between legal authorities and the population and that legal socialization is the primary manner in which the values that form the basis of assessing such fit are imparted onto citizens.

THE COERCIVE SYSTEM: FORCE AND INSTRUMENTALITY

In a coercive system, people who are authorities tell others what to do and motivate compliance with their directives in an instrumental manner. This system is founded on the use of force to compel people to obey. If authority is exercised by using power, rather than exuding legitimacy, people come to be motivated by implied or explicit threat, or by use of reward and punishments. In fact, the exercise of power in a coercive system is predicated on the display of dominance and control, which can include humiliation or status degradation of those being subjected to it. Under those conditions, people react to their assessment of the power of the authority, rather than on whether that authority is acting in accordance to societal values concerning the way power is appropriately used. At its core, this is authority based upon coercion.

While people are responding to authorities based on their coercive power, they may also make legitimacy-based judgments. They may react to the low quality of treatment they are receiving by making negative motive-based trust judgments, and may develop the sense that an authority is not acting in ways that would lead them to want to have a relationship through which there could be trust. They may also react to the lack of voice and explanation in the authority's decision-making in this same way. Consequently, the autocratic exercise of authority can both undermine legitimacy among those who have a framework for evaluating legitimacy, and lead their behavior in relationship to the authority to be based solely or largely upon cost–benefit calculations.

This coercive style of authority is recognized in most discussions of legal socialization as an initial orientation frequently found in young children, who expect to be directed and shape their behavior primarily by thinking about costs and benefits (Freud, 1930; Kohlberg, 1963, 1981; Tapp & Levine, 1974). It is possible for children to develop this type of relationship to authorities, whether parents, teachers, or the police and courts. If so, their orientation toward rules is consistent with a deterrence model: they obey rules when they fear punishment. Some children do not move beyond this initial orientation as they age, and remain instrumentally-focused as adults. Such a view of law and legal authority is associated with higher levels of criminal behavior in both adolescents and adults given the reality that legal system cannot maintain constant surveillance of all wrongdoing.

While it is clear that rule through coercive power occurs, and that sometimes as Thucydides famously said centuries ago, "The strong do what they will and the weak endure what they must," there are constant reminders that even in power-based relationships people seek to inject legitimacy issues into the exercise of power and that those subjected to power react to those legitimacy issues even while contending with issues of control and dominance (Tyler, 2006a).

A good example is the development of the "rules of war": the ethical rules that govern how soldiers should behave when fighting others. For many people war is the ultimate example of an arena ruled through force, but still even in war issues of appropriateness in the exercise of authority arise (McMahan, 2004). For example, killing people without reasons that people can see as appropriately linked to military goals (illegitimate decision-making) or in especially and unnecessarily cruel ways (illegitimate treatment of and disrespect for the dignity of others) or for reasons that ought to be outside the concern of soldiers such as when the people involved are not enemy combatants, but rather civilian women and children (illegitimate boundaries), is viewed as more heinous and is punished, when the opportunity arises, more severely even when the rules of war are generally governing conduct. Thus, legal values are always in play when it comes to assessing the exercise of authority and issues of legitimacy are never totally absent in any social relationship (Brickman, 1974).

CONSENSUAL SYSTEMS: MUTUAL RESPECT AND LEGITIMACY

For legal socialization to provide the basis for a consensual system of law, young people must both develop a framework of attitudes and values defining ideas of legitimate authority, and within that framework, must have supportive attitudes and values toward legal authority. As we described in chapter 1, this framework is structured around three dimensions of legal values that include issues of quality of treatment, fairness of decision-making, and appropriateness of boundaries. Having the opposite of these experiences can also create values, but values of alienation and cynicism that undermine legitimacy. If individuals simply fail to internalize such values then their only connection to the law must necessarily be based on coercion. However, if individuals experience forms of authority that facilitate the acquisition of legal values, then the law can rely on those values as a means to encourage deference. In this case, individuals are consenting to the authority of the law rather than being coerced through the exercise of force.

The idea of consensual commitments reflects the suggestion that people have a conception of "the right way for a society to be organized" (Flanagan, 2013, p. 12). As an example a key element in legal socialization is the shift from the early adolescent view that government authority should be limitless, to a belief that it is acceptable to question the power and decisions of leaders, and to believe in a sphere of individual freedom and separation from government (Helwig, 1998). In the case of law, there is an increasing cynicism about the normative basis of law as children grow older (Fagan & Tyler, 2005). Adolescents feel that "the fact that a law is on the books does not, in itself, mean that a law is right or just" (Flanagan, 2013, p. 129). The recognition that law and government are not necessarily due their deference means that adolescents must make decisions about whether or not they *consent* to supporting the law and government that they experience in their lives.

DEVELOPING CONCEPTIONS
OF LEGITIMATE AUTHORITY

An interest in consensual authority leads to a focus on legitimacy, which is central to deferring to authority. Legitimacy means that a person believes that it is appropriate and right for some external authority to make decisions about law and legal policy and that they ought to voluntarily follow those decisions, without concerns about reward and punishment (Tyler, 2006b). Legitimacy is found to be the core judgment about legal authorities that supports law (Jackson, Bradford et al., 2013; Tyler, 2006a).

There are other values (e.g., moral values, social norms) that can also promote support of the law, but those are rooted in factors external to legal authority. Morality is linked to nonstate authority, for example religion, and to the individual judgments of right and wrong that are linked to these other values. Social norms are linked to the views of family, friends, neighbors, or others in the community. And legitimacy is linked to the operation of state authorities. Hence, one challenging problem for children, adolescents, and adults is deciding when to defer to which external authority. And as a sense of self with personal autonomy develops, a person can simply follow their personal conscience, which will of course reflect the residues of socialization more generally.

Legitimacy reflects a consensual relationship between the people and legal authority in that people readily accept the law's possession of power in society. Without legitimacy that relationship will likely depend on coercion and force to motivate the public to defer to the law. As we argued in chapter 1, there are a number of gains for the system when it is consensual and based upon legitimacy. In short, legitimacy creates a superior form of legal system made possible by developing a trusting relationship, in which people believe that their needs and concerns are being taken into account by benevolent and sincere authorities that are trying to do what is best for those over whom they are exercising authority (Tyler, 2009).

Most children evolve beyond their initial instrumentality stage and develop conceptions of legitimate authority based on their values about the proper relationship between the people and agents of the law (Tapp, 1991; Tapp & Levine, 1974). To develop a framework of legitimacy, children must have a conception of what makes an authority or institution legitimate. This conception is based on the legal values they internalize concerning the appropriate role for the law in society as a source of formal social control.

We suggest that the three key issues already outlined must be addressed: What is the range within which an authority can legitimately act? What characteristics of decision-making lead rules and decisions to be legitimate? What types of treatment by authorities are associated with legitimacy? Using their evolving conceptions of legitimacy, children then have a framework through which to determine whether the particular rules and authorities they deal with are legitimate, and ought to be obeyed.

In a consensual system, young people need to develop a view about what legitimate authority is, so that they have a way to determine when others are appropriately exercising authority over their behavior. Is the person or institution that is giving directions or making rules entitled to direct the behavior of others? Are they doing so within a sphere where they have a right to be acting? And are the actions they direct others to engage in reasonable and appropriate within the framework of shared community values? These questions are moot if the relationship is grounded on instrumental terms, since in that case, people are reacting to threats or incentives. But before they are willing to voluntarily defer, people evaluate the authority they are dealing with through their framework for understanding what legitimizes and thereby entitles someone to tell them what to do.

BOUNDARY CONCERNS

People put limits on where and when authorities have a right to exercise their power, and ask whether authorities are respecting those boundaries of their position (Huq, Jackson, & Trinkner, 2016; Smetana, 2002; Trinkner, Jackson, & Tyler, 2016). No authority is allowed to wield power in all cases at all times for all behaviors. In some instances, particularly where a sense of personal jurisdiction is strong, individuals even reject the right of an authority to make or enforce rules. When an authority tries to impose rules in such cases, individuals will be less likely to recognize their legitimacy, regardless how fairly that authority makes decisions or treats people. Trespassing on the part of the authority will only serve to erode trust rather than build it. Range matters. For example, people who will accept their responsibility to fight and die based upon a person's command may rebel at the suggestion that they make that person coffee. It is not the magnitude of the potential commitment that matters. It is whether that commitment falls within a domain where it is appropriate to accept the decisions of authority.

Connected to the concept of appropriate range is the issue of conflicting authorities. As children develop, they increasingly recognize that the questions of who is entitled to exercise authority and when they are entitled to exercise it are important (Tapp & Levine, 1974). Among adults, issues requiring judgment to be made about conflicting authority may occur between church and state. With children, conflicts can occur between different parents, or between parents and teachers. Just as an adult has to decide to which authority they will defer in such conflicts, children too have to learn how to make these decisions. Moreover, there is continuity in the legal socialization process (Tapp, 1991). The decisions we make during childhood to resolve such conflicts has a direct influence on how we understand our relationship with the law as adults.

FAIRNESS OF DECISION-MAKING

Another important issue that informs our perception of the legitimacy of an authority is how that authority is using the authority inherent in their position of power to make decisions as they work to create, implement, and enforce rules (Fondacaro, Brank, Stuart, Villanueva-Abraham, Luescher, et al., 2006; Thibaut & Walker, 1975; Tyler, 2006a). There is wide variation in the manner in which authorities make and implement rules, and there is no single, common feature that shapes everyone's conception of the proper use of authority.

Some authorities make decisions without discussion or explanation, while others consult, share power, deliberate, and explain. Again, in the case of decision-making, people develop expectations about what characteristics are associated with legitimacy. Should an authority provide an explanation for the rules they create? Do they need to involve others in joint efforts to decide what the rules will be? Is it best to create rules that affect everyone equally? To what degree should an authority's decision be shaped by their own personal preferences and biases?

There are examples of authorities that rule autocratically, without shared participation or explanation. However, those authorities are generally not considered legitimate, and so need to credibly threaten punishment or promise reward to gain compliance with their rules (Beetham, 1991; Lewin, Lippitt, & White, 1939). It is often possible for authorities to regulate order in this way, although this can be a more costly and less effective model for social order than one based upon consent. It is also incompatible with a democratic system of government.

FAIRNESS OF INTERPERSONAL TREATMENT

An additional concern affecting judgments of legitimacy involves whether people feel authorities are treating them appropriately as people and members of a community when rules or decisions are made or are implemented (Lind & Tyler, 1992; Tyler, 1997). Each individual has status as a human being and as a member of a community, which carries entitlements about quality of treatment. In political communities there are formal conceptions of appropriate treatment, which are expressed as rights. Everyone who is a citizen is entitled to dignity and respect from their community (Tyler, 2006a).

Belittling or humiliating treatment, in particular, is inconsistent with the expectations that people have about how they should be treated by authorities, both as a person and as a member of a group, organization, or community. For example, the United Nations *Universal Declaration of Human Rights* addresses the rights to which all human beings are inherently entitled, including the right to treatment with dignity. When people have an expectation of this or any other right as an entitlement of their membership in a group, not receiving it raises questions about the legitimacy of an authority or institution.

Discussions of legal authority often relegate quality of treatment issues to a secondary status. The law is frequently defined in terms of decision-making procedures. However, studies of people consistently find that quality of treatment issues are central to their reactions to their experiences and in defining their relationship with society (Jackson, Bradford, et al., 2013; Tyler, 2006a; Tyler & Huo, 2002). The reason that people care about quality of treatment is that many connections to authorities and institutions are relational in character (Tyler & Lind, 1992). This means that people's identity and their feelings of status and self-worth are linked to their position in society.

Parents, teachers, police officers, and judges—as authority figures regulating behavior— all communicate information about standing and status through their actions. When they fail to respect someone's rights they communicate messages of exclusion (Tyler, 1997, 2011; Tyler & Blader, 2003). Equal rights are a hallmark of democratic societies and equal standing is associated with social harmony in groups. So lack of respect for a person's rights suggests that they are not fully included in society. They are marginal members and lack equal standing. When authorities fail to respect personal status they send signals of a marginal position in society. People's status is reflected by politeness, courtesy, and treatment with dignity on the part of others, especially authorities. When people do not receive those types of treatment it suggests that they lack status within their group. Such disrespect undermines identification with society, which is central to viewing authorities as legitimate and deferring to them.

The centrality of respect to group membership is illustrated by a study on group deviance. Huo (2002) asked people to react to a group that espoused opinions they disagreed with in a university context. They could respond in three ways: by denying the group material resources, by denying them procedural rights, or by treating them disrespectfully. The study found that people regarded denial of respectful treatment as the most serious harm that could occur. Denial of material resources was the least serious harm. This study demonstrates experimentally what is repeatedly found in surveys: disrespect by police officers and judges has the strongest negative impact upon people dealing with those authorities (Tyler & Huo, 2002).

EXPERIENCING CONFLICTING APPROACHES

So far, we have presented two different approaches to legal socialization, one emphasizing compliance in response to coercion and the use of force, and the other emphasizing deference through consent and the promotion of legitimacy. Although we have presented these two systems as distinct and independent, it is likely that they are not as cleanly separated in the real world. We do not want to give the impression that people either exist within a coercive system or a consensual system. In actuality, people encounter many different types of authorities throughout their life experiences, each of which can utilize coercive or consensual tactics based on their internal dispositions or the situation at hand. Indeed, nowhere is this more true than during adolescence, when youth are surrounded by different authorities from the moment they wake up to the moment they go to bed.

Each of these authorities is likely to use different styles to enforce their rules. As we will discuss in later chapters, the interplay of different types of authorities is an essential feature that propels the legal socialization process. However, because legal socialization is dependent on experiences with many authorities, it is likely that children will encounter both continuity and discontinuity across these different authorities in terms of the styles and approaches that are used to regulate behavior and enforce control. This could involve differences between parents; among teachers, or in varying encounters with legal authorities. Or it may involve a disjuncture between spheres, as when a child raised using physical discipline encounters a teacher who tries to manage authority through discussion and reasoning, or a child who is accustomed to reasoning and explanation from their parents suddenly being treated in a forceful and domineering manner by a teacher or police officer. If coercive strategies are more likely to lead to the rejection of legal authority and consensual strategies are more likely to produce consent and deference, then the question becomes, how do people reconcile these two qualitatively different experiences when it comes to understanding their relationship with the law?

An example of this issue of discontinuity can be found in the way in which people, especially children and adolescents, learn about the law. Young people are presented with two different perspectives. One is the formal civics education that people learn in school and through government pronouncements and the speeches of leaders. Another is the reality of their everyday interactions with legal authorities. In minority communities these two sources of information commonly conflict (Justice & Meares, 2014). In particular, law enforcement strategies of control and dominance convey a message of distrust and social marginality that leads to popular distrust of the law and legal authorities (Carr, Napolitano, & Keating, 2007). Such treatment differs from the promises of rights and respectful treatment that make up the bulk of formal civics education.

The idealized vision of law presented in the type of formal education found in civics classes can clash with the reality of law enforcement on the street. For example, consider a recent essay on raising a black son. The author notes that "we teach our son to respect authority," but also that we teach "lessons passed down from our parents: if you are stopped by the police, keep both hands in plain sight on the wheel, respond respectfully and make no sudden moves" and "we are teaching [our children] to fear law enforcement officers" (Maltais, 2014). While legally people are entitled to question officers and refuse to answer questions or allow searchers, in reality people almost never do so (Kessler, 2009).[2] Their idealized vision of what they might be entitled to do differs from their pragmatic sense of what can be done.

One challenge during legal socialization is integrating these two levels of understanding of law: the idealized and the experienced. We will consider this issue in part by contrasting formal ideals versus informal realities which often differ, sometimes in dramatic ways. Youth must reconcile the ideal of democracy and rule of law which they learn in their civics classes with the discordant realities of how authority is often exercised without reference to either of these ideas. For example, if a youth told a police officer that the officer was not legally entitled to search them, he or she would most likely immediately experience a sharp clash between law in civics books and law on the street. Nor is this limited to experiences with the law. Children often experience some legal and nonlegal authorities as authoritarian and directive, offering little opportunity for understanding, and tinged with disrespect and hostility (Carr et al., 2007; Humes, 1997; Straus & Donnelly, 2001). On the other hand, they often experience other authorities that are benevolent and caring, encouraging participation and discussion, showing mutual respect and understanding. Of particular interest to us, is examining how such mismatches influence legitimacy judgments and behavior, especially in legal contexts.

Fundamentally, this challenge emerges throughout the legal socialization process because authorities vary in their use of coercive and consensual approaches. A child who is raised in a democratic home managed with a consensual approach utilizing discussions and explanations or has been in a school that is focused upon helping children develop models of civic leadership may find their first encounter with a police officer surprising. Being treated as a suspect who might be dangerous and who needs to be dominated and controlled can be upsetting and create fear and resentment. That child might be surprised, for example, to have the police officer approach them with their gun drawn or by being told to lie down on the street with their hands out when they are not violating any laws.

Conversely a child raised through physical discipline and authoritarian parenting may be confused in school when asked to be involved in discussions about why rules exist or when expected not to use physical aggression and the threat of force toward classmates to resolve disputes, for example by bullying them. In both cases these conflicts put a person in a situation in which their accustomed frameworks for understanding authority and rules are thrown into question. For example, children raised by authoritarian parents value power and use it when dealing with their peers by bullying (Knafo, 2003).

BEHAVIORAL CONSEQUENCES

As we document throughout this volume, studies demonstrate clearly that the civic attitudes and values that children and adolescents hold shape their behavior toward authorities and rules both immediately and through their lasting impact during adulthood. A key focus of much of the currently available research is on delinquency and the values of children and adolescents are clearly implicated in their self-reported and externally measured criminal behavior. Of course, such behavior does not appear from nowhere and studies show a trajectory from childhood interpersonal aggression to school bullying and school rule infractions to contact with formal legal authorities and a potential for incarceration for juvenile crimes (Moffitt, 2007). This pattern then forms a framework for adult behavior.

The opposite trajectory, and the one most common within our society is the development of favorable civic attitudes and values early in life which supports rule abiding behavior in school and law-abiding behavior in society and leads to an emergence in adulthood as a person who trusts and supports the police, the courts, and the law and feels a responsibility and obligation to defer to the law and cooperate with the legal order. The feelings of safety and reassurance that flow from these dispositions supports not only compliance with the law but also engagement in society and its institutions, leading to personal success and to support for the well-being of one's community (Tyler & Jackson, 2014).

This is the legal socialization success story and the story behind viable and flourishing democratic societies. Of course, not everyone experiences this success story. Variations in race, social class, income, and neighborhood all shape the actual nature of each person's socialization experience. These differences aside, one of the most important findings of the research that we will highlight throughout our discussion of legal socialization is that above and beyond such differences coercive systems usually become associated with rejection and alienation from authority, while consensual systems promote acceptance and social cohesion.

SUMMARY

A viable democratic society needs two things: First, it needs a population which has internalized the values that lead to a certain amount of loyalty to the ideals of law and government. Second, it needs a government that is upholding and respecting those values and principles that are deemed important by society. These two criteria are better met with a consensual approach of legal authority than a coercive one. As Mansbridge (2014) suggests, coercion alone is not enough for effective governance; there needs to be "legitimate" coercion. She notes that "less legitimate coercion throws sand in the cogs, the system begins to grind more slowly and less well, and the product becomes more expensive—sometimes too expensive to compete" (p. 11). Our argument here is that society works more effectively when the population has the supportive attitudes and values that are instilled during the legal socialization process and the need for coercion is minimized.

Legal socialization minimizes the need for coercion, legitimate or otherwise, because it leads to a populace more supportive of and cooperating with the legal system because they want to, not because they are being forced to (Tyler, 2006a; Tyler & Fagan, 2008). Gibson (2004, p. 289) similarly suggests in a "political system few resources are more coveted than political legitimacy. Legitimacy is an endorphin of the democratic body politic; it is the substance that oils the machinery of democracy, reducing the friction that inevitably arises when people are not able to get everything they want from politics. Legitimacy is loyalty; it is a reservoir of goodwill that allows the institutions of government to go against what people may want at the moment without suffering debilitating consequences."

People are not born holding these attitudes and values. Rather, they need to develop them during the preadult years, and experience a system of government that behaves in a way that embodies them during adulthood. Although they are socialized to accept the need for authority and rules in order to have a functional society, they are also socialized to expect a certain type of relationship with the legal system. People learn that authority must involve attention to the views of the public, who need to believe that legitimate authorities listen to, consider, and take account of their views and their needs. Unless people think that authorities are doing these things, they are unlikely to view them as legitimate and to defer to the decisions they make and the rules they create. Thus, their acceptance of legal authority is contingent on whether legal actors are wielding their authority in appropriate ways. This is the basis of a consensual system: to utilize power in ways that leads others to consent and voluntarily defer to authority.

Our focus throughout this volume will be on showing the benefits of using a consensual approach of authority. In particular, we will suggest that a consensual approach is more desirable because it promotes voluntary deference and willing cooperation with the law and the actions of legal authorities by establishing their rightful claim to hold power and wield authority. In Part II we will make this argument by reviewing the different models that have been proposed to explain the legal socialization process. In Part III we will show the benefit of consensual authority across a range of different authority types.

CHAPTER 3

༒

Legal Socialization across
the Life Course

In studying legal socialization, we will adopt a life-course perspective to help frame our understanding of how the socialization process unfolds. This perspective views legal socialization as central to development where law-related values, attitudes, and competencies are formed and refined over a life time in response to the interplay between natural maturational growth and an ever-expanding and increasingly complex social environment. This framework considers change over time from the perspective of balancing forces of continuity against the possibility of change.

This approach has been quite useful in studying related areas (e.g., political socialization, Hess & Torney, 1967; Sears & Brown, 2013). In another example, criminology has used a life course perspective to map the occurrence and desistance of criminal behavior across different ages and life events (Laub & Sampson, 2003; Sampson & Laub, 1993). While such work is useful to our discussion here, our approach will examine the emergence of legal values, attitudes, and behavior both within and outside of the legal world.

There has been a long history of using a life-course framework to better understand legal socialization (Hogan & Mills, 1976; Tapp, 1987; Tapp & Levine, 1977). Legal socialization is not a static process, but rather is continuously shifting. For one, people constantly change, especially early in their lives, a process that is only compounded and accelerated as they encounter a wider variety of rule systems and forms of regulation. Nor is the legal system itself stationary, but rather necessarily changes with the ebb and flow of time as new issues emerge and old issues fade away. From the social upheaval in the 1960s and 1970s to the rise of the drug war and calls for community policing of the 1980s and 1990s to the technological breakthroughs in a post-9/11 era, the legal system as continually changed its goals, approaches, and strategies (Reiner, 2010; Sklansky, 2005, 2006). As a result, it is only natural that how people relate to the law as a social institution—the very essence of the legal socialization process—will also shift and change over time.

This approach raises several interrelated core issues about how and to what degree legal socialization occurs throughout the life cycle. One important issue is whether children develop an initial orientation toward rules and authorities that persists and shapes later relationships with other authorities. For example, to what degree does experiences with parental authority shape the way in which people expect to behave with teachers during adolescence or legal authorities during adulthood? How is this initial orientation subsequently molded or changed as individuals experience other types of authority that exercise their power in similar or different ways?

A second issue to emerge from the adoption of a life course perspective is the degree to which there are distinct features at each life stage in terms of how individuals typically understand and define their relationship with authority. For example, young children have particular difficulty conceptualizing abstract ideas and legal principles. Rather than viewing their relationship with legal authority as about rights and reciprocity where authorities are supposed to respect their rights and they are supposed to follow the law, they tend to view the relationship in unidirectional and instrumental terms (Tapp & Levine, 1974). Legal actors are seen as absolute, free to make laws and rules and enforce them as necessary. As a result, children follow rules and obey authority because they understand that authorities are in a position to punish them. However, these features generally—but not always—fall away in later years, only to be replaced by other outlooks that are more nuanced and sophisticated.

Another important issue concerns the role and importance of critical periods. Are individuals more or less open to change during particular developmental periods? When are those periods, and how long do they last? Psychologists argue that most socialization occurs during childhood (Grusec & Hastings, 2015). Furthermore, adolescence is widely believed to be an especially important period for legal socialization because it is a time when adolescents are trying to understand their place in the social environment and also a time when they are most likely to have their first contact with the formal legal system (Tapp & Levine, 1974). As a result, much of our focus throughout this book will be on adolescence. While psychologists view these years as crucial to the development of predispositions, they also emphasize that emerging cognitive, neurological, and biological features and limits mean that at any given age a child or adolescent has limited capacities relative to a mature adult (Grusec & Hastings, 2015).

A fourth important issue concerns the domains of different authorities. If legal socialization is a lifelong process that begins during early childhood, then this means experiences with nonlegal authorities and rule systems are also a source of legal socialization, given that the vast majority of individuals do not explicitly encounter tangible representations of the law until later in life (Levine & Tapp, 1977; Trinkner & Cohn, 2014). Indeed, as we will explain in later chapters, there is a tremendous amount of research showing that encounters with nonlegal authorities during childhood and adolescence facilitate the acquisition of legal values, formation of law-related attitudes, and development of legal competencies. We choose to focus on three domains of authority that are particularly salient in terms of legal socialization: parents in the home, teachers in the school, and legal authorities in the juvenile justice system.

A final issue concerns the transition into adulthood. During this time, people evolve from being the targets of legal socialization (children, adolescents) to being the agents of socialization (parents, teachers) (Luong, Rauers, & Fingerman, 2015). How do legal values, attitudes, and capacities change during this transition? Although our attention will be focused on childhood and adolescence, we also recognize that to some degree legal socialization occurs throughout the life cycle (Tapp, 1987). If legal socialization drives the way in which people understand their relationship with authority, then it is likely that such an understanding will go through some type of a shift when people become adults and are no longer the subject of authority, but rather find themselves being an authority (Tapp, 1991).

HISTORICAL SHIFTS ACROSS GENERATIONS

A life-cycle approach recognizes that development occurs within a unique cultural environment of historical events. This approach considers legal values, attitudes, and reasoning as they develop, grow, and change across the life cycle, while recognizing that such development occurs in the framework of generational development, with each generation being uniquely shaped by cultural and historical events and their own collective values.

In addition to these life-cycle influences, the large literature on generations suggests that the particular events—such as wars, natural disasters, and economic catastrophes—experienced by a common age group create a distinctive orientation toward rules that persists over time (Alwin & McCammon, 2003; Leisering, 2003). Irrespective of whether we are talking about baby boomers or the millennial generation, we recognize that each era produces children, adolescents, and adults of distinctness. Our argument is that these events will necessarily shape the way people think about their relationship with the law. After all, many of the most important historical events that emerge explicitly or implicitly relate to issues of the law and legal system.

Inevitably for each generation, there always seems to be a particular image or representation of the law that emerges in popular culture. From Rockwell's "The Runaway" to Bull Connor's dogs in Birmingham to the beating of Rodney King to the current policies of stop-and-frisk, mass surveillance, and unmanned drones, each generation's experiences with the law have undoubtedly influenced the way in which they define and understand their relationship with the legal system and police officers. Part of the challenge and intrigue of studying legal socialization is not only identifying these historical shifts, but also capturing how they are influencing individuals as well as society at large. As researchers, the difficulty lies in not only being able to identify those historical events that created similar experiences for a group of individuals, but also separating those individuals from other groups of individuals who had a different set of experiences.

THE CASE OF THE MILLENNIALS

A good example of how historical events can shape the way an entire generation relates with the law is the current millennial generation (roughly those born from the early 1980s to the early 2000s). Millennials have grown up in a heavily policed world that has seen a dramatic increase in the use of force and punishment to combat crime and other social problems (Fagan, Geller, Davies, & West, 2010; Goff, Epstein, & Reddy, 2013; Kraska, 2001) and the encroachment of legal authority into traditionally nonlegal domains (e.g., the school, Arum, 2003; Mukherjee, 2007). In large part, this only got worse after 9/11. After the terrorist attacks, significant changes were made to the law (such as passage of the Patriot Act) and legal policy (the emergence of the War on Terror). These changes fundamentally changed the relationship between the criminal legal system and the public. Of course, everyone in our society experienced these changes, but millennials experienced them at a time during which their attitudes and values concerning their relationship with the law were being initially formed.

Many of the abstract ideas that people held about the appropriate exercise of authority shifted in the context of the belief that America was at war. This is not a new phenomenon, as every era of war has brought forward the idea that leaders must exercise authority in ways inconsistent with traditional democratic processes. In the civil war Lincoln put dissenters in jail; during World War II Roosevelt interned Japanese Americans; post-9/11, the government began a broad program of preemptive surveillance. However, unlike Lincoln and FDR, the post-9/11 War on Terror has not had an end date, and so none of these things that changed how people related with the law have concluded (nor likely will they anytime soon). On the contrary, the United States seems to have entered into an era of perpetual if undeclared war against vaguely defined enemies who are "terrorists." This war has justified a number of modifications in traditional law, allowing unprecedented levels of surveillance and control, much of it autocratic and nontransparent.

Research suggests that such changes in social conditions, in particular instability and threat, shape law-related views. For example, using National Election Study data from 1992, Feldman and Stenner (1997) found that societal threats increased the desire for authorities to use harsh punishment and to support order and security over freedom and liberty. More broadly, Stenner (2005) used General Social Survey data collected between 1972 and 1994 to demonstrate that the strength of the impact of support for coercive authority on punitiveness (e.g., attitudes toward capital punishment) and for lowered support for the democratic principle of civil liberties is shaped by the instability of social conditions related to societal threat, especially normative threat. She concluded that societal threats lead to a rise in authoritarianism and support of leaders that "prove to be relentlessly sociotropic boundary maintainers, norm enforcers, and cheerleaders for authority" (p. 32). The desire for authority is important because it leads to attitudes such as the support for the aggressive use of military force (Herzon, Kincaid & Dalton, 1978; Kam and Kinder, 2007; Barker, Hurwitz, & Nelson, 2008; Hetherington & Weiler, 2009). Such results support the speculation that events such as the 2001 terrorist attacks on the United States might be particularly likely to provoke an influence of the desire for strong authority on policy decisions.

Of course cohort differences are usually not tied to a single distinct event. Rather, they represent a progression of experiences that slowly change the relationship between authorities and individuals. This more general process of change can be seen in how the current millennial generation has responded to the explosion of technology over the last twenty years. Already a number of changes in technology have pressed society's understanding of laws and authority, as well as its relationship with the law. From issues about pirated software and illegal downloading of music and movies, to questions about privacy rights in a world of social media and cyber mass surveillance, it seems that there is an endless stream of new technologies that are forcing society to reevaluate what is the appropriate role and scope of legal authority.

These are all issues and questions that earlier generations have not had to face at such a young age. One wonders how this generational cohort that views these innovations as second nature and integral to their lives will respond to and defer to laws that are created and enforced by authority figures that are not accustomed to participating in this online world.

Further, not everyone in any given generation faces the same challenges or has the same experience. During WWII German immigrants faced hostility and discrimination; today, Muslim children experience distrust. At other times Asian immigrants, Irish Catholics, or other groups were viewed with particular suspicion. Just as there are cohort effects across generations, within each generation some groups have had particular types of experience with society and law.

Not all such challenges are linked to a particular period of time. Throughout our history African Americans have consistently been the target of policing and incarceration in a variety of forms, as have Native Americans. For these groups a legal socialization experience of marginality has been long-term and continuing.

Potential generational effects can also be seen in the millennials in terms of the changing nature of the legal climate in schools that have been brought about over the years as court rulings increasingly give children more rights (Arum, 2003). For example, children have won the right to due process when they are facing suspension from school. This includes knowing the school's rules prior to the infraction, a detailed notice of the charge against the child, an explanation of the evidence, and a hearing where the child can tell their side of the story. At the same time there has been an unprecedented surge of law enforcement presence in schools, coupled with coercive styles of authority and zero-tolerance policies (Arum, 2003; Hirschfield, 2008; Mukherjee, 2007; Rios, 2011). In some respects this transition was in response to the increased legal rights afforded students, which implicitly assume that school infractions and the regulation of them are legal matters subjected to legal principles. Where behavior was once regulated and handled within the purview of school administrators, now individuals are being brought into the criminal justice system for infractions that occur in school. The often more informal discipline of administrators is replaced by the more formal processing by legal authorities.

This evolving legal climate has led to changes in children's legal consciousness for all future generations of children that go through the educational system. In particular, it has served to make school authority less absolute by placing heavier restrictions on the ability of school authorities to infringe on students' rights. As a result, the relationship between students and school authority has changed. However, this change was not sudden, as was the case in 9/11, but rather a more gradual change that has occurred over many years. This generational change in school authority occurred within an overall climate of declining authority support for most social institutions and for national government (Gallup, 2015; Smith & Son, 2013). In general those children socialized at later times have experienced authority at a time when institutional authority was more openly questioned and less willingly accepted and obeyed.

Discussions of younger generations echo this theme of declining institutional legitimacy by arguing that people are becoming more focused upon friendship networks, preferring transitory and peer-based relationships (Pew Research Center, 2014b; Shore, 2011). They are more mistrustful of institutional loyalties and often show a lack of respect for traditional hierarchical authority. This does not necessarily mean disrespect for the idea of authority, but rather for a style of authority that expects deference simply because of its position. Younger generations seem to be rejecting that notion and supplanting it with the idea that obedience and deference is earned. Authorities need to build credibility through their behavior in order to be followed rather than relying upon age or position as a symbol of authority. Credibility is built by acting in accordance with the way society expects authorities to behave and make decisions.

A key issue in this discussion is isolating where this declining institutional legitimacy is coming from. On the one hand, it may be that younger generations truly have a different set of values concerning the appropriate role of authority. Because they have a different set of values, they define their relationship with authority differently. Subsequently, authorities are no longer viewed as appropriate because their behavior and policies no longer fit with these new values. On the other hand, it may be that values about the appropriate use of power by authority have not changed in younger generations. Instead, the young may have changed their beliefs about whether existing authorities match those values. In this case, the declining legitimacy is more an issue about whether institutional authorities are still upholding societal values about the proper way to exercise power.

A NOTE OF CAUTION

Irrespective of whether all members of a generation shape a set of common legal values, the point is that the larger environment within which a cohort is socialized changes their general concerns and impacts upon their attitudes and values. Legal socialization is not simply what happens within a particular family, school, or juvenile justice system. These systems are affected by larger events and additionally people experience these larger events as part of the society to which they belong. For example, young people who are not Arab Americans are not the target of antiterror surveillance and infiltration of youth groups, but they are influenced by the climate within which the police engage in these activities (Sunshine & Tyler, 2003a; Tyler, Schulhofer, & Huq, 2010).

An illustration of the problem of separating age from cohorts is presented by the data from the European Social Survey.[1] People in the survey were asked about the importance that they placed upon "following rules" and "behaving properly and following traditions and customs." When the sample was broken down by age it was found that the proportion of people holding these values changes across age groups. In the case of following rules, for example, 31.1% of 14- to 16-year-olds said following rules was important; 26.2% of 17- to 18-year-olds said it was important; 28.2% of 19- to 29-year-olds; 32.7% of 30- to 41-year-olds, 35.4% of 42- to 53-year-olds; 40.0% of 54- to 65-year-olds; and 50% of people over the age of 65. Similar results were obtained for other questions. There were clear differences in which older individuals were more likely to believe it was important to observe laws and social norms than younger individuals.

What are the implications of this finding? It would be tempting to infer that as people get older they are increasingly likely to view following rules as more important to their sense of self, with the ages of seventeen to eighteen reflecting the time when people are least likely to endorse this value. This would support the argument that adolescence is a time of particular instability with regards to legal socialization. However, it must be recognized that in this analysis age and cohort are confounded. The older people interviewed have lived through different events and may be different because of those events, and not due to age. For example, many of the older European respondents were young during the cold war period with some actually living in or near the Soviet bloc, factors that might have heightened their belief that following rules is important (Finckenauer, 1995; Gibson, Duch, & Tedin, 1992). It is always difficult to separate out the particular experiences of a generation from people's age.

EVOLVING ORIENTATIONS TOWARD THE LAW

A core question in legal socialization is the degree to which there is an evolution in a person's general orientation toward rules and authorities over their life course. Generally, it is suggested that the early years of life are central to establishing the basic values, attitudes, and capacities for processing information from later life experiences (Renshon, 1977; Sears, 1975). People might not be willing or able to change once they reach adulthood. This suggests that early legal socialization experiences likely persist later into life. As a result, however their orientation to authority during childhood will remain with them throughout adulthood. On the other hand, even if people can change in response to new experiences, those experiences will still be interpreted to some degree through a framework of legal competencies that was established early in life.

In this regard, early legal socialization experiences will persist into adulthood as a sort of lens through which people see and react to the world as they grow older. While we would not argue that such experiences become crystalized to the point that they cannot change, we do acknowledge that they strongly shape later legal behavior and attitudes during adulthood because they experience these later events through the framework of the attitudes and values they already hold. Indeed, our argument is that early socialization experiences impart a set of values on individuals concerning their expectations about the behavior of authorities, their decision-making, and their recognition of boundaries. These values then act in concert with attitudes and competencies as a lens through which people interpret their direct and vicarious experiences with legal authorities as adults (Cohn & White, 1990; Tapp & Levine, 1974). Given this focus, much of our emphasis in this volume is on examining how attitudes and values emerge and morph during early childhood and how those changes subsequently orient individuals to an increasingly formalized and complex set of rules.

The evolution in children's' understanding of rules changes its focus during their life as the nature of the rules and authorities that are most central to their lives changes. Over the life cycle young children move from having the primary authorities that are central to their lives be their parents, and the primary institution they are involved in of the family, to a broader view of authority. Later children become more heavily involved in school and in their interactions with teachers and peers. During the transition into adulthood, as people become increasingly engaged in their community, they deal with legal authorities such as police officers and judges.

As the range and formality of the rules that a developing child deals with enlarges, children have to face an increasingly complex set of issues about rules. First, they have to reconcile issues of divided authority. They deal with parents, teachers, peers, and legal actors such as police officers. Each has some claim to authoritativeness, and children have to decide when to defer to each type of authority. Further, with all authorities children have to manage their growing sense of autonomy and the concept of rights against obedience. They have to determine when they are entitled not to obey.

As children develop they also become more aware of issues of discretion. Authorities have flexibility when implementing rules. A parent can excuse a child who takes an extra cookie, just as police officers ignore many minor crimes committed by juveniles. Such discretion can be viewed as either an appropriate or an inappropriate action. Central to legal socialization is the development of a conceptual framework for evaluating these everyday actions of legal actors.

However, as individuals age their views of authority become more complex and abstract, especially during adolescence (Adelson & O'Neil, 1966; Adelson, Green, & O'Neil, 1969; Tapp, 1991; Tapp & Levine, 1974). During this time adolescents begin to interact with many different types of authority figures. They come to understand that there is a larger social world around them, and that they are only a piece of that world. These experiences change the way they define their relationships with authority figures.

Adolescents are no longer content with allowing authorities to control all of their behavior. Instead, they begin to exert their autonomy, to test the boundaries and the limits of both governmental authority and state power (Casey, 2015; Emler & Reicher, 1995). They may be particularly likely to rebel against rules or authorities' directives. This includes laws, but also family and school authorities. It reflects the general tendency of adolescents to engage in unconventional and illegal behavior involving a wide variety of mostly minor infractions of rules and laws but some potentially more major types of transgression, including the use of drugs, shoplifting, and vandalism (Moffitt, 1993).

This is also a time for adolescents to refine the values and attitudes that were initially formed during childhood. Given their increased likelihood of coming into conflict with various authority figures, individuals experience different modes and styles of authority. This provides an opportune moment to make comparisons between how they think authorities are supposed to treat them and how they are actually treated. In essence, they are trying to come to grips with what they want, what they should have authority over, and what external authorities want and should have authority over. Who should be allowed to decide what is acceptable under different circumstances? It is these comparisons that then lead to judgments about the legitimacy of external authorities.

As adults, as is true of children, individuals are especially likely to be imbedded in a stable framework of family and work in which their environment is generally composed of people who share their preexisting values. Hence, there is typically less change during this period in terms of core values about the role of the legal system. On the other hand, it is clearly possible that people can have important personal experiences with the law and legal authorities that can potentially have drastic effects on their attitudes and perceptions of legitimacy.

Further, the legal system itself is not static, but rather it continuously changes over time (Reiner, 2010). The result is that people also continue to evaluate its policies and laws in terms of whether the legal system is behaving in accordance with their values concerning the proper role of the legal system in terms of its relationship with citizens. While the values that are instilled during childhood and reinforced in adolescence likely remain stable during adulthood, the degree to which people see the law, its policies, and authorities as legitimate may potentially change as police behavior changes (Trinkner & Tyler, 2016). Indeed, there have been times in this country where at least some citizen's views of the legal system were quite negative, such as during the civil rights movement or following the Rodney King beating. Today we can see backlash against police policies like stop and frisk or concerns over police adopting mass surveillance strategies of mostly law-abiding citizens.

These historical periods in which people had negative views of the legal system as illegitimate do not reflect instances where Americans suddenly had different values about the appropriate behavior of police and the legal system. Rather, the tactics and policies being implemented (in other words, what legal authorities are actually doing "on the ground") are clashing with societal values about the way police officers and the law are supposed to interact with citizens. In other words, it is often the case that Americans' values concerning what legitimacy is do not change, but rather legal policy and procedure changes and clashes with existing values. Authorities do not act in ways that accord with the principles reflecting the basis for popular legitimacy.

It is also important to note that people's concerns about legal authority or not just personal or group-based. If the white adult population believes that minorities are treated unfairly by the police, their sense of legitimacy goes down (Tyler & Fagan, 2008). If the non-Muslim population believes that the police mistreat Muslims, their views about police legitimacy decline. People, in other words, judge the police in terms of their actions toward everyone in the community, even when unfair actions are unlikely to touch them personally.

EVOLVING DOMAINS OF LEGAL SOCIALIZATION

As individuals age, they deal with issues of authority in a series of different spheres or domains. These experiences are vital to their developing a conception of how they interface with authority and rules systems and what is appropriate within that relationship, both in terms of their responsibilities and the responsibilities of the authorities. Early on children deal with a relatively small number of authorities, typically with whom they have a long-term relationship and strong emotional attachment. These early foundational experiences can either be reinforced by later contacts with different authorities from different domains or they can clash. In either case, the important thing is that in each stage of their evolution children are presented with the challenge of learning how to relate to rules and authorities in a different context.

What domains are the most important? We identify three important contexts: the family, the school, and the legal system. As we will detail extensively in Part III, interactions with authorities in each of these contexts impact the development of legal values and competencies, as well as engagement in both positive (e.g., participation) and negative legal behavior (e.g., delinquency). Additionally, these contexts are dynamically related. For example, parenting shapes children's behavior in educational and legal contexts (Hoeve et al., 2008, 2009; Parker & Benson, 2004). On the other hand, schooling has traditionally been viewed as a way to socialize citizens so that they exemplify the values needed for a healthy democracy to survive, like deference to the law and legal authorities (Campbell, 2006; Dewey, 1916). As children grow and move through adolescence into adulthood, these different domains of life are experienced both sequentially in that parents are encountered first, then teachers, then the legal system and simultaneously in that children still interact with their parents after they encounter school authorities and so forth.

As children and adolescents evolve through a series of phases of learning about authority each is characterized by a system of authority which has particular features based upon its context. The first is the family. Children's first experience with authority comes through their interactions with their parents and siblings. Parental authority involves a long-term relationship with authority figures with whom the child has an emotional connection and upon whom they are strongly dependent.

Of the various type of experience that people have with authority, their initial experience with their family is most likely the most important. It creates a framework for authority dynamics within which (or against which) all later authority systems are integrated. Parents are the authorities with whom a person has the longest relationship; they are the ones with whom children are typically the emotionally closest, and they are the first authorities people experience. Family dynamics are pivotal to later rule relations and authority dynamics.

When they begin school children must learn to adapt and manage their relationships with authorities with whom they do not have a long-term personal or emotional connection or a close familial bond. Although they may have a single teacher for an academic year, they will likely switch to another the next year. In most cases, they will retain little if any contact with the prior teacher. As children progress in the educational system, they will begin to take more specialized classes and experience contacts with different teachers in any given day, not to mention other school administrators. These contacts introduce children to the idea of impersonal authority and to the concept of institutions. Here the power of the authority comes from their role within the institution, rather than their relationship with the individual.

For the first time in school, children are interacting with authorities whose role is linked to a particular environment or location. Prior to this, parents were able to exert their authority to some degree across all of the situations a child was in and over time. However, during school children begin to understand that despite their ability to shape behavior on school grounds, teachers have little authority over behavior when children are not at school (Laupa & Turiel, 1986, 1993; Tisak, Crane-Ross, & Maynard, 2000; Yariv, 2009). They begin to realize that the range of the responsibility to obey an authority can be limited to particular domains or situations. Beyond those domains they are free to make autonomous decisions. This will have important ramifications concerning their values about what types of behaviors authorities are allowed to control and when such regulation is acceptable.

Typically, people first come into direct contact with legal institutions and authorities during adolescence. Contact with these types of authorities is different from prior experiences. In most cases, these individuals will be acting within an institutional capacity. Adolescents will likely have no prior contact with them, not know who they are, not have a long-term contact, nor will they establish some type of bond. Instead, they will probably have a single encounter in which some problem or conflict is resolved through the exercise of formal procedures after which both the individual and the authority will go their separate ways. In many cases, these contacts can then initiate other contacts with other institutional authorities, such as social workers, that will follow a similar trajectory. In each case, individuals have expectations about how these authorities should interact with them. The nature of these expectations is powerfully shaped by the values, attitudes, and competencies imparted on them in prior experiences with parents and teachers.

This progression of evolving domains of authority suggests that issues concerning the management of authority and rules changes in a variety of ways from childhood to adolescence to adulthood. As they age, individuals have to deal with more remote authority figures. Instead of developing long-term bonds, these relationships increasingly are with strangers or people they barely know. Authority also becomes gradually more impersonal over time. This is especially pronounced within educational contexts. Rules and institutions slowly begin to replace people. As a consequence, dealing with the concept of rules and authority relations increasingly requires one to balance issues of autonomy and rights against obligations to authorities and judgments about their character, motives and intentions.

CONSENT VERSUS COERCION REVISITED

In the last chapter, we outlined two general approaches to legal socialization: the coercive and the consensual. In particular, we emphasized that consensual systems are more effective in developing the type of attitudes and values that are central to creating positive relationships between citizens and legal authorities that are based on legitimacy and mutual trust. Throughout this volume we will compare these two systems across each of the three domains highlighted above. We argue that within each domain, young people can experience two competing models of authority: one that can create frameworks for understanding legitimacy and support the development of positive attitudes about authority and rules, and another that serves to undermine attitudes and value development by wielding power in domineering and forceful ways.

As we will demonstrate later, consensual approaches are more effective across each of the three authority domains we examine. Exercising authority in this way serves to internalize a set of values through which people can understand and evaluate authority rules and decisions and in doing so evoke voluntary compliance and cooperation so long as those rules and decisions are being made in appropriate and legitimate ways. Irrespective of whether the issue is parenting practices (Trinkner & Cohn, 2014), school climate (Resh & Sabbaugh, 2014b), or patterns of interaction with the police (Fagan & Tyler, 2005), the courts, or incarceration programs (Buss, 2011), studies demonstrate clearly that supportive civic attitudes and values are shaped by childhood and adolescent experiences and that consensual systems of authority lead to the incorporation of those attitudes and behaviors into the child's own framework or identity.

Unfortunately, there are strong cultural traditions within the United States in favor of directive models of authority, despite the compelling evidence for the value of consensual and legitimacy-based authority. The idea that using strict and harsh discipline leads to law-abiding behavior has deep roots within American culture and can dominate thinking about how to manage disruptive children. This can be seen across parenting, educational, and legal contexts. A substantial minority of family dynamics are found to be heavily directive, and sanction-based strategies such as spanking are widely used (Straus, 1991). Schools often adopt strict rules and harsh punishments in efforts to manage order (Arum, 2003). And the criminal justice system has become increasingly punitive in its orientation toward juveniles (Slobogin & Fondacaro, 2011), with programs such as "scared straight" and incarceration boot camps being popular (Petrosino, Turpin-Petrosino, & Buehler, 2004; Vignati, 2011).

However, research consistently highlights that strict and punitive discipline actually has the opposite effect in relation to its goal of promoting rule-following. Harsh parenting leads to mistrust, rejection, and antisocial behavior (Hoeve et al., 2008; Straus & Donnelly, 2001). Harsh zero-tolerance policies in schools actually do not manage order effectively or efficiently (Arum, 2003; Kupchik, 2010). Punitive criminal justice programs increasingly are being found to be counterproductive in that they make people's relationship with the law more antagonistic and adversarial (Aizer & Doyle, 2015; Stoudt, Fin,e & Fox, 2011–2012). Rather than producing individuals that respect and trust authority figures, these approaches actually serve to delegitimize these institutions and create youth that function outside of these formal and informal social control mechanisms (Petrosino, Turpin-Petrosino, & Guckenburg, 2010). Whether the authority is a parent, teacher, or police officer, a punitive and demeaning interpersonal style coupled with inconsistent, harsh, and physical discipline does not motivate the adoption of supportive attitudes and values toward rules and authorities, and is associated with a variety of types of undesirable behaviors including interpersonal aggression, bullying, school rule infractions, and illegal behavior.

SUMMARY

A full understanding of the legal socialization process is only possible with the incorporation of a life course perspective. Our basic argument is that children evolve through a set of distinct-but-interconnected authority systems (family, school, legal authority) as they undergo common processes of cognitive, neurological, and biological development. On the other hand, these institutions do not all operate in the same way, and across these three authority systems any given child can have very different socialization experiences. In particular, their experiences vary in terms of the degree to which they are coercive or consensual. Every child has both common and unique socialization experiences.

Further, on a macro level the process of legal socialization is not static. Trying to understand the socialization process is complicated by the reality that children grow up in a particular era, and their socialization is shaped by societal and cultural changes within the overall society. Every generation has a common set of experiences that differ from those of other generations, but are common to a particular cohort.

However, despite recognizing the dynamic nature of legal socialization and its inherent complexity, we will show throughout this volume that certain consistencies emerge. A healthy and effective relationship between the law and public is most likely to arise when people internalize supportive legal values and attitudes and when the legal system acts in accordance with these values. The legal values that frame one's relationship with the law concern issues of quality of treatment, fairness of decision-making, and appropriateness of boundaries that are imparted on individuals as they mature.

PART II

Models of Legal Socialization

Our goal in this part of our discussion is to examine the different theoretical perspectives that have been used to explain the legal socialization process. In large part, this field has been dominated by two prior literatures. The first is concerned with the mechanisms that drive the internalization of values and formation of attitudes. This outlook is largely rooted in social psychology and learning. It emphasizes the interactions that youth have with social institutions and authorities as a means to acquire notions about what are appropriate and inappropriate legal behaviors. The second perspective is concerned with evolution of reasoning and the cognitive abilities that enable abstract thinking. This outlook is rooted in cognitive developmental psychology. It emphasizes that people naturally acquire more advanced cognitive abilities which then fundamentally alters the way that they view their relationship with the law.

In addition, we will consider research on neurological development and how general biological and cognitive growth during childhood and adolescence can put limits on their understanding of the law, legal procedures, and appropriate legal behavior. Although such an area has not been incorporated within prior discussions of legal socialization, we include it here for two reasons. First, legal socialization has always in some respects been tied to biological development and maturation (Tapp & Levine, 1970); however, that association has been given only cursory insight. Second, neurological research has had a tremendous impact on the legal system over the last fifteen years as it has challenged many of the notions upon which the juvenile justice system is founded (Scott & Steinberg, 2010). We include a discussion of neuroscience and youth development here in that hopes that it will spur others to integrate this work into legal socialization scholarship.

In the ensuing chapters we will look closely at the literature on the mechanisms of attitude and value socialization, as well as the literature that examines the evolution of reasoning and the cognitive abilities that enable abstract thinking. The first of these literatures is concerned with the taking on of values that are initially not part of a developing child's value system, but which become part of the self during the legal socialization process. Value incorporation is linked to work inspired by Freud (1930) and Durkheim (1973). This research is primarily concerned with whether or not young people take on the values that help society function.

Another line of research within this literature addresses the development of supportive attitudes through the study of the socialization of political and social attitudes (Sears, 1975; Sears & Brown, 2013). This research examines variations in the favorability of the attitudes that are adopted by young people during legal socialization. For example, it finds that minority children are likely to develop less favorable views about the police, the courts, and the law. The concern in these studies is with the factors that shape the favorability of the attitudes that young people develop.

A second tradition of legal socialization research is concerned with the development of cognitive reasoning and reflects evolving models for thinking about legal authority and the appropriate relationship between the law and citizens. The key idea underlying this literature is that people's ability to understand concepts of authority and rules depends upon their ability to think at particular levels of abstractions. This tradition is associated with Kohlberg (1963, 1981) and Tapp (1966, 1991). The key underlying model is one of an evolving thinker actively constructing, critiquing, and reconstructing increasingly complex views of law and legal authority (Cohn & White, 1990; White, 2001). This effort is not unique to law. Children and adolescents are viewed as seekers of understanding about all aspects of their lives, ranging from the physical to the social world. But they are motivated to develop models that they believe reflect truth and coincide with their lived experiences. They are naïve scientists seeking accuracy and through interaction with the world developing more nuanced and sophisticated models to explain it (Kelley, 1973).

As this discussion suggests, it is important to distinguish between the ideals of law and government and the practicalities of how legal and government authorities manage social order in reality. This distinction makes the degree to which people are active and critical thinkers about the law a fundamental issue within legal socialization. People need to have a model of appropriate authority against which to evaluate the authorities they deal with.

Authors such as Kohlberg (1963) and Tapp (1991) emphasize that children and adolescents are trying to make sense out of the legal world, to understand why there are rules and when and why they should follow them. It is a natural part of social development to seek and to develop conceptions of appropriate authority and rules that will inform that understanding. If people experience existing authorities as departing from their ideals, they may be unwilling to trust them or voluntarily defer to their authority (Jackson, Bradford, et al., 2013).

In contrast, other models of socialization, such as that of Freud, place less weight upon active reasoning and suggest that at least some children adopt social values unthinkingly and without a critical perspective. These models present a more passive view of the child. For example, models of identification emphasize accepting rules to preserve relational bonds, not because of their content.

A new and important literature within legal scholarship concerns biology and neuroscience. This literature emphasizes the limits of the developing child (Scott & Steinberg, 2010). Children and adolescents have limited abilities to control their emotions and make independent judgments. They are not simply miniature adults. Hence, while they may be active seekers of knowledge and may be working to construct ever more complex and sophisticated models of the world, they are also fundamentally limited in their capacities until they become fully functioning adults. How neurological development shapes the legal socialization process is an open question at this time. Our discussion is largely an opening salvo with the hopes that it will promote further inquiry into this important area.

CHAPTER 4

᠕

Developing Values and Attitudes
about the Law

During earlier scholarly eras, an understanding of the processes of legal
socialization was considered central to discussions about law and the
development of legal culture. It was assumed that the effectiveness of law in
a society depended upon the existence of a supportive legal culture among
adolescents and adults (Easton & Dennis, 1969; Hess & Torney, 1967;
Hyman, 1959; Tapp & Levine, 1977). Research on how people develop
the civic values and supportive attitudes that influence their orientation
toward the law are distinctly addressed in the literatures on value socialization and socialization of political attitudes.

VALUE SOCIALIZATION

The degree to which people accept and internalize societal values is an
important area of traditional socialization research. During the formative
years of modern social science, classic social theorists (Durkheim, 1973;
Freud, 1930; Parsons, 1937; Weber, 1968) argued that a central element
underlying the success or failure of modern societies was their ability to
encourage members to widely adopt norms and values, leading people to
place loyalty to the society above the pursuit of their own personal self-
interest. Efforts to inspire voluntary commitment to the goals of society are
important because the "only obedience worth soliciting and maintaining is
one born of love not fear. The [most desirable motivation for obedience]

is not money, legislation, or conscription ... but the people's attachment to their government from the sense of the deep stake they have in such a glorious institution" (Samet, 2004, p. 7). This type of obedience is "freely given and inspired by love of country" (p. 7).

Authors such as Durkheim (1973) and Weber (1968) focused on this issue in the more mundane context of everyday law. They were preoccupied with the issue of managing social order in an era of large nation states, which could no longer be bound together by shared customs and personal relationships. For example, Weber (1968) contrasted traditional authority to a new form of authority more suitable for nation states: rational bureaucratic authority. This type of authority requires people to view often physically remote leaders as legitimate, and suggests that such legitimacy flows from those authorities being perceived to exercise their power justly or in legitimate ways. Such judgments reflect the individual's conception of the appropriate nature and range of a particular authority's power. It is not an accident that national leaders surround themselves with symbols of legitimacy, and emphasize that they are entitled to obedience because they are making decisions and creating rules appropriately—in ways that exemplify societal values concerning the proper exercise of authority. Similarly judges wear robes and sit under symbols of justice, while police officers wear badges and uniforms. All of these classic theorists are united in viewing the ability of a society to socialize loyalty in citizens as central to its viability.

INTERNALIZATION OF VALUES

Rather than focus on the appropriate exercise of authority as Weber did, Durkheim (1973) and Freud (1930) both believed that the key issue in terms of societal viability was the widespread acceptance of moral values among the members of the society. Durkheim referred to the idea of moral solidarity, and argued that the community needed to share common values about right and wrong. Although Freud focused upon the individual rather than on the community; he also emphasized the internalization of moral values. Weber (1968), in contrast, was more directly concerned with the legitimacy of rules and authorities, and so had a stronger legal focus. His concern was with developing the governmental and legal institutions required to allow a capitalist economy and a democratic polity to flourish.

Our own perspective is more in alignment with Weber. As we have noted, moral values are values, like legitimacy, and they are found to influence people's behavior (Beerthuizen, 2013; Blasi, 1980; Hoffman, 2000;

Stams et al., 2006), but they do not necessarily support the law or the state. In fact, in many cases moral beliefs can lead people to reject the laws of the state (Kohlberg, 1963). Weber's views are especially relevant to legal socialization scholars because of his focus on building mutually beneficial relationships between citizens and legal institutions and authorities. People in diverse societies do not necessarily share a set of moral values, although they can share a common understanding that societies work best under a strong rule of law and a common commitment to defer to legal authorities and institutions.

An underlying assumption of these theorists is that value socialization is about the incorporation of societal values into the person's own motivational framework. If successfully socialized, young people take on the personal responsibility for obeying the law and legal authorities, because they think it is the right thing to do. Much of the general socialization literature is about the socialization of moral values, with children accepting societal standards of right and wrong. The legal socialization literature distinguishes itself with its focus on children internalizing societal values about how it should exert its authority through legal institutions to restrict and regulate people's behavior. However, because most illegal actions are also viewed as immoral, these two motivations frequently complement each other in supporting law and legal authorities.

Early psychological research focused upon the acquisition and internalization of moral values. The quintessential approach in this regard is found in the work of Freud (1930). Although he did not specifically address legal values, his insights are still applicable to legal socialization theory. The Freudian approach, which rested on moral values, defined the issue of value acquisition as central to general socialization, and also identified psychological mechanisms through which that socialization occurred.

Freud suggests that there is a fundamental tension between society and the individual. The individual wants freedom, and society wants conformity to societal standards. This suggests a fundamental conflict between a self-interested child and society. Early theorists in the Freudian tradition have argued that children begin their lives acting out of instrumental self-interest (Hoffman, 1977, 2000), while later psychologists have suggested that children are born with at least some innate tendencies toward moral behavior and begin to show signs of moral concerns early in their lives (Bloom, 2013).

Regardless of whether children are born with their core reason for acting being self-interest and are then socialized toward a broader set of social motivations, or born with pro-social tendencies toward empathy and morality that can be built upon, it is agreed among psychologists that children acquire the values that underlie morality during their early socialization experiences (Killen & Smetana, 2015). Research suggests that environmental factors associated with socialization can enhance or degrade such innate tendencies. One key environmental factor is the behavior of agents of childhood socialization (Chang, 1994; Hoffman, 2000). Their actions supplement or undermine the influence of social motivations linked to empathy and virtue (Krevans & Gibbs, 1996).

FROM MORAL VALUES TO LEGAL VALUES

While we distinguish between moral values and legal values, we can examine the development of legal values through Freud's (1930) model of moral value socialization. Socialization in the Freudian model can be motivated in two ways. One way is through the internalization of moral values, in which societal values become personal values, and people follow them because they believe that they are right. Another way is through identification. In the case of identification, people take on values to maintain social bonds, initially with parents and other caregivers. Over time people forget why they follow these values and they become functionally autonomous, which means that the child follows them because they have come to believe that the values are intrinsically appropriate and ought to be followed. They no longer connect the values to the parents and teachers from which they originally acquired them. Overtime these values become their values with their own justification. They become part of a person's identity, and they self-generate negative emotions of guilt or shame when they fail to live up to these standards.

An important point emerging from these studies is that it is not foreordained or inevitable than any given individual will evolve into an adult whose motivations are linked to values. It is possible for children to have experiences that either enhance or diminish the role of values in shaping their behavior (Colvin, Cullen, & Vander Ven, 2002; Unnever, Colvin, & Cullen, 2004). Additionally, to the degree that their behavior is based upon values, children can be socialized to develop either an antisocial, oppositional orientation or a supportive orientation toward existing authorities.

Whatever their innate tendencies, children can grow up to become adults who go through life with positive supportive social values; conversely, they can become people whose behavior is primarily shaped by negative oppositional values. This is both true of social interactions and of people's relationship to the law. And of course they can be individuals who have no values, favorable or unfavorable, and who orient toward authority and rules instrumentally, obeying when the risk of punishment is high and disobeying when it is low (Kroneberg, Heintze, & Mehlkop, 2010).

Studies of the general population suggest that some small proportion of adults lack the ability to reason or to form the type of close attachments which lead to empathy with or concern about the opinion or well-being of other people (Coid, Yang, Ullrich, Roberts, & Hare, 2009; Neumann & Hare, 2008). This group has no mechanism through which it might develop values and therefore lacks the set of internal values that lead to guilt or remorse over actions that are inconsistent with social rules, whether formal laws or informal norms (Blair, 1995, 2005).

Moral development is distinct from legal development, but they can separately and jointly enhance compliance and cooperation when the behaviors involved are immoral as well as illegal. For example, people do not commit murder because it is against the law, and also because they think it is morally wrong. In many situations, societal values and personal moral values converge in supporting common actions, but it is also possible that there may be conflict. For example, in the United States abortion is legal, but many people consider it immoral.

There are also cases in which societal rules make behavior illegal, but some group in the public does not consider it immoral; for example, drug use. In such situations, whether or not people obey the law depends heavily upon whether or not the law is viewed as legitimate. In the simplest case morality is viewed by a person as irrelevant. In a more complex situation they may regard the actions dictated by law as contrary to their moral values. For example, in the case studied by Kelman and Hamilton (1989) soldiers were ordered by a legitimate authority to engage in acts that many thought were immoral (in this case killing civilians).

SOCIAL NORMS

Other approaches to value acquisition highlight the role of social norms, and how their expression and maintenance in society can also lead to the internalization of civic values (see Tyler, 2011, for a discussion of this literature). Again, these perspectives are not specifically focused on law or legal institutions, but have the potential to make important contributions to an understanding of legal socialization nonetheless.

Here values are reflected in the customary rules governing behavior in groups and societies (social norms). Like legal and moral values, social norms define appropriate behavior in social situations. However, they are more informal and develop within communities, rather than being imposed through formal structures such as laws. The type of norms that are of concern in this discussion are those linked to internalized feelings of responsibility to others and the group, not rules that are enforced through fear of sanctions.

A key mechanism underlying the desire to follow norms is the desire to have the esteem and approval of other people, in particular one's parents or other significant authorities (teachers, neighbors, coworkers, etc.). Hence, shame—the thought of how other's would negatively evaluate a person—that is often suggested to be the emotional involved in the motivating influence of norms. And, like moral values, social norms generally work in support of the law. However, there are circumstances under which community norms can be apart from or even contrary to formal legal rules.

As an example, in northern American cities snow often covers parking spots during the winter. People who dig out a parking spot may put a chair in that spot to mark it for their own use. The local social norm is that making the effort to clear a spot confers some entitlement to it. While this entitlement is generally recognized within the community, it has no basis in law; by law, parking spots are available to anyone who wants to use them. Therefore, when people defer to such chair placement because they accept the underlying idea of entitlement, they are conforming to a social norm (Silbey, 2010). Of course, people sometimes seek to protect "their" parking spots by extralegal actions such as damaging other cars, which throws personal perceptions of entitlement into conflict with legal rules and authorities. If people follow these norms because they are concerned about the disapproval of others, that reflects norms. If they fear retaliation that is an example of coercion.

Like moral values, social norms are a source of the motivation to obey or disobey the law that is distinct from legitimacy. When the law prohibits behavior that is also disapproved of by one's family or friends, this adds additional internal motivation to a person's decisions to obey the law. On the other hand, the opinion of one's social network can be a factor supporting lawbreaking, as when people act to gain the respect of other's in their gang. Hence, it is again legitimacy that is central to law.

SUPPORTIVE LEGAL ATTITUDES

Research on how people develop the supportive civic attitudes that influence their orientation toward the law is addressed in the literature on political socialization (Hess & Torney, 1967; Hyman, 1959; Tapp & Levine, 1977). This work suggests that children are socialized to have attitudinal dispositions about governance and government institutions, of which the law is a part, and explores the degree to which those dispositions are favorable or unfavorable.

Attitudes are defined by psychologists as general orientations toward people or groups that are both cognitive and affective (Eagly & Chaiken, 1998). For example, a generally negative attitude about criminals combines negative feelings with beliefs, as in the belief that criminals are dishonest. Attitudes are expected to shape behavior, with those who have negative attitudes toward criminals avoiding contact with them, or behaving with hostility when interacting with them.

Our primary concern is attitudes toward law and legal authority. However, we recognize that such attitudes are themselves a product of evolution. Children initially experience informal rules and later as adolescents they deal with more formal laws. Similarly, they first experience authorities in the form of their parents, then their teachers, and later police officers and judges. With these experiences children evolve from dealing with informal rules and decisions to dealing with more formal laws and procedures, and with the decisions of first informal authorities and later formal authorities.

The results of studies indicate that individuals' development of attitudes toward law and legal authorities are not solely dependent upon their interactions within the formal legal system, but are also dependent upon their experience with other more informal rule systems early in their life (Levine & Tapp, 1977, Rios, 2011; Trinkner & Cohn, 2014). Legal socialization is ubiquitous in that there is continuity between the different contexts of family, school, and the community such that interactions with authorities and rules from a variety of earlier (family, school) contexts all serve to shape attitudes toward laws and the legal system (Tapp, 1991; Trinkner & Cohn, 2014). In other words, the way that children learn to deal with authorities and rules when they deal with their parents sets the stage for their later orientation toward school and society.

Early attitudes are also focused upon individuals, primarily parents. Later trust and confidence in formal legal authorities reflects attitudes about such authorities as individuals and over time increasingly about the institutions behind these authorities. It would seem strange to say that a child has an attitude toward the family as an institution, but clearly adolescents and adults develop attitudes toward institutions such as the police. When a police officer steps out of a police car wearing a uniform and carrying a badge, they are a stranger but they represent an institution. In contrast, a community police officer or a school resource officer interacts with people over time which promotes the development of interpersonal relationships. This serves to give the officer a distinct trustworthiness in their community that is separate from citizens' general views about the institution they represent.

ATTITUDES TOWARD AUTHORITY

A second theoretical framework relevant to law is the study of the development of general attitudes toward accepting the directives made by authorities. One important illustration is authoritarianism, a psychological model which defines what people have as their orientation toward authority (Adorno, Frenkel-Brunswik, Levinson, & Sanford, 1950). For someone with an authoritarian personality, obedience toward authorities is viewed as reflecting a general value—that obedience is important. The importance of obedience can be contrasted to the importance of other values, such as thinking independently. Models of authoritarian attitudes ask people how important it is to obey authority and how important obedience is as a value to teach children. These questions can be asked in and of themselves, or in contrast to the importance of other values, often reflected by judgments about the importance of autonomy or self-expression. The core argument is that people learn a general orientation toward authority, and that this orientation shapes their behavior toward legal and extralegal authorities. People with an authoritarian personality would be expected to be more likely to both think it is important to obey and to actually obey all types of authority.

A second attitude linked to authoritarianism is punitiveness, which is the desire to punish those who break rules (Adorno et al., 1950). This attitude expresses one's view about whether and how much to punish people who commit crimes. There are striking differences in people's reactions to rule-breaking, which range from emphasizing the need to punish violators to emphasizing restoration of the bond between the violators and society through some kind of restorative or reconciliation process. The restorative approach is based upon the assumption that the offender has attitudes and values that can be appealed to for change (Braithwaite, 1989: "good person, bad behavior"). The punitive model does not make this assumption and, on the contrary, is often linked to the belief that offenders do not share commonly held values or, in the extreme, may not hold any values (Tyler & Boeckmann, 1997). As a consequence, punishment is regarded as the only mechanism of social influence that could work.

People also differ in how they believe that rule-breakers should be dealt with and punished (Cohn, Bucolo, Rebellon, & Van Gundy, 2010; Cohn &

White, 1990). In the case of law, punishments generally occur after the occurrence of some type of due process of law (for example, a trial). The courts not only enforce this legal order, they also protect people's rights and allow them redress, even against the government. This means that a trial involves efforts to determine facts, but also a consideration of values. Defendants have the chance to speak and to raise arguments and objections. They can seek to mitigate or excuse their rule-breaking behavior. Such procedures take time and limit the ability to swiftly respond to wrongs.

The delays associated with the rule of law are frustrating, more so to some people, and they can be unsettled by the complexities arising in legal procedures such as trials where discussions about what is and can be known, or about the appropriate punishment for a crime. Authoritarians are more likely to endorse the idea of short-circuiting such procedures and trusting the judgments of strong leaders to determine guilt and to implement severe punishment.

ATTITUDES TOWARD DEMOCRACY

Attitudes toward democracy involve shared democratic commitments which shape people's willingness to cooperate with others in society to achieve collective solutions. The key to societal effectiveness is a shared view about what is appropriate as a response to problems or issues that arise in everyday life. For example if someone feels cheated by a neighbor, it is a shared understanding that they do not pick up a gun and confront them. Similarly if someone is a victim of a crime, they do not personally seek revenge against the perpetrator. Society in the United States (as in most democracies) is based on the principle that people seek help from recognized authorities, who follow mandated laws and procedures to determine issues of justice and guilt. People's willingness to defer to legal authority is linked to whether they share this common commitment to the rule of law.

Similarly, people share views about the values that the community and legal authorities should uphold. If the public believes that they have the same sense of what is normatively appropriate for their community as do the courts and the police, then this shared vision motivates cooperation with the legal system (Tyler & Jackson, 2014). The idea of shared values has emerged as a central component of the relationship between citizens and the legal system in recent work on the police. In a study based in the United Kingdom, Jackson, Bradford, and colleagues (2013) articulate the idea of "moral alignment": the belief that the public and the police share core values about community goals and values. More recently Tyler and Jackson (2014) have used this idea to talk about "normative alignment" in the United States. In both cases, the key idea is that people are sensitive to whether legal authorities are exerting power and regulating citizens' behavior in way that conforms to the norms and values within their community.

ATTITUDES TOWARD LEGAL PROCEDURES

Shared attitudes also reflect a commitment to procedures over outcomes. The idea underlying the rule of law is that disagreements and conflicts are resolved through a set of generally accepted procedures. Trial by jury is an iconic ideal in Americans' conception of the legal system and reflects views about how legal decisions should appropriately be made. It embodies a particular set of American values and provides support for the general idea of the legitimacy of the law. If the law follows the rules of law, it is judged to be legitimate (Tyler, 2006a).

An important part of civics education is the development of such concepts as having rights when dealing with legal authorities, being innocent until proven guilty, being entitled to have a lawyer and being entitled to the due process of law (Center for Civic Education, 2010). These concepts then provide a basis for the public to decide whether or not the system is acting fairly in its treatment of people in ways that reflect these ideals. And, importantly, these are procedural ideas, shaping attitudes about how decisions should be made. In most cases, we can never know for sure if someone is guilty, but we can know whether they received due process and a fair trial. A jury trial, as a deliberation, requires people to be willing to listen to and think about the views of others.

DEMOCRATIC ATTITUDES RELATED TO CITIZENSHIP

Another type of attitude is centered on the concept of "good citizenship" in a democratic society, beyond the direct issue of law and obedience to legal authority. A broader analysis of government implicates attitudes toward rule of law and toward democracy as important in the viability of democratic communities (Almond & Derba, 1963; Hess & Torney, 1967; Lipset, 1959; Sears, 1975). Such support goes beyond simply obeying the law, although it certainly includes it. It is particularly important in terms of accepting a role for the law and legal authorities and not supporting individual or collective extralegal actions, in particular violence. For example, when a person's preferred candidate is not elected rioting is not the appropriate response. Similarly, people are expected to participate in the political process in conventional ways such as going to rallies and donating money, and not unconventionally, by burning down the office of one's opponent or harassing and demeaning their supporters. These are affirmative norms of conduct for a democracy. Violent actions may be wrong because they are illegal, but they also more generally violate the common understanding of what it means to be in a democracy: winning by persuasion and seeking willing acceptance.

The political science literature identifies several key attitudes toward the rule of law and democracy: (1) support for pluralism and competitive elections; (2) rights consciousness; (3) support for civil rights and dissent; (4) support for the rule of the people; and (5) commitment to equality of citizens (Almond & Verba, 1963; Dalton, 1994; Gibson, 1996). The general argument underlying the importance of these attitudes is that democratic governance depends upon the norms of democracy being widely held by the population. If they are, then people engage in lawful activities such as competition in elections after campaigns in which all points of views are reflected and respect the rights of minorities to hold and express their views, even when they disagree with those views. Without such civic attitudes democracies do not function well.

There are many attitudes relevant to law and governmental authority. Narrowly conceived, people learn an attitude related to the police and courts, an attitude that influences the acceptance of legal authority. Broadly conceived, they develop a general view of authority and citizenship. Should authorities be unquestionably obeyed, or is discussion and questioning desirable? Are people entitled to an explanation when they deal with a legal authority and do decisions have to be justified? Can they be questioned or appealed? Do people who differ in their views need to work together to establish a consensus in a trial or a community meeting? Is it acceptable for people whose views differ to express and lobby for their views by holding protest rallies? Is it appropriate to determine who governs us by elections, and, if so, should people defer to the winner? All of these types of attitudes are result of early legal and political socialization (Flanagan, 2013). They directly and indirectly shape later attitudes and behaviors as adults.

THE CENTRALITY OF LEGAL SOCIALIZATION
TO DEMOCRATIC VIABILITY

The classic literature on value socialization explores how young people internalize social values, and assumes that the content of the internalization process will be supportive of existing authorities and institutions (Durkheim, 1973; Freud, 1930). The later literature on political attitudes recognizes that attitudes about social institutions taken on through the socialization process can vary in favorability, and considers the factors that lead to supportive or defiant attitudes (Almond & Verba, 1963; Lipset, 1959). How people's values and attitudes shape their relationship to societal institutions and interactions with the authorities that represent them is an additional area of focus.

Many twentieth-century social theorists view the socialization of norms, values, and attitudes as essential to a democratic society. In social psychology a key figure holding this view was Kurt Lewin, who contrasted democratic models of authority to autocratic forms. Lewin argued that the social value of legitimacy encouraged the voluntary acceptance of authority, with the result that people voluntarily accepted directives and followed them irrespective of whether or not their work was under the surveillance of a leader (Lewin, Lippitt & White, 1939).

The underlying assumption in this model is that supportive attitudes and values are important because they lead people to willingly cooperate with authority. In a healthy and viable society, a substantial proportion of the adult population must hold those values. In addition, social institutions must embody those values.[1] It is the match between personal values and institutional values that motivates voluntary deference and willing cooperation. Therefore, attention has been directed to understanding the conditions under which these values and attitudes are acquired and activated.

A focus on the socialization of supportive legal attitudes and values is consistent with models of social evolution, such as that articulated by Donald Campbell (1975). These models suggest that societies can develop a variety of styles of social functioning, some of which are more flexible and adaptive than others. In other words, alternative types of social arrangements are differentially effective in motivating successful forms of social coordination and regulation.

This argument further follows the theoretical reasoning of Lewin in suggesting that the most superior forms of social organization rely upon people's voluntary behavior. In other words, it particularly focuses on *why* people obey the law. As we have noted, the focus on why people cooperate is hardly a new one. In his pioneering book *The Spirit of the Law*, Montesquieu distinguishes societies in which members are motivated by fear from societies in which people are motivated by civic spirit (Shackleton, 1961).

Voluntary behavior in turn requires that the people within a group, organization or society have supportive attitudes and values. They need to believe that they should—and more generally want to—cooperate with authorities and institutions (Tyler, 2011). If societies based upon shared attitudes and values are more viable and effective, then the ability of a society to successfully socialize its members is an essential component of a strong society. In terms of legal socialization, an additional and equally important characteristic is the creation of a social institutions that embody and abide by the shared values concerning the application of power with regards to enacting social control. It is only when a society can create values that are supported by and shared among citizens and the social institutions with which they interact that the self-regulatory benefits of attitudes and values can be realized (Tyler, 2011).[2]

LEGAL SOCIALIZATION AND NORMATIVE ALIGNMENT

Of course, we are not suggesting that democratic societies should simply seek to socialize the value of obedience, nor is that the argument of social scientists like Lewin. Instead, successful democratic societies are based upon a set of shared values, which define what constitutes the legitimate exercise of authority (When is authority entitled to be obeyed?), and the idea that authorities and institutions must abide by those values in their dealings with the public (When is authority acting appropriately?).

The acceptance of rules is based upon the concordance between the values of society's members and its social institutions. A system and its authorities are entitled to obedience only so far as they embody societal expectations about the appropriate exercise of authority. This idea has been labeled "moral alignment" or "normative alignment" to reflect the idea that people are strongly influenced by whether or not they believe that authorities, such as the police and the courts, are motivated by values that reflect those of the community (Jackson, Bradford, et al., 2013). So it is important both that people incorporate a set of shared attitudes and values about law and legal authority, and that the legal system reflects those values through the laws that it enacts and implementation of those laws on the street and in the courthouse. Perceived normative alignment is one element of legitimacy, along with feeling and obligation to obey and having trust and confidence in authorities.

Appeals to values are not only the province of existing authorities. Critics typically appeal to these same values, arguing that existing authorities and institutions do not embody them. For example, in his book *An American Dilemma*, Gunter Myrdal (1995) framed the treatment of African Americans as a contrast to the legal ideals of the United States. The law and society movement developed "gap studies," which highlighted the deviation of the actual operation of legal institutions from the ideals enshrined in legal documents and traditions. Thus, while existing authorities would like cooperation from the public, there is always a question of whether the institutions they represent are aligned with the ideals that lead to their being viewed as legitimate, or whether loyalty to those ideals leads to the need and desire for social change.

The challenge of legal socialization is especially pronounced in diverse settings whose population does not have a common cultural, religious, or geographic ancestry, such as that of the United States. As a consequence, societal institutions need to work harder to build national solidarity and create shared commitment to legal institutions and authorities. Building this solidarity takes many forms: children take civics classes in school, people sing the national anthem at sporting events, flag lapel pins are worn, and national symbols ranging from Mt. Rushmore to the Statue of Liberty are widely featured in the media in association with political events. All of these incorporate or are symbols of the shared values that our society and its legal system are based upon—values like fair treatment, due process, representative lawmaking, and equal opportunity.

In the case of law, the classical architecture of buildings that house our courts, the ubiquitous image of the balanced scales of justice, and even the black robes worn by judges are symbols that serve to evoke and reinforce shared American legal values (Gibson, 2015). These uses of unifying symbols and rituals reflect the recognition that the health and viability of our society is linked to creating national solidarity, and ensuring that the public is aligned with and supportive of existing authorities and institutions.

The benefits of alignment and support through shared values can be illustrated using an example outside the realm of legal authority. Democratic armies are evaluated as superior fighting forces because their soldiers are more highly committed to their cause, and more able and willing to exercise voluntary initiative when fighting (Reiter & Stam, 2002). Autocratically led armies fight in a more regimented and rule-bound way, with soldiers following orders and complying with authorities. Internally motivated soldiers want to win, and exercise their creativity and initiative to do what is needed to best defeat their opponents. It is suggested that this latter motivational approach is the better one from a perspective of military effectiveness. Similarly, societies benefit when they are organized to maximize the degree of self-motivated behavior among citizens.

As noted in Chapter 2, although coercion can work as a social control strategy it is resource intensive and hence counterproductive for societies. And societies are least able to motivate people during times of crisis when the capacity of government to create deterrence threats or provide for cooperation is weakest. Ironically, it is usually during this time that the government is most in need of people's cooperation and support. Take the current climate, for example. Right now the United States has an extraordinary level of national debt (Fisher, 2010); many municipalities and states are quickly running out of money if they have not already (e.g., Borney, Snavely, & Priddle, 2013; Tillman, 2010), and an unprecedented number of people are incarcerated (Travis et al., 2014). Fiscally speaking, regardless of whether deterrence and coercion works, it is impossible to sustain the current deterrence-focused strategy without drastically cutting back on other programs and services.

This argument suggests that the legal system has both superior and inferior types of authority. A culture based on compliance like the type that currently dominates the system today is capable of working, but it typically does not work well. It requires continual surveillance of the population and consistent enforcement of sanctions for noncompliance in order to secure compliance in the rest of the public (Garland, 2001). As a result, it depends on continual levels of gross expenditure and ever-expanding surveillance mechanisms to motivate people to comply. The practical problem, however, is that these exorbitant levels of resources actually secure low levels of compliance at best, providing society a fairly low bang for its buck. And ironically, this system of authority can actually exacerbate the problem of noncompliance because it does not build, but rather undermines, the very attitudes and values that shape and promote law-abiding behavior (Colvin et al., 2002; Kroneberg et al., 2010; Unnever et al., 2004).

An example of this type of argument is provided by Axelrod (1984) who suggests that people can best serve their own interests in negotiation by being initially cooperative. Why? Because they can identify those others in the population who are also cooperative and can engage in mutually beneficial exchanges with them while managing their interactions with people who are competitive. Competitive people, in contrast, compete with others and in so doing turn all their interactions into competitive ones. It is the ability to identify and profit from working with those people who are also cooperatively motivated that leads to overall superior outcomes for the individual—and, we argue, for societies as well.

Of course, in any society not everyone is capable of acting via socially motivated cooperation. As we will discuss later, children can grow up without adopting supportive legal attitudes and values. Such children may best be controlled through the threat or use of sanctions, although these children are in the minority. The majority of children, we argue, grow up to have respect for and to follow the law, so long as the law respects them and recognizes its boundaries. Hence, a desirable form of social organization takes advantage of those who can act on values, but responds to others with force. In this regard, it seems especially pertinent for societies to plan to first treat people in ways that are rooted in values; if people fail to respond to these means of social control, only then should society deal with them via sanctions (Axelrod, 1984; Ayres & Braithwaite, 1992).

Traditionally the goal of law has been to obtain compliance. This restraint orientation is directly linked to values, which are internal factors restraining the exercise of self-interest. However, as the scope of desired actions has moved to cooperation and engagement (Skogan & Frydl, 2004; President's Task Force on 21st Century Policing, 2015), models of motivation in law have increasingly come to resemble those talked about in management. Management models are concerned about how to motivate willing and enthusiastic work behavior from employees. While employees need to be motivated to obey rules, this is only one aspect of what is desirable from a good employee. A good employee needs to be inspired to do what is needed to help their organization succeed. Sanctions, and even incentives, have been found to be inferior mechanisms for motivating such willing and cooperative "extra-role" behavior (Tyler & Blader, 2000; Tyler, 2011).

SUMMARY

Our concern in this chapter is with the content of legal socialization. What is it that people need to have to be able to engage consensually with law and legal authority? First, they have to have feelings of obligation and responsibility to defer to external authority. One of the core questions that people, young or old, ask about others is why they should obey them? Obeying an external authority limits personal freedom and the ability to act completely in terms of personal self-interest. So why would someone do it? This question has preoccupied many social scientists over the years, and as we have outlined, mechanisms of value internalization have been identified and shown to be effective.

Of course, as we have emphasized, for authorities to gain deference they have to fit the framework that people develop for recognizing legitimacy. They have to be legitimate to gain deference. It is not simply a matter of being a particular authority. For example, in the case of the police, an officer can step out of a patrol car wearing a uniform and carrying a badge, but will this mean that they will have authority that is recognized by those they deal with? Of course they also carry a gun, but the point is to look for consensual bases of deference.

Finally, although people may have a conception of legitimate authority, they also need to evaluate the authorities that actually exist in their political and legal world. This leads to favorable or unfavorable attitudes about authorities, institutions, and procedures. If people have favorable, supportive attitudes, then their values lead them to feel an obligation to defer to those authorities if they are acting in appropriate ways.

Ultimately there are two distinct issues. First, the question is whether people have values and are not simply reacting to legal authority in terms of its coercive potential. People can act based upon risk alone, and if they do so because they have no law-related values or see them as irrelevant, then they act based upon gain or loss. Second, if people have values, then the question is whether the authorities can engage with those values. As we have noted, values are a double-edged sword. A legitimate authority can engage them, but an illegitimate authority is harmed by recognition that they are failing to act appropriately. Ultimately the desirable combination is a framework for assessing legitimacy and an authority who, when viewed from that framework, is evaluated favorably.

CHAPTER 5

⌀

The Development of Legal Reasoning

Another important element of legal socialization is the capacity to think and reason about legal issues and the law. Much of the initial work on legal reasoning (and legal socialization) was inspired by Kohlberg's seminal research (1963, 1981) on morality and the cognitive developmental approach to socialization (e.g., Piaget, 1932). Thus, any reader familiar with Kohlberg will likely see parallels in the ensuing discussion. Our purpose in this chapter is not to survey the tremendous amount of literature on moral reasoning or moral development more generally,[1] but rather focus on the role of *legal* reasoning in the legal socialization process specifically. To be sure, these two areas are intricately related (Tapp & Kohlberg, 1971) and references will be made to the moral reasoning literature when appropriate. However, legal socialization, particularly the work on reasoning, has always been distinguished from the moral development literature in terms of content and focus (Tapp, 1991; Tapp & Levine, 1974). As such, our goal here is to take stock of the work specifically focused on legal reasoning as it pertains to the field.

Central to this approach are people's cognitive schemas which contain information about their conceptions of laws, rights, the exercise of power, and the relationship between citizens and legal institutions (Cohn & White, 1990; Finckenauer, 1990; Tapp & Levine, 1974). These cognitive schemas are not static, but rather are transformed over time through natural maturational processes, as well as interactions with the various rule systems contained within everyday social institutions. This reasoning ability provides a means to conceptualize, interpret, and interact with both the formal legal system and other rule-based institutions. In particular, people develop an understanding of their standing as citizens and the position of the law as a source of social control. This serves to add meaning to their relationship with the legal system, both in terms of their own responsibilities and the responsibilities of legal actors as regulation agents. It provides a means to make decisions about when and why people should cooperate with or disobey the law.

A reasoning approach to legal socialization has traditionally focused on identifying variations in the ways people understand the role of the law in society and how this thinking changes over time (Tapp & Levine, 1974). The majority of this work has focused on how such thinking shapes legal judgments about the purpose of laws, how legal authority should be used, and whether people should feel obligated to obey legal institutions. In this regard, the development of legal reasoning is central to legal socialization because it provides a means to make sense of one's sociolegal environment and stimulates the formation of legal attitudes and beliefs (Cohn & White, 1990).

Surprisingly, there has been little work examining the degree to which legal reasoning actually predicts law-related behavior, despite theoretical arguments for such a link (Tapp & Kohlberg, 1971; Tapp & Levine, 1974). However, more broadly, the development of cognitive reasoning capacities has been linked to delinquency and other disruptive behavior (Paternoster & Pogarsky, 2009; Morgan & Lilienfeld, 2000; Scott & Steinberg, 2010). Furthermore, studies of moral reasoning, which much of the legal reasoning literature is based upon, has also shown that more advanced cognitive skills are associated with law-abiding behavior among people of all ages (Bear, 1989; Eron, 1987; Galen & Underwood, 1997; Guerra, Nucci, & Huesmann, 1994; Jurkovic, 1980; Kowalski & Wilke, 2001; Laible, Eye, & Carlo, 2008; Raaijmakers, Engels, & van hoof, 2005; Tisak, Tisak, & Goldstein, 2006), although that association is not as powerful as once thought (Haidt, 2001). For example, Stams and colleagues (2006) report that a meta-analysis of fifty studies finds that juvenile delinquents generally have a lower level of moral reasoning than nondelinquents. They report that "developmentally delayed moral judgment is strongly associated with juvenile delinquency, even after controlling for socioeconomic status, gender, age and intelligence" (p. 697).

REASONING ABOUT LAW

By its very nature, legal socialization is not a passive process. Individuals are not empty vessels waiting to be filled up with values and attitudes.

Instead, they engage with the social world around them, including the legal system. People are active thinkers in that they are continually trying to make sense of their surroundings. This is true of their legal environment as well. During childhood and adolescence, individuals interact with a number of rule-based social institutions across a variety of situational contexts. These experiences serve to develop a more nuanced understanding of their relationship with authorities in regards to their rights and obligations (Helwig, 2006). How they understand their role in regard to the law and the law's role in regard to society provides an important influence in developing and explicating both their expectations of appropriate conduct on the part of legal authorities, and also their own obligations and responsibilities as members of society.

These reasoning capacities are especially important because they represent a way of providing meaning to one's social and legal environment that makes sense of one's lived experiences (Cohn & White, 1990; White, 2001). "Legal reasoning creates a link between one's sense of self and group norms, between one's moral/legal identity and the social environment" (Cohn & White, 1992, p. 109). As we have explained previously, value internalization and attitude formation play a fundamental role in shaping the way that individuals interact and interface with the legal system. It is people's reasoning capacities, however, that allow them to use those values and attitudes to make sense of their legal environment. In doing so, these reasoning abilities can play an important role in making judgments of legitimacy and whether legal authority is behaving in appropriate ways (Cohn, Trinkner, Rebellon, Van Gundy, & Cole, 2012). Law involves rule-based reasoning, and without an understanding of that reasoning, people cannot critically relate to rules and authorities.

While accepting that the idea of the rule of law is central to the effectiveness of the legal system, an equally important part of legal socialization is the development of critical noncompliance (Hogan & Mills, 1976). It is important not to assume that the unthinking acceptance of any rule or decision is desirable. Studies of adults, for example, typically suggest that they recognize that there are circumstances under which they ought not to accept rules or the decisions of authorities (Bocchiaro & Zimbardo, 2010; Kelman & Hamilton, 1989). This recognition can be brought about through the use of critical and deliberative thinking. In these instances it is not only important to have a set of internalized legal values and attitudes, but also the means to understand how those values should be represented within the social environment. This framework tells people whether or not legal authority is behaving appropriately and is therefore "legitimate." Legal reasoning, therefore, is an important component in recognizing when the legal system should be obeyed and when it should not.

Individuals begin to reject legal authority and withhold their compliance when they believe that the legal system, its laws, or authorities are not representing the values upon which individuals base their understanding of and relationship to the system (Jackson, Bradford, et al., 2013). For example, rules or decisions may be deemed illegitimate because the person enacting them is not entitled to exercise authority or does so unfairly (Huq, Jackson, & Trinkner, 2016). This is also the case when the decisions themselves are contrary to principles of distributive fairness, or to moral values defining right and wrong (Sunshine & Tyler, 2003b).

In each case, the essential element driving the nonconformity is the critical understanding that the system or its authorities are not abiding by the values upon which their authority is supposed to rest. Therefore the nonconformity is not resulting simply from pursuit of self-interest, but from criticism of the values underlying the system, the way the system represents societal values, or both. Indeed, even young children understand that in some circumstances it is all right to break a rule (Tapp & Levine, 1974); for example, when one is starving and steals a loaf of bread or if you steal medicine to help a sick family member. Similarly, four-year-old children distinguish the idea of "personal issues" about which they should have freedom of choice from legitimate exercises of parental authority (Nucci & Weber, 1995).

Most adults believe that there are times when it is justified to disobey the law or the directives of a legal authority, and an important part of legal socialization is developing a framework for determining when circumstances support this view. As an example, Kelman and Hamilton (1989) studied a situation in which soldiers were ordered to kill civilians during the Vietnam War. They found widely varying public views about whether refusing an order that was subsequently recognized to be illegitimate was an appropriate action. Some people said that soldiers were not responsible, since a person is obligated to obey legitimate authority. But others used a framework of "just orders" to distinguish the circumstances under which obedience is appropriate.

Beyond the extreme situation of wartime, people generally recognize an obligation to refuse to obey unjust rules or decisions (e.g., Bocchiaro & Zimbardo, 2010). Take, for instance, the civil rights movement during the 1960s. During this time, the legal system was being used to enforce what many people regarded as unfair laws. Their unfairness flowed from their discriminatory nature. Many people recognized that the legal system in this instance was not representing the social norms upon which it was founded, such as equality and liberty for all. In response, they felt an obligation not to comply with the laws or defer to legal authorities.

Despite this noncompliance, most would say their behavior was consistent with a model of consensual legal authority, precisely because the legal system was not representing the values upon which it was founded. These decisions about responding to authority can also be made in response to everyday situations, such as when an adolescent sneaks out of the house because he views being grounded as unjust, or workers go behind the back of a manager whom they view as autocratic and unreasonable. In other cases, they can involve much more consequential events, such as the refusal to follow the commands of a military leader or to be drafted to fight in an unjust war.

Moreover, it cannot be automatically argued that people were defying legal authority out of pure self-interest, as many whites flocked to the hotbeds of civil rights tension even though the injustice involved targeted minorities. As such, legal reasoning not only provides a means of understanding why individuals defer to laws and legal authorities, but also why individuals may decide to reject and resist laws and legal authorities (Cohn & White, 1990; Hogan & Mills, 1976; Tapp & Levine, 1974). And that basis is not the failure of legitimacy. People are not acting out of self-interest. They are responding to legitimacy and the idea of consensual legal authority, but they are applying a reason-based model of legitimacy.

It should be noted that while situations of resistance are important, they do not typify the general experiences people have with the law. Higher levels of reasoning have been associated with less delinquency and crime (Cohn & White, 1990; Morgan & Lilienfeld, 2000; Stams et al., 2006). As we describe below, more advanced forms of reasoning that move beyond simple instrumental concerns foster the understanding that societies work better when people follow the law and accept the legal system as a means to maintain social order, both of which have been shown to motivate willing compliance and support of the legal system (Jackson, Bradford, et al., 2013, Tyler, 2006a; Tyler & Huo, 2002).

COGNITIVE DEVELOPMENTAL APPROACH
TO LEGAL SOCIALIZATION

As has been noted early legal socialization theory has been strongly influenced by the cognitive developmental approach, which has its roots in the work of Jean Piaget (1932) and Lawrence Kohlberg (1963, 1981). This approach assumes that individuals' thought processes are organized into cognitive schemas that produce characteristic patterns of thought. These patterns of thought, in turn, create a lens through which people process and interpret the world around them. These thought processes are a general property of the person, and as a consequence, have a stable influence across situations and over time.

Reasoning capacities evolve as children develop, moving from simple rudimentary patterns of thought to more complex ones, in an interactive process between people and their environment. This process is assumed to largely be driven by natural maturation. As individuals age, their patterns of thought evolve as a part of general efforts to understand the world and create cognitive representations of it that can guide their actions. As they become older, children develop ever more complex thought processes, meaning that they increase their cognitive ability to problem solve, integrate different viewpoints and incorporate more logical, rational, and abstract concepts into their reasoning abilities.

Although the development of more complex cognitive abilities is largely driven by naturally occurring biological events, this progression is molded and shaped by the environment in powerful ways. In particular, the environment continually presents people with new information about their social world. Usually, this new information is incorporated into their existing cognitive structures in a process called assimilation. However, in situations where the information is incompatible, people are forced to modify their existing thought patterns to account for the discordant information. This is called accommodation. From this perspective, a person develops new ways of thinking that are ever more complex, by assimilating and accommodating new information.

KOHLBERG AND MORAL DEVELOPMENT

Piaget's work was largely concerned with the general process through which individuals develop their "pure" cognitive abilities. Kohlberg (1963, 1981) took Piaget's ideas and applied them to the specific topic of moral development. He was interested in how children developed the capacity to reason about moral issues and make judgments about moral behavior. To Kohlberg, the development of this capacity was vital to children being socialized into society and adopting the values that indicate how people should and should not behave in society.

Kohlberg's model assumes that people will behave based upon their beliefs about what is appropriate or inappropriate. As a consequence, the key issue is *how* children make moral judgments and how this process changes over time, as they become adults. The reciprocal process of reasoning back and forth about appropriate rules shapes the child's evolving ability to think about moral questions.

The central element of Kohlberg's model is his articulation of a series of progressively more complex ways of reasoning about morality. These are generally summarized into three stages: preconventional, conventional, and postconventional. A detailed discussion of these stages is provided below, in the context of their extension to legal socialization by Tapp (1991; Tapp & Kohlberg, 1971; Tapp & Levine, 1974). However, a simplified presentation is that preconventional reasoning is motivated by self-interest where moral judgments are largely determined by what will be punished or rewarded. Conventional reasoning shifts to view moral behavior as that which upholds social conventions and norms. Here, following rules is an end it itself because it is recognized that it promotes social order. Finally, more judgments at the postconventional level are shaped be individually internalized principles about justice, ethicality, and equality. Individuals are motivated to engage in prosocial behavior to the degree that it accords with their moral principles.

While Kohlberg's theories apply to moral reasoning, he emphasizes several points relevant to law and legal socialization. First, as children's cognitive abilities grow and became more complex, they are better able to take in multiple perspectives on any given issue. As they are more able to put themselves in other people's shoes, they consequently begin to understand that there are multiple perspectives on any given issue. This accelerates the development of moral reasoning because it forces them to view issues from perspectives that they may not have accounted for, or that may have been incompatible with their previous views. Such social development is central to the ability to understand and support democratic values such as tolerance for undesirable opinions and the need to compromise with others (Miklikowska, 2012; Morell, 2010).

Second, Kohlberg emphasizes that the social institutions surrounding children can accelerate the development of moral reasoning. To Kohlberg, complex moral reasoning is dominated by notions of equality, justice, and reciprocity. To reason at a high level means to think about an issue from the perspective of an impartial observer. To the degree that the social institutions that come into contact with children exemplify these principles of complex moral thought, they can facilitate the development of moral reasoning.

LEGAL DEVELOPMENT

Starting the early 1960s, June Tapp took the core ideas underlying Kohlberg and Piaget and applied them to legal socialization (Tapp, 1976,

1991; Tapp & Levine, 1970, 1972, 1974). More than any other, she helped to ground the field within a cognitive development perspective and helped to distinguish it from other related areas associated with attitude and value socialization (e.g., political socialization and moral socialization). In Tapp's (1991, p. 334) view, legal socialization "overlaps the realms of political and moral socialization, but differs by context (e.g., court), agent (e.g., judge), and topic (e.g., rights)."

However, in drawing from Kohlberg, she explicitly recognized that law and morality are fundamentally intertwined because laws and the legal system are formalizations of the moral principles that define society (Tapp & Levine, 1974). The task of law is maintaining and enforcing societal perceptions of appropriate and just behavior (Tapp, 1987). In this regard, the law serves as a framework that guides how individuals should interact with others, particularly in terms of resolving conflicts. The primary purpose of the legal system is to uphold the moral values and norms of society, and it plays a vital socializing function in teaching individuals the ethical codes of conduct valued by society. To be socialized into the legal system is to understand the moral code embedded within it, as well as the purpose of the system in regulating social behavior within society.

An important goal of research on legal socialization is to understand how individuals come to develop their orientation toward the law and the legal system, and to understand the role they play within that system. Central to this undertaking is examining how people's conceptions of basic legal principles—such as justice, rights, and the rule of law—both form and change over time as people age. However, Tapp and Kohlberg (1971) recognized that moral development and legal development are intricately linked. Laws are based on fundamental moral principles that are embedded within society. Understanding how a person's orientation to the rule of law changes over time is necessarily tied to how their orientation toward moral norms also changes.

SCOPE OF LEGAL DEVELOPMENT

Despite the label of "legal" socialization, individuals' legal development is not strictly linked to the formal legal system and interactions with its authorities (Tapp, 1991; Trinkner & Cohn, 2014). Legal development is both ubiquitous and continuous. First, while interactions with laws, the legal system, and its authorities is central to legal socialization, the precursor of such socialization is learning about the conceptions of rules and authority per se, concepts central to all social systems. In this respect, legal socialization begins long before individuals come into contact with the formal legal system. Experiences with other rule-based social institutions, like the family and school, all reflect general ideas about rules and behavioral regulation and thus are central to learning about the position and purpose of the law within society.

The legal system is one fundamental part of the broader social environment that is made up of many different institutions that are intricately related. Together they functionally create a "network of rule systems that are in practice 'legal' in nature" (Tapp & Levine, 1974, p. 35). In this regard, there is continuity among the many different social environments in which people interact and develop their understanding of rules, laws, justice, and authority. What children learn about exercising power and behavioral regulation in one arena will necessarily shape their understanding in other arenas. For example, when children are reprimanded by a parent for inappropriate behavior or rewarded by a teacher for following the rules, they are in essence being socialized into the legal system in so far as those encounters provide information about how external entities will attempt to control their behavior. Will they explain, discuss, and reason or will they compel using their power and control over resources?

Although legal socialization transpires across the entire lifespan, there are a number of points that have received particular emphasis within the cognitive developmental approach (Tapp, 1987, 1991). The first is when a child begins attending school and has to interact with and distinguish between two separate rule systems for the first time. Children are especially likely to encounter new or different authorities and ways of creating and enforcing rules during this time. The second is during adolescence, when teenagers begin to exert their autonomy and are likely to have their initial contact with the formal legal system. The third is later in life, when individuals move from being the ones socialized to the ones doing the socializing (e.g., become a parent, teacher, or police officer).

ENVIRONMENT AND LEGAL DEVELOPMENT

From a strict cognitive developmental perspective, legal socialization is largely a self-motivated process (Tapp & Levine, 1974). People are predisposed to develop their conception of and orientation to the legal system, and they engage in a continual effort to interpret their experiences and use them to develop increasingly complex cognitive models of the world. This argument reflects the key underlying assumption of cognitive developmental models: that people are naturally motivated to develop an increasingly sophisticated understanding of the world in which they live (Thomas, 2005).

Despite this assumption, the role of the environment also powerfully shapes legal development (Tapp, 1991; Tapp & Levine, 1974). The legal system, much like any other rule system, is designed to help lubricate and facilitate human interaction by formally establishing how people should and should not behave when interacting with each other. Children are more likely to learn appropriate behaviors and how inappropriate behaviors will be handled by others when they interact with the authorities around them, especially as they move into environments not controlled by their parents. These interactions will serve to accelerate or decelerate people's legal development depending on their tenor and quality.

In particular, two aspects of the environment are especially likely to influence the legal socialization process. The first concerns the role of legal poverty (Tapp & Levine, 1974). The ideal of "being poor" in this sense is not defined strictly along monetary lines, but rather in terms of rights deprivation and lack of legal participation that is typically found in areas of concentrated disadvantage, something other authors refer to as having a "legal consciousness" reflecting an awareness of low status and social marginality (Ewick & Silbey, 1998). This definition expands poverty to those individuals who may not experience financial hardship, but nonetheless may lack rights or legal status (e.g., children, prisoners, or soldiers). If people are legally poor in this respect, then their ability to interact with the legal system is severely hindered, resulting in stunted legal development. On the other hand, those who do not experience this deprivation have more opportunities to interact with their legal world, which accelerates the process of developing legal consciousness.

Authority figures are a second source of environmental influence on legal development. Because they are tasked with creating and enforcing laws and rules, authorities serve as the lynchpin of the entire legal socialization process. They facilitate the formation of legal values and attitudes and stimulate the growth of legal capacities by providing a venue for people to acquire, apply, challenge, and refine their understanding of justice, rights, and the rule of law (Fagan & Tyler, 2005; Tapp & Levine, 1974; Trinkner & Cohn, 2014). The ways in which rules are either created or enforced gives meaning to societal norms of conduct (Cohn & White, 1990) and clarifies one's relationship with the legal system (Trinkner & Tyler, 2016).

When authorities interact with people in fair, ethical and democratic ways, the development of legal reasoning is accelerated; when they do not, it is hindered (Levine & Tapp, 1977; Tapp, 1987; Tapp & Levine, 1972). In this respect, the cognitive developmental approach to legal development is consistent with the value- and attitude-based approach that we reviewed in the previous chapter. Discussion, explanation, participation—all of these features of democratic rule implementation are argued to accelerate legal development more generally and legal reasoning in particular (Tapp, 1991). However, befitting the cognitive nature of this approach, there is little emphasis placed on nurturance, benevolence, and respectful treatment that was so central to the discussion in chapter 4. However, the placement of authorities within the legal socialization process fits well with the general outlook articulated throughout this volume.

STAGE THEORY OF LEGAL DEVELOPMENT

As we noted, the development of legal reasoning is premised on people having a set of legal schemas or cognitive structures that contain information about the way they conceptualize rules, laws, the legal system, rights, and responsibilities (Cohn & White, 1990; Tapp & Kohlberg, 1971; Tapp & Levine, 1974). These structures serve to organize their thoughts and knowledge concerning the law. In doing so, they provide a cognitive framework through which people process and interpret their sociolegal environment. Everything in a person's experience is interpreted and given meaning through these legal schemas. This ability to use one's cognitive capacities to organize and make sense of the legal world is the primary function of legal reasoning.

Legal reasoning determines how people both conceptualize legal issues and make legal judgments, thereby giving them the tools to understand the basic principles and values that underlie the legal system (Tapp & Levine, 1974). It provides people with the ability to develop rule-based codes of conduct that help them in gathering information, making decisions, guiding interactions, and clarifying rights and responsibilities within the law and legal system of which they are a part (Tapp, 1987). Ultimately, a fully developed legal reasoning capacity leads to "an ethical jurisprudence, a moral abidingness, a fair or just legal consciousness, for self and society" (Tapp, 1991, p. 332).

There are three levels of reasoning about law. For most people, development follows a sequential trajectory in which their reasoning begins at the first level, moves to incorporate characteristics from the second level, and so forth. However, an invariant sequential progression is *not* a requirement (Tapp, 1991). In fact, this is one of the important ways in which Kohlberg's (1963) perspective on moral reasoning development differs from the development of legal reasoning. Moreover, the stages are not mutually exclusive, another deviation from Kohlberg. People are not stuck in a particular stage, but instead can use multiple modes of thought simultaneously. As people progress and gain the ability to think at more complex and abstract levels, they are still able to think about legal issues using a more rudimentary level of reasoning. Indeed, a hallmark of higher levels of legal reasoning is the ability to think about and incorporate a multitude of different perspectives concerning a particular issue.

In this respect, each level of legal reasoning reflects a different way of thinking about the relationship between the law and people in society in terms of the position and duties of the law and the responsibilities and obligations of citizens. The first level is the preconventional level, where reasoning is primarily structured around compliance with authority. The second is the conventional level, where reasoning is based on issues of conformity to society. The third and most advanced level of reasoning is the postconventional level, which is structured around internalized abstract principles concerning individual rights and justice.

Generally speaking, everyone has the ability to use all three levels of legal reasoning by adulthood. However, the capacity to use higher levels of reasoning is not reflected in the frequency with which each level is used (Tapp & Levine, 1970, 1972, 1974; Tapp & Melton, 1983). For example, in the United States, most adults typically use conventional reasoning when making legal judgments, hence the name "conventional." Few adults use postconventional reasoning on a frequent basis. However, those engaged in postconventional reasoning are still capable of thinking about issues at a preconventional or conventional level. Alternatively, conventional thinkers may utilize postconventional thinking depending on the situation or issue at hand.

LEVEL 1: PRECONVENTIONAL REASONING

At its core, preconventional reasoning is motivated by instrumental hedonism and a focus on external consequences of behavior. This focus is largely expressed in personal and material terms. Individuals using this kind of thinking are concerned about the tangible rewards and punishments that will affect them directly. This produces apprehension and fear, leading to the avoidance of punishment. The relationship with legal authority at this level is sanction-orientated, conceptualizing the law and legal system in absolute terms given its power to create and enforce legal rules. Citizens' obligations in this respect are to follow the law, not because they believe in it or because it is good for society, but rather because not doing so would evoke punishment.

In this sense, preconventional reasoning leads to a general acquiescence to legal authorities, given that they hold absolute power to punish behavior. Not surprisingly, preconventional reasoning is associated with a strong motivation to comply with whatever the legal system dictates, regardless of extenuating circumstances or individual feelings. However, this compliance is contingent on the degree to which people believe they will actually be rewarded or punished for upholding or violating the law.

LEVEL 2: CONVENTIONAL REASONING

This type of reasoning is based on the understanding that the individual is embedded within a larger society or community. Society has norms that dictate appropriate and inappropriate behavior and social roles that embody those expectations. These norms and social roles form the basis of societal harmony and must be upheld in order to maintain social order. As a result, people have a strong commitment to the community. They are motivated to fulfill role expectations and behave like good people "ought to" behave. This level is oriented toward law-and-order. It is recognized that the law and legal system are dictated by social norms. In this regard, one's relationship with the law is driven more by an attachment to society rather than any power that is given to the legal system to enact social control. The law is a representation of social convention and hence should be followed for the good of society.

Obedience and compliance are motivated by personal duty to conform to society by following laws rather than a fear of punishment as is the case in preconventional reasoning. Above all else, social role expectations must be maintained for the betterment of all, even at the expense of the individual. Justice is largely a question of a majority vote, and equality is nothing more than the impartial interpretation and application of rules. Individual rights are viewed as subservient to the group. Often they are attached to one's social role and are easily confused with privileges attached to one's social station.

LEVEL 3: POSTCONVENTIONAL REASONING

Postconventional reasoning is characterized by principled thought and action. Individuals using this level of reasoning understand the role of social norms and values and the need for social order. At the same time, they are more inclined to view the world from multiple perspectives that inform their understanding of the relationship between society and the law. The values of a particular social order can be differentiated from the values and ethical rights of individuals. They are able to recognize that the majority's wants and needs are not always the same as the individual's, and that the former should not necessarily override the latter. This level of reasoning is more advanced in that it uses basic and abstract legal principles—such as the social contract, civil rights, democracy, and mutuality—to guide judgments, behavior, and social interactions.

Postconventional thought conceptualizes the law in regard to legal and ethical principles. Like conventional reasoning, laws are understood to be not the products of unilateral authority dictating to the masses, but rather societal products stemming from democratic participation among members of society to create a set of shared expectations. The legal system is appreciated as a social institution with the task of upholding societal norms through the enforcement of laws, and the importance of following the law as a means to sustain law and order is understood.

However, unlike conventional reasoning, postconventional thought also recognizes that individuals must make their own ethical and legal choices congruent with the principles discussed above. Individuals using postconventional reasoning do not engage in blind conformity to group pressures or legal authorities. Instead, they can differentiate between legal principles and how they are expressed in terms of the concrete laws, rules, and enforcement strategies of the legal system. As a result, compliance, obedience, and participation are largely motivated by these guiding principles, even if it goes against the current social mores of the majority, as expressed through the legal system.

This differentiation is also reflected in how one's relationship with the legal system is understood. Unlike preconventional and conventional thinking, which conceptualizes the relationship in terms of force or social conformity, postconventional thinking is based on consent. Because of its emphasis on legal and ethical principles, postconventional thinkers have expectations about how the legal system is supposed to wield its authority with regard to regulating behavior. When the system meets these expectations, people consent to their authority and recognize their position of power. Postconventional thinking stimulates deference, but only to the degree that the legal system is upholding its end of the social contract.

Ultimately, the development of a fully formed legal reasoning competency leads individuals to form a principled ethicality of law where their thoughts about and interactions with the law are guided by ethical principles of morality and justice (Tapp, 1991; Tapp & Levine, 1974). This principled legality is important to the legal socialization process because it allows for the continual evaluation and maintenance of the legal system. If the legal system is the formal embodiment of society's moral norms concerning the exercise of power for the purposes of social control and order, then having a fully formed and functioning legal reasoning ability allows an individual to continually evaluate that system in terms of whether it is still properly representing those norms. In essence, it gives people the capacity to differentiate between the physical manifestation of societal values (i.e., the legal system) and the values themselves, and to judge whether those two things are in congruence.

IMPLICATIONS OF A REASONING PERSPECTIVE

The cognitive reasoning perspective makes several important contributions to our understanding of legal socialization. An important theme running throughout this literature is the evolving person as an active participant in efforts to understand the law and develop sociolegal schemas which make sense of their relationship to that institution. Because the person is actively seeking to acquire knowledge, all of their experiences are important. For example, children playing together on a playground learn about basic principles of distributive justice through give and take (Damon & Killen, 1982; Rosen, 2014). This area of active interaction is an important counterpoint to instruction from hierarchical authorities such as parent and teachers. It foreshadows the importance of peer groups during adolescence.[2] Even as children, people can actively draw their own lessons from their personal experience and learn about the social world in ways which are outside the formal hierarchies of family, school, and government.

LEGAL REASONING AND LEGITIMACY

The capacity to evaluate the system is an integral part of legal socialization. As we noted in earlier chapters, legal systems are most effective when they are viewed as legitimate by the population (Tyler, 2006a), and when perceptions of their legitimacy come from a sense of shared values between citizens and legal authorities (Beetham, 1991; Jackson et al., 2013; Tyler, 2006b). In addition, legitimacy represents both an evaluation about whether the law and its agents are using their power and station in an appropriate manner and ought to be obeyed and an expression of trust and confidence in their actions. In order for legitimacy judgments to be made, people must have a framework for assessing the appropriateness of legal authorities and their use of power. The capacity to think about the law with regard to its position and function within society provides such a framework.

Given that each level of legal reasoning conceptualizes the relationship between individuals and the law in a different way, judgments about legitimacy should be driven by different factors depending on one's level of reasoning. For example, from a preconventional perspective, the legal system is seen as legitimate because of its absolute position in society to regulate people's actions, through force if necessary. At this level, legitimacy comes from the laws that give the police and courts power to control other people's behaviors. Conventional reasoning, on the other hand, with its emphasis on social roles and societal harmony, would see the legal system as legitimate to the extent that it creates a social order aligned with the majority's expectations about appropriate behavior. Within postconventional reasoning, the legal system is legitimate to the extent that it conforms to the ethical and legal principles that it is founded upon and is supposed to embody, such as humane treatment, democratic participation, and the recognition of civil liberties and rights.

In this sense, postconventional reasoning paints a similar portrait of legitimacy to that of the literature on value internalization reviewed in the previous chapter in that people support the law when they believe it is fair and just, and reject it when it is not (Jackson, Bradford, et al., 2013; Tyler, 2006a; Tyler & Huo, 2002). In other words, their own developing reasoning has led them to conclude that they ought to accept the values underlying law and legal authority. They have thought about and recognized through discussions that accepting these values makes sense and is appropriate. The values are not experienced as being externally imposed. Later we will discuss the associations between reasoning and compliance behavior. Before that, we want to address another important contribution from the legal reasoning literature concerning people's reactions to a legal system when they believe it is not living up to its principles and obligations.

PROACTIVE PARTICIPATION AND CRITICAL NONCOMPLIANCE

One of the most important outcomes of the legal socialization process is the idea that postconventional reasoning can stimulate proactive participation within the legal system through social action (Cohn & White, 1990; Finckenauer, 1995; Tapp & Levine, 1974). If the legal system is failing to uphold the basic moral norms of society, then by extension it needs to be changed so that it aligns with societal moral norms. In this way, postconventional reasoning motivates individuals to try to change the system for the betterment of all. Traditional models of values and attitudes often adopt compliance as their primary and even only criteria. Does the person obey the law? Yet we as a society also hope that people will take action to uphold the principles of the law.

An example of this approach in action is provided by a study of adults. Haan, Smith, and Block (1968) studied the engagement of people in the Berkeley free speech movement, which involved breaking laws. They found that participation in such illegal collective actions was higher among those who were postconventional in their reasoning. Members of this group were more able to justify violating laws than were those motivated by conventional reasoning. In the case of postconventional reasoning, participation was motivated by the desire to oppose laws viewed as unjust. Conversely, participation was high among the pre-conventional because they thought they were unlikely to be caught and punished for breaking the law, but were likely to receive other material benefits.

This study illustrates the way that a model of legal reasoning can provide a framework for understanding issues that are harder to explain using other models. If our focus is on supportive attitudes and values, it is hard to explain how people can know whom to obey or when to disobey. Discussions of authority recognize that people do not view all rules or directives as equally appropriate. But how do they make this decision? Their ability to do so implies that they have some underlying understanding of the idea of rules as social creations designed by humans and potentially flawed.

We can contrast this view to an alternative view about attitudes and values articulated by Kelman and Hamilton (1989). These authors argue that obedience involves the resolution of a conflict between attitudes about competing authorities. Historically, for example, people felt conflict when one authority (e.g., the king) and another (e.g., the pope) disagreed. In that case, two sets of values (the legitimacy of the law and the legitimacy of moral values) were in conflict. They argue that people's behavior was a reflection of the strength of their identification with these distinct legitimate authorities. This view contrasts with that of Tapp because it does not view the issue as being about reasoning based upon one's own values, so much as determining the strength of one's identification with two external authorities and the values they promote.

The capacity to evaluate the legal system that comes with postconventional reasoning has a possibility of ignoring or defying rules built within it. It is widely recognized that the goal of legal socialization is not to create individuals who blindly follow legal authorities or society. Rather, the goal is to create individuals that understand the principles underlying the law, so that they can recognize when those principles call for both compliance and noncompliance. There will always be certain situations in which *not* following the law is the right thing to do. Any complete model of legal socialization must address the emergence of this type of behavior (Hogan & Mills, 1976).

Generally speaking, many protest movements incorporate the violation of laws that are viewed as unjust. For example, the 1960s ushered in monumental social change in the United States precisely because people recognized that the existing laws were not championing basic legal principles of justice and equality for all, and thus should not be followed. Today similar change is occurring in the area of the rights of homosexual and transgender people, who experience discrimination in employment, housing, and marriage laws, because increasing numbers of people are viewing these laws as unjust. The content of contested laws changes over time but in each case a willingness to break those laws is linked to the view that they are unjust, not just to estimate that they can be broken without a risk of punishment. In fact, often the risk of punishment is high but people are still motivated to disobey.

Such critical noncompliance is vital to the health of any legal system in a democratic society. Developing the ability and competence to use postconventional reasoning directly leads to this important attribute of successful legal socialization. And again, it is hard to explain how people can make a decision about when it is appropriate to disobey without some set of underlying principles. Of course, people may not agree. Whether the issue is regulating gay marriage or abortion rights, reasonable people may disagree. This leads to another concept: developing a consensus about how society should respond to disagreements about what is the best way to enact formal social control. People need to both have values and understand the principles behind them. They also need to have the principles of democratic governance available so that they can manage differences of opinion.

Underlying both of these suggestions is the argument that postconventional reasoning provides the individual with a principled basis for standing outside of and independently evaluating systems of law and authority. It is important to recognize, however, that preconventional reasoning also provides such a basis, because people are evaluating the system through a prism of self-interest. The Haan, Smith, and Block (1968) study of the engagement of people in the Berkeley free speech movement also found that participation in illegal collective actions was high among preconventional reasoners too. Both groups were more able to justify violating laws, although they did so for different reasons. Preconventional reasoning led to a motivation by estimates of the likelihood of instrumental gains (making friends, having a good time) or costs (getting caught) from illegal actions. Postconventional reasoning led to protest to uphold the principles behind law.

LEGAL REASONING AND BEHAVIOR

One of the biggest limitations of the reasoning approach to legal socialization is that little attention is given to the behavioral consequences of legal reasoning (Cohn & White, 1992; Finckenauer, 1990; Hogan & Mills, 1976). Underlying much of the early theoretical work is an implicit assumption that psycho-legal judgments cause behavior. The focus is on identifying how people come to make those specific judgments, relying mostly on cognitive interviewing techniques that ask people what they think about the law, its purpose in society, and when it is okay to break laws. For this work, legal reasoning is the outcome of importance, not behavior.

Due to the focus on the development of legal reasoning, few studies have specifically examined its role in producing or inhibiting law-related behavior. Some supporters point to the literature linking higher levels of moral reasoning to lower delinquency (e.g., White, 2001), given the high degree of similarity between Kohlberg's account of moral development and Tapp's perspective on legal development. Indeed, numerous studies support such a link (e.g., Stams et al., 2006), although it is generally recognized now that moral reasoning ability is not the only or even the best predictor of moral behavior (Haidt, 2001). However, Tapp (1991) was adamant that despite their similarities legal reasoning—and legal socialization more generally—is distinct from moral reasoning and development, a position that requires empirical research specifically linking legal reasoning to behavior.

Studies examining a direct link between legal reasoning and legal behavior have found mixed support. Early work by Morash (1978, 1981, 1982) showed that delinquents did not fail to develop more advanced levels of legal reasoning as implied by Tapp and Levine (1974). Moreover, she found no differences in legal reasoning between serious or chronic offenders and first-time offenders. She concluded that lower levels of legal reasoning were not associated with delinquent populations. However, in a sample of Russian boys and girls aged ten to seventeen, Finckenauer (1995) found lower levels of legal reasoning among delinquents compared to nondelinquents. Additionally, self-reported delinquency was negatively correlated with legal reasoning level regardless of sex or delinquency status. More recently, Grant (2006) found a strong negative association between legal reasoning and self-reported delinquency in a large sample of secondary students in Mexico (equivalent to ninth graders in the United States).

Other researchers have attempted to address this issue by arguing that legal reasoning has an indirect, rather than direct, effect on delinquency and law-abidingness (Cohn & White, 1992; Grant, 2006). This work emphasizes that legal reasoning is a mechanism by which societal norms about legal behavior and social control are internalized. Different levels of legal reasoning provide alternative lenses to analyze one's sociolegal environment, which help to form attitudes about laws, legal authorities, and behavioral obligations. Such attitudes connect the abstract and general nature of reasoning to one's tangible and immediate environment, thereby having a stronger effect on behavior.

This argument has found empirical support. In her studies of college students (Cohn & White, 1990) and middle and high school students (Cohn et al., 2010, 2012), Cohn found that higher levels of legal reasoning were associated with less normative approval of illegal behavior, greater belief that such behavior should be punished, and greater likelihood of viewing legal and nonlegal authority figures as legitimate. Further, each of these factors was associated with less concurrent and future illegal behavior. In Finckenauer's (1995) study of Russian youth, the significant link between legal reasoning and self-reported delinquency disappeared once he accounted for attitudes concerning the importance of following the law, the fairness in which laws were enacted, and the degree to which laws were viewed as moral. Although mediation was not tested, legal reasoning was correlated with each of these attitudes suggesting a mediational path (Baron & Kenny, 1986). Similarly, Grant (2006) found that the association between legal reasoning and self-reported delinquency was mediated by felt obligations to obey the law and responsibilities to maintain citizen commitment. He concluded that stimulating the development of legal reasoning was an essential component of creating a culture of legitimate legal order.

OTHER LIMITATIONS OF A REASONING APPROACH

The reasoning approach to legal socialization has other limitations in addition to issues over its equivocal connection to behavior. Because it is grounded in Kohlberg's (1963, 1981) moral development theory, it suffers from some, but not all, of the same problems.[3] Unfortunately, while criticism of Kohlberg has pushed the field of moral development forward to create a more expansive area of study encompassing a range of perspectives and contexts (see Killen & Smetana, 2006), a similar movement has not occurred within the work on legal reasoning. Most, if not all, of the work in this area is grounded in a cognitive developmental approach.

On the one hand, the development of legal reasoning was never positioned as sequential (i.e., a person must move from preconventional, then to conventional and so on) or invariant (e.g., when at the convetional stage of reasoning, a person cannot use preconventional or postconventional reasoning), two requirements of the cognitive developmental approach to moral reasoning that has generally not received strong support (Killen & Smetana, 2015). Research has shown that even young children can and do think about complex moral issues, including psychological versus physical harm (Smetana, Campione-Barr, & Yell, 2003), concepts of rights (Helwig, 2006), fairness and justice (Bloom, 2013), and social inequality (Brown & Bigler, 2004), with at least a rudimentary understanding of the principles underlying them. This refutes the notion that children are incapable of complex or principled reasoning until later in life.

However, similar to Kohlberg, the development of legal reasoning is, at least implicitly, largely discussed as a global theory. In other words, people are thought to reside within a particular stage or level of legal reasoning that shapes the way they look at and understand legal issues. One problem with this approach is that there is no evidence that people only use one mode of thought when examining legal issues. Indeed, Tapp and Levine's (1972, p. 241) original investigations showed that "youth recognized that their daily behaviors were guided predominantly by a law-and-order maintaining frame [preconventional], although they realized purpose and principle [postconventional] should determine compliance." Moreover, across a wide variety of issues, there were large differences within and between groups in the degree to which they used different levels of reasoning, indicating that the development of legal reasoning ability is issue specific to a greater extent than is typically presented.

Legal reasoning research has also given only cursory attention to contextual and environmental aspects of legal development. Legal reasoning is said to develop primarily through a natural process that transpires as people mature (Tapp & Levine, 1974). Situational and environment factors (e.g., authorities, poverty) are important only to the extent that they hinder or accelerate this growth. Thus, much of the attention has been focused on simply identifying the different modes of thought and how their frequency of use varies with age (Tapp & Levine, 1970, 1972, 1974). Such an outlook is overly simplistic and narrowly focused at the individual level. Research on moral judgments has shown that as children develop they increasingly incorporate contextual information into their inferences (Killen & Smetana, 2015). Moreover, decades of research in sociology and criminology have highlighted the importance of macro-level factors in the production of law-related behavior and in creating people's views about their relationship with legal authority in their everyday lives (Justice & Meares, 2014; Sampson & Bartusch, 1998; Sampson, Raudenbush, & Earls, 1997).

Additionally, this approach is overly focused on developing an increasingly abstract and intangible understanding of the purpose and function of the law centered on justice and the use of power to control social behavior (see Gilligan, 1982 for a similar argument with regards to Kohlberg). While it could be argued that these topics should be at the foreground of legal development because they are central functions of a working legal institution, it is also the case that the function of the legal system goes beyond behavior regulation and meting out justice. Indeed, legal socialization is founded on the notion that the law is an integral part of the social environment because of its diffuse impact on human interaction. For example, community policing initiatives emphasize working together to solve neighborhood conflicts and address community problems (Cordner, 2014). These initiatives are built on displaying empathy and benevolence toward the public more than abstract legal principles or social contracts. Relatedly, as currently conceptualized, legal reasoning has difficulty separating legal philosophy from legal reality. Although many aspects of law (e.g., court proceedings, legal policy, dispute resolution) are grounded in esoteric legal principles, most people do not actively think or interface with the legal system in this way as they go about their daily lives (Ewick & Silbey, 1998). Thus while legal reasoning does capture an important element of how people think about the law, one cannot shake the feeling that it is also missing a great deal more.

SUMMARY

In this chapter we examined a reasoning approach to legal socialization. This approach is grounded in the notion that people are active agents in the socialization process, continuously trying to make sense of their socio-legal world. Assisting them in this endeavor is the development of increasingly sophisticated cognitive legal schemas concerning the position and purpose of the legal system within society. Together, these schemas shape people's understanding of their obligations as citizens with regards to following laws and deferring to legal authorities, as well as the duties of the legal system with regards to its exercise of power and regulatory authority. Ultimately, legal reasoning provides the ability to think about and understand one's relationship with the legal system, gives meaning to one's legal world and social position, and fosters the creation of legal attitudes and the perceptions of legitimacy. Legal reasoning has the power to promote both rule-following and rule-breaking. While reasoning based on conventional norms and principled ethics is generally associated with compliance, it can also stimulate critical noncompliance when people believe the law violates their principles of jurisprudence.

The legal reasoning perspective paints a similar picture to the value-based perspective discussed in chapter 4. It emphasizes that some individuals think about the law in fairly instrumental and absolute terms. However, it highlights that this type of thinking is typical of younger children and that the most people outgrow this view. As people obtain more complex reasoning abilities they develop internalized responsibilities concerning their behavior. Importantly, those obligations are not driven by fear of punishment or avoidance of authority, but rather on a normative and principled understanding of what is appropriate legal behavior on their part and in regards to the legal system. People will be motivated to uphold and support the law to the extent that the legal system follows societal norms and embodies democratic legal principles.

As we noted at the outset of this volume, our overall goal is to talk about legal socialization by moving beyond instrumentally-based approaches that feature coercion, dominance, and punishment to approaches that feature securing consent through respectful treatment, fair decision-making, and acknowledgment of personal boundaries. Societies work better under the latter approach because they promote the legal system as a legitimate source of authority and motivate people to voluntarily follow the law.

In this respect, the literature on legal reasoning fits nicely with this goal. The natural growth of legal reasoning leads to the internalization of social conventions and legal principles that guide prosocial behavior. Legal authorities and institutions can accelerate or impede this trajectory based on the manner in which they use their power. As Tapp and Levine noted

(1970, p. 581), "emphasizing the trust-affiliative characteristics of authority figures, increasing the consensual or participatory nature of encounters with the authority system, and creating a sense of civic responsibility for maintaining order appear to be more powerful than the threat of sanction or the risk of legal penalty in internalizing compliance. Ultimately, the model of the persuasive socializer may achieve greater success than the coercive one."

CHAPTER 6

✌

Neurological Development
and Legal Competency

In the last two decades, there has been an explosion of technology that has helped researchers in understanding the intricate relationship between our brains, the environment, and behavior. These technologies allow researchers to gather an ongoing record of mental activity as revealed in biological and neurological processes. As a result of these new technologies our knowledge of how the brain governs behavior, especially social behavior, has grown exponentially. While there has been a concurrent surge in this work as it applies to the legal world (e.g., Grisso et al., 2003; Scott & Steinberg, 2010; Steinberg, 2009), there has been little focus on understanding the role of the brain, and biology more generally, in the legal socialization process. This is a severe limitation in the field, since understanding any type of socialization process requires "a consideration of how biological and sociocultural factors interact in a complex and intertwined manner" (Grusec & Hastings, 2015, p. xii). This is especially poignant within the legal socialization context as biology—in the form of maturation—has always been a central component of most models of legal socialization (Tapp, 1991; Tapp & Levine, 1974). Our goal here is to begin to address this limitation by reviewing recent work on the neurological development of youth and its implications for their legal socialization.[1]

It is not a new insight to recognize that biology shapes and therefore limits developmental capacity.[2] The cognitive developmental approach to socialization incorporates the idea that biology, in the form of natural maturation in cognitive ability, is a vital aspect of that process (Grusec &

Hastings, 2015). Legal socialization is simply a specific aspect of general maturation (Tapp & Levine, 1974). However, at the time of this earlier writing, researchers were severely restricted in their ability to investigate how biological processes actually influenced behavior. Instead, they examined how people thought about the law and how those cognitive representations influenced the way in which they interacted with the legal world. Although it was understood that cognitive abilities were rooted in and driven by biology (i.e., the brain), the tools to understand how neurology controlled behavior were not yet available.

DEVELOPMENT OF NEUROLOGICAL NETWORKS

A number of studies have provided a neurological map of the networks that drive the development of reasoning capacities in adolescents. The first network to fully mature is the "pure" reasoning capacity that relies on logic, abstraction, and rationality. Recall from the previous chapter that legal reasoning has traditionally been defined along these terms (Tapp & Levine, 1974). Youth begin to exhibit cognitive competencies of adult levels in formal reasoning by early adolescence (Spear, 2000). Although adult-level reasoning is *possible* by early adolescence, this does not mean that teenagers are adept at using this capacity when thinking about the law and making legal decisions (Steinberg, 2008, 2009). The effective use of complex reasoning to make sense of one's legal world takes more than logic and abstraction. It also depends on the incorporation of social and emotional information. However, the neural networks that are primarily responsible for processing this kind of information are distinct from those that give rise to pure cognitive ability; moreover, these systems follow different developmental trajectories.

THE SOCIOEMOTIONAL SYSTEM

The next important neural network is the socioemotional regulatory system (Steinberg, 2008, 2009), which resides in the limbic area of the brain. This is considered the emotional life center because it is the primary part of the brain responsible for emotional expression, arousal, and reactivity (Bonnie & Scott, 2013). This system also plays a vital function in processing social information and engaging in social behavior because of its importance in processing emotions. Humans are inherently social creatures who have a fundamental need to understand their social environment (Baumeister & Leary, 1995), including the legal system, which is the formal expression of society's rules governing interpersonal behavior. Our ability to make sense of this social world, and hence the legal system, is intricately linked to our ability to understand and process emotional cues in our environment. For that reason, this neural system is important to processing both emotional and social information.

This system also contains the brain's reward circuitry (Steinberg, 2009). Neurochemicals that are associated with the experiences of pleasure and elevated mood are found in high concentration in this part of the brain.[3] When individuals engage in behaviors that give them a reward, there is a subsequent increase in these pleasure-based neurochemicals. This neural activation underlies people's understanding of the consequences of their behavior, a key component of their legal competencies.

With the onset of puberty, there is a sudden and rapid increase in neural activity in the socioemotional system (Steinberg, 2014). This dramatic shift in activity leads to an increase in emotional arousal and reactivity. Youth's emotional states begin to have a larger impact on behavior and cognition. At the same time, they become more sensitive to their social environment (Bonne & Scott, 2013). Situational cues and other forms of social information play a more prominent role in the way information is processed and how the world is represented within the mind. Young people become more susceptible to social influence and peer pressure when trying to make decisions (Chein, Albert, O'Brien, Uckert, & Steinberg, 2011). Many facets of adolescence, ranging from acquiescing to peer pressure to joining gangs, are easier to understand when this increased susceptibility to social influence is recognized. There is also a dramatic increase of neurochemicals in the reward circuitry, resulting in greater sensitivity to pleasurable activities. This increase is associated with more thought and behavioral activity being directed toward the pursuit of short-term goals and rewards (Steinberg, 2014).

Overall, these changes in the way teenagers process emotional and social information fundamentally alter the way they represent and think about their world. It follows that the increased activity of the socioemotional system in early adolescence is important in terms of developing legal competencies above and beyond the ability to use complex abstract thought, which forms the basis of the cognitive developmental approach. Reasoning is not solely being driven by logic; a deluge of emotional, social, and sensational information is also involved. In many ways, the increasing importance of these factors in the reasoning process serves to undermine pure cognitive ability, like logical and rational thought, pushing individuals to engage in behavior or think about the world in ways that they may not have previously considered.

THE COGNITIVE CONTROL SYSTEM

The final important neural network is the cognitive control system (Steinberg, 2009). The control system is also essential to processing social and emotional information; however, not in the same ways as the socioemotional system. Rather than instigating emotional reactivity and situational impulsivity, this system acts as a parachute of sorts through the use of advanced cognitive processes, such as foresight, planning, and impulse control (Bonnie & Scott, 2013). It is responsible for developing strategies to solve complex problems and for working with multiple pieces of information simultaneously (Stuss & Knight, 2002). As a result, it is considered the seat of executive functioning in the brain and plays a central role in deliberative thinking and decision-making (Casey, 2015).

The cognitive control system serves two important functions. First, it plays a vital role in detecting the complex relationships between situations, actions, and consequences, and storing them in memory for use in decision-making (Miller, Freedman, & Wallis, 2002). This system organizes experiences from specific interactions within the environment into common themes, which are then used to develop rules of how one should behave in the social environment, thereby shaping our understanding of the world around us. Second, because of its ability to develop behavioral scripts for proper behavior, the cognitive control system is primarily responsible for the inhibition of behavior, especially the kinds of behaviors that violate formal or informal rules (Bonnie & Scott, 2013). This is largely because it controls the evaluation of risk and reward, determining the weight given to the future consequences of behavior. In doing so, it makes goal-directed behavior possible. Individuals rely on their control system when they visualize a goal and initiate the behaviors needed to achieve it.

The neural areas underlying the cognitive control system develop throughout childhood into early adulthood (Blakemore & Mills, 2014), and are some of the last parts of the brain to reach full maturity (Gogtay et al., 2004). A key aspect of this development is forming neural connections between the areas of the control system and the areas of the socioemotional system (Steinberg, 2008). The emergence of the socioemotional system serves to undermine the ability of adolescents to use rational and deliberative thought, while at the same time increasing their propensity to behave and think in highly impulsive ways. The development of the cognitive control system specifically counters this influence, hence its name. As development progresses, individuals are increasingly better able to incorporate social and emotional information from the world around them into their reasoning processes, without it overwhelming their executive functioning or deliberative behavior.

However, unlike the socioemotional system which undergoes a sudden and exponential shift in activity with the onset of puberty, the development of the cognitive control system is more linear and gradual (Steinberg, 2009). As a result, during early adolescence behavior is more influenced by emotional arousal and social reactivity. As the cognitive control system matures, individuals' ability to limit this reactivity improves. While social and emotional processing still influences behavior and thinking, it becomes more difficult for it to override decision-making capacities (Chein et al., 2011).

Anecdotally, it is as if the engine has started, but there is an inexperienced driver behind the wheel (Dahl, 2001). In much the same way, adolescents have the pure cognitive ability to think about their legal world in complex and abstract ways; however, it is not until the maturation of this last neural system that they can use these advanced cognitive abilities appropriately and efficiently (Steinberg, 2009). There is more to developing legal reasoning than mastering the ability to think about the law. The ability to process and control other factors, such as emotion, is also required.

THE NEUROLOGICAL UNDERPINNINGS OF LEGAL REASONING DEVELOPMENT

As we described in the previous chapter, the cognitive developmental approach to legal socialization (Tapp & Kohlberg, 1971; Tapp & Levine, 1974) emphasizes that youths' ability to think about the law and their relationship with it becomes increasingly more sophisticated as they mature. Whereas younger children are most likely to understand the law in instrumental and concrete terms, during early adolescence they begin to recognize the important social function of the law and align their behavior with social conventions. During late adolescence and adulthood they become better able to understand the role of the legal system through multiple viewpoints and to separate their ideas about appropriate behavior from social norms and expectations. This improves their ability to control their own behavior so that it aligns with their internalized legal values and principles.

The neuroscience literature reviewed earlier sheds light on the neurological growth that is likely driving the development of legal reasoning. For example, as Tapp and colleagues show (1970, 1971, 1972, 1974), conventional modes of thinking begin to dominate conceptions of the legal system during early and mid-adolescence. Conventional reasoning distinguishes itself from preconventional reasoning because it incorporates the understanding that the individual person is part of a larger social community. Its emergence during early adolescence coincides nicely with the increased activity of the socioemotional system that is responsible for incorporating information from the social environment into decision-making and thought.

A key tenet of legal competency from the cognitive developmental viewpoint is the ability to understand and integrate multiple perspectives concerning the purpose and function of the law. This is most apparent in postconventional reasoning when people are motivated to separate and balance the needs of society with the wants of the individual. Perspective-taking is a central component in this mode of thought. However, postconventional reasoning is the last stage to fully emerge, usually during late adolescence (Tapp & Levine, 1974). Although young children are capable of postconventional reasoning (Tapp & Levine, 1972), it is not until young adulthood that postconventional reasoning becomes the dominant model of conceptualizing one's relationship with the law and legal system.

Again, this developmental trajectory of legal reasoning coincides with a similar trajectory in terms of neurological development. Executive functions such as being able to infer the mental states of others, understand intentionality, and incorporate multiple perspectives are the responsibility of the cognitive control system (Blakemore & Mills, 2014). While these functions emerge early in childhood, they go through immense improvement during middle and late adolescence (Dumontheil, Apperly, & Blakemore, 2010; Güroğlu, van den Bos, & Crone, 2009), becoming fully developed in early adulthood (Mills, Lalonde, Clasen, Giedd, & Blakemore, 2014).

Although the neurological development literature has yet to be specifically applied to questions of legal socialization, there appear to be many similarities between the development of legal reasoning from a content perspective and the development of neurological networks during adolescence. This suggests that there may be biological limits with regards to the emergence of legal reasoning capacities that become less important as people age. This may explain why even though young children are capable of using postconventional reasoning, this tendency is stunted until later in life.

The argument that there may be biological limits constraining the development of legal reasoning is in contrast to the view espoused by the cognitive developmental approach. Proponents of this view argue that legal reasoning development could be artificially accelerated by exposing (young) individuals to more complex forms of legal reasoning via opportunities to take on different roles, participate in efforts to resolve interpersonal conflicts, solve complex problems, and participate in decision-making (Tapp & Kohlberg, 1971). Presumably, such exposure highlights the shortcomings of less sophisticated forms of legal thought and pushes people to think of the law in different terms. Ultimately, this facilitates the development of more nuanced legal schemas leading to more complex thought.

While a neuroscience perspective does not necessarily contradict these arguments, it does suggest that the effectiveness of these interventions will be dependent on one's age. Exposing young children to complex reasoning may have little influence on their legal reasoning capacities if they lack the neurological hardware to work with that information in an effective and efficient manner. Behavioral research seems to bear this contention out. For example, past interventions with young juveniles aimed at increasing their reasoning capacities through exposure to more complex forms of reasoning have largely failed to have much of an influence on legal reasoning ability or legal behavior (Morash, 1978, 1981, 1982).

THE CAPACITY TO SELF-REGULATE

One of the most important outcomes of the entire legal socialization process is developing the capacity to regulate one's own behavior. The entire framework constructed by writers such as Freud (1930), Durkheim (1973), and Weber (1968) that we reviewed in chapter 4 is based upon the assumption that the key element of general socialization is the ability to develop mechanisms of self-control, in particular those based upon adherence to internal values. Although the cognitive developmentalists (e.g., Tapp, 1991) do not place as much focus on what people do as on their *reasons* for what they do, a central theme running throughout their perspective is that the way in which people understand the purpose and function of the law in society will either promote or hinder their self-regulatory capacity within the legal realm.

Neuroscience research links the development of self-regulation with changes in the neural networks during childhood and adolescence. As activity in the socioemotional system spikes during puberty, children become increasingly sensitive to socially rewarding behavior (Chein et al.,

2011). This neurological immaturity limits the ability to control impulses, especially when it is tied socially or emotionally rewarding consequences. Unsurprisingly, engagement in risky and sensation-seeking behavior, including antisocial behavior, are especially common during this developmental period (Bonnie & Scott, 2013), leading some to blame the developing brain for the drastic increase in criminal behavior found during adolescence (Scott & Steinberg, 2010; Steinberg, 2014). The important thing to understand, however, is that for most, the emergence of this increased frequency of offending is a normal part of growth and maturation (Moffitt, 1993). In tandem with their efforts to reason about law adolescents also test limits behaviorally and learn through their errors and successes what is and what is not desirable behavior. This testing is a necessary part of growing up and coming to understand the value of rules and of self-limiting strategies in the fact of excitement and temptations.

At the same time as this exponential increase in activation of the socioemotional system, the parts of the brain that manage executive functioning and cognitive control develop more slowly and incrementally (Miller et al., 2002). The neural networks responsible for inhibiting behavior according to the social norms of the community at large are not yet strong enough to control the increased activity in the socioemotional system. This is especially true for the cognitions related to whether or not to commit a variety of types of antisocial behavior. We have a developmental period here where teenagers are especially inclined to engage in impulsive behavior precisely at a time when their ability to control such behavior is curtailed. Given this, it is no wonder that a lack of impulse control has been argued as the central element leading to criminal and delinquent behavior (Gottfredson & Hirshi, 1990). More recent work has tied this lack of control directly to an underdeveloped or damaged prefrontal cortex, the part of the brain responsible for cognitive control (Brower & Price, 2001).

This situation provides an explanation for why so many crime-committing adolescents go on to live adult lives as law-abiding citizens. The age-crime curve is probably the closest thing to a "law" that criminological science has (Steffensmeier & Ulmer, 2002). Interestingly enough, when one looks at frequency offending by age, there is a sharp increase during early adolescence which coincides with the sharp increase in activity of the socioemotional system. Frequency of offending then slowly and gradually declines as people age until it becomes stable during early adulthood. This trajectory coincides with the development of the cognitive control system. In this regard, it is not surprising that fourteen- to twenty-five-year-olds commit the majority of crime, as they are still maturing at both a neurological and psychosocial level.

THE CAPACITY TO PARTICIPATE IN THE LEGAL SYSTEM

In addition to its influence on self-regulation, research also shows that neurological development plays an important role in determining one's capacity to participate in the legal system. Earlier we discussed legal impoverishment in terms of rights deprivation and legal consciousness (Ewick & Silbey, 1998; Silbey, 2005; Tapp & Levine, 1974). Such social impoverishment serves to restrict one's ability to interact with the legal world. However, neurological development represents a different kind of legal impoverishment altogether. Here people are not restricted because they lack rights or legal status, but their participation is restricted because they lack a fully-developed brain to process the information that is necessary to participate appropriately in the system.

Nowhere is this more apparent than in the juvenile justice system. For example, as is true with adult courts, juvenile courts also require adolescents to be competent to stand trial. Generally speaking, competency is determined by whether they can appropriately participate in the legal proceedings, so that their due process rights are not violated (Scott & Grisso, 2005). Such participation is based on their ability to factually and rationally understand the proceedings, as well as the ability to assist in their own defense. This involves issues like awareness of the charges, understanding the consequences of legal pleas or possible penalties, and comprehension of the trial and its consequences. The latter includes the ability to receive and communicate information to counsel to prepare a defense, and the capacity to make decisions about pleading and the waiver of constitutional rights.

Studies suggest that many adolescents do not have these capacities (Grisso, 1997; Scott, 1992; Scott & Grisso, 2005; Scott & Steinberg, 2010; Woolard, Fried, & Reppucci, 2001). In a large study of adolescents and young adults, Grisso and colleagues (2003) found that adolescents younger than sixteen were more likely than those sixteen or older to be cognitively impaired to the point where they were not competent to stand trial. Not only did the younger adolescents show deficits in understanding and reasoning concerning their participation in the trial, but they also showed a marked degree of psychosocial immaturity. For example, they were less able to assess the risks that could result from their decisions, and had difficulty understanding long-term consequences as opposed to immediate rewards. Many of these deficits can be traced directly to their still-developing brain, especially those areas that constitute the socioemotional and cognitive control systems (Steinberg, 2009).

NEUROLOGICAL DEVELOPMENT AND DETERRENCE

Long ago, Tapp (1966) suggested that the developmental trajectory of legal reasoning points to problems with legal strategies that rely on deterrence and punitive policies. Given that most people base their understanding of the legal system on conventional or postconventional reasoning, a legal system reliant on rewards and punishments to encourage compliance with legal authority would fail because it was rooted in the principles of a type of thought (preconventional) that most people do not generally utilize. In essence, she argued that deterrence-based strategies treat adult (and adolescent) offenders as young children, capable only of understanding that illegal behavior is bad because it leads to negative consequences.

In a similar way, a neuroscience approach to legal socialization also calls the utility of deterrence into question, although for different reasons. Until adulthood, people are not capable of acting like the fully functioning, rational decision makers that deterrence models assume them to be. A still-maturing brain hinders adolescents' ability to think about the future consequences of behavior, especially the punishments associated with that behavior. At the same time, they are highly sensitive to the emotionally gratifying and socially rewarding behaviors that deterrence is designed to prevent. As summarized by Slobogin and Fondacaro (2011, p. 14), "the most significant traits of adolescent immaturity are not compromised cognitive abilities but rather impulsivity and a tendency to give in to peer pressure." These elements are important both as explanations for lawbreaking, and also because the characteristics of adolescents (impulsivity, attraction to risk, and peer driven behavior) make it more difficult to manage adolescent behavior through the application of formal sanctions and punishments.

Many of the forms of limits testing common to adolescents are part of a more general process of learning about rules, by testing limits and making mistakes (Casey, 2015). It is for this reason that the overwhelming number of adolescents who commit minor crimes mature and become normal law-abiding adults (Moffitt, 2007). Part of the normal process of growth is testing limits to build internal models of risk assessment and to understand how values interact with social environments. It would be wonderful if adolescents could learn about limits without sometimes going too far, breaking rules, suffering consequences, and becoming more mature, but that is unrealistic given their social, emotional, and cognitive growth.

The way in which adolescents make decisions increases the likelihood and frequency with which they will come into contact with the formal legal system. This is a substantial problem given that the juvenile justice system as grown exponentially more punitive in the last thirty years as a result of crime control policies rooted in deterrence (Slobogin & Fondacaro, 2011). Punitive legal policies have lasting, potentially damaging impact on individuals who are still developing neurologically (Petrosino, Turpin-Petrosino, & Guckenburg, 2010).

As a result, it is important to try to manage rule-breaking in ways that maintain a normal developmental trajectory rather than changing that trajectory. Widespread minor criminal conduct by adolescents brings many into contact with various elements of the criminal justice system. Those who are not drawn into that system generally mature out of crime (Steffensmeier & Ulmer, 2002), while greater contact with it is associated with declines in the perceived legitimacy of the law (Fagan & Tyler, 2005) and a greater likelihood of future criminal conduct (Petrosino et al., 2010). Hence the developmental neuroscience literature makes a powerful case for diversion away from formal legal processes (Scott & Steinberg, 2010).

SUMMARY

Neurological research represents a new frontier in legal socialization research. Our goal in this chapter was to review this work and highlight ways in which this emerging literature converges and diverges with more traditional perspectives on this field. This work points to a developmental trajectory where children continually acquire greater internal resources through which to understand and manage the issues associated with the law, authorities, and the self-regulation of behavior. In this respect, it coincides with many of the arguments made by the cognitive developmental perspective. However, unlike the cognitive developmental approach, this trajectory is not a global one fully transforming youths' mental abilities. Instead, neural networks vary in degree with how quickly they develop. Importantly, this limits youth in important respects that is largely not captured by either of the other two perspectives we have reviewed in previous chapters. Depending on their age, they can struggle with inhibiting immediately rewarding behavior and have difficulty understanding the consequences of their actions, increasingly, the prevalence of negative contact with the legal system.

The neurological perspective is especially important because it highlights two key issues related to adolescents and law. First, adolescents commit crimes because they are struggling to manage the cognitive and social skills needed to understand rules and to be able to self-regulated based upon consensual values such as legitimacy. It is important to recognize this when considering issues of responsibility, and when thinking about issues of treatment and rehabilitation. Adolescents are in the midst of the ongoing process of growing out of the cognitive and biological limits that promote their criminal behavior. Hence, treatment should encourage that process.

Second, neurology provides an explanation for why diversion makes sense of juveniles. It is fashionable to view rehabilitation of adults as unrealistic. However, that is not the case with juveniles. On the contrary the best solution for most juvenile offenders is to divert them out of the juvenile justice system and focus upon rehabilitation, not criminalization, and punishment. Almost all adolescents mature out of crime if simply let alone. Conversely, contact with juvenile justice processes undermines this natural development process. This is especially true when that contact undermines the development of natural cognitive development, and emotional and social maturation. The most desirable approach is to maximize opportunities for natural development through minimizing exposure to criminalizing processes and by maximizing efforts to assist natural development through various forms of rehabilitation. Those rehabilitation efforts can involve enhancing opportunities for reasoning and can be linked to the development of strategies for emotional control and more effective decision making.

PART III

cℵɔ

Legal Socialization across the Spheres of Childhood and Adolescence

In this part of our analysis we examine the legal socialization process across three important domains: family and parents, schools and teachers, and legal institutions and authorities. Our goal is to assess the degree to which experiences with authority and rule-making and enforcement influence the acquisition of supportive legal values, formation of law-related attitudes, and development of legal reasoning competencies. Although researchers in each of these phases of legal development (family, school, legal authority) use different terminology and theoretical frameworks, similar themes and core issues emerge concerning the various ways authorities can engage with youth and how their actions are understood by children and adolescents. Beyond differences in terminology and perspective, we aim to show that the literature in each domain tap into common ideas about how legitimacy is created and maintained among youth.

Children first begin to learn about rules and authorities from their parents, and, while family socialization is crucial, it is the phase over which the state has the least control. Children can learn to obey authority, or they can develop an oppositional orientation toward rules and authorities in their relationship with their parents. Whatever they learn in their early family experiences, it shapes their later attitudes, values, and behaviors about rules and authority. As a result, children enter school with an orientation about what to expect from authorities. This involves, first, a framework that defines their relationship to authority as being about coercion or consent. To the degree that they have a consent based model of authority, they then have views about whether the authorities they have dealt with are entitled to legitimacy when viewed through this framework.

School provides a second sphere of learning about rules and authority. It is one that is more formal and complex, but in some ways family-like in that students have long-term relationships with teachers (particularly during the early years). This is a time when children begin to compare the behavior of different authority figures to their prior experiences and expectations concerning the way authorities should behave, which are initially rooted in family socialization patterns. To the extent that their interactions with teachers are similar to their interactions with their parents, the values and attitudes that were instilled and formed in the family will be reinforced.

Adolescents then move into the larger world in which they might potentially have contact with many legal or quasi-legal authorities, police officers, judges, social workers, and corrections officers. Given that a large proportion of crimes committed are committed by adolescents (Steffensmeier & Ulmer, 2002) and that many people who commit crimes only commit them when they are adolescents (Moffitt, 2007), the likelihood of such contact is highest during this period. When they deal with legal authorities, adolescents are drawn into a complex and formal set of juvenile justice procedures. Additionally, unlike parents and teachers, in this context youth deal with strangers on a (typically) one-time basis.

Irrespective of whether we are discussing the family, schools, or legal authorities, the models of authority that children and adolescents encounter are frequently models that have been shown to be less than optimal mechanisms for developing supportive legal attitudes and values. Many times they feature practices (e.g., physical or inconsistent discipline, lack of empathy, rejection, and humiliation) that can actually encourage the development of the negative attitudes and values that are precursors of antisocial behavior (e.g., delinquency, bullying). The developing child learns to view authority through an instrumental lens, viewing power and force as the mechanism through which people influence (in this case control) others. In addition, to the degree to which they have values related to authority, they view authorities in negative terms, and develop cynicism and alienation, not consent and legitimacy.

On the other hand, there is the clear possibility of engaging in policies and practices that will lead children to internalize supportive values and develop positive civic attitudes that become part of their identity and sense of self. Our argument is that such policies and practices need to consider three essential dimensions of authority relations: quality of treatment, fairness of decision-making, and recognition of appropriate boundaries. These dimensions form the basis for how people understand their relationship with authority and their expectations concerning their interactions with those that hold power. As we will discuss in the ensuing chapters, the importance of each dimension consistently emerges within the research on parenting, school climate, and the policing of juveniles. However, as a preview, we summarize the three dimensions below and in Table 1.

The first element is the quality of the relationship between the young person and authority and of the social bonds and identification that

Table 1. THE ANTECEDENTS OF LEGITIMACY

	Family dynamics	School climate	Policies and practices of the juvenile justice system
Treatment	• Create socioemotional bonds; avoid rejection • Show concern and caring • Address needs • Treat respectfully	• Care about and show interest in students • Avoid humiliating or demeaning actions • Listen to students and show they are heard • Praise and respect students	• Respect people and their rights • Be benevolent by acting in ways that show concern about people • Show concern and consideration of views when explaining policies and actions and the reasons for them • Avoid stigmatizing behavior/stereotyping
Decision-making	• Apply rules consistently • Be transparent • Allow voice and dialogue • Explain actions	• Apply clear rules in a consistent and transparent way • Allow voice and discussion about rules • Explain punishment	• Apply legal rules in a consistent and transparent way • Allow input and explanation about applications • Be transparent • Explain actions
Boundaries	• Differentiate domains of personal and parental control • Respect spheres of personal autonomy	• Discuss public and private spheres of authority • Recognize domains of personal autonomy • Understand situational restraints on school authority	• Recognize that intrusions into personal sphere must be justified and explained

come from it. The focus here is on how authorities treat the individuals over whom they exercise their authority both in terms of what authorities do and how their actions are understood by young people. Objectively, it involves whether there are caring actions such as being aware of and responsive to a child's needs, paying attention to where they are and what they are doing, and treating them and their concerns respectfully. These actions shape whether a child or adolescent infers that the authority has a trustworthy character, benevolent motives, and is sincere and caring.

The second element involves the quality of the way in which an authority exercises their authority and makes decisions. Here, the focus is on how the authority creates, applies, and enforces rules and how those decisions are understood by those affected by them. This involves issues of consistency in rule application, explanation for decisions, willingness to discuss reasons for decisions, and openness to input and to the possibility of correcting errors. These actions are understood in the framework of what it means for an authority to be fair and just, and whether a particular authority exhibits these characteristics.

The third element involves the appropriate scope of rightful authority given to any particular authority figure. Here the focus is on what kinds of behaviors individuals believe an authority has a right to restrict and in what situations. The important thing is how behaviors are defined along different domains (e.g., personal versus public), which flows from a cognitive understanding of the nature of rules and authority. Regardless of whether authorities treat people with respect or make fair decision, they will not be given control over certain parts of people's lives. When they try to encroach on these areas, people will not recognize their legitimacy and resist their attempts at control. Ultimately, the conflict over boundaries leads to the development of autonomy and self-regulation.

The values internalized during prior experiences with parents and teachers form the basis for how individuals initially understand their relationship with the law, as well as their expectations concerning the way the legal system should interact with them. It is this continuity among different phases that explains why, for the most part, people want and expect police officers to behave in similar ways to how students want teachers to behave and how children want their parents to behave. The subsequent interactions they have with legal authorities will serve to further shape and modify their values and attitudes about the law and the application of power by legal authority.

People who simply defer to any command from an authority without evaluating it can be a danger to themselves and to society. Models of effective authority therefore focus on reasoned acceptance of legitimacy, not

blind compliance. When legal authorities behave in ways that are consistent with individuals' values concerning the appropriate use of authority,
they judge them to be legitimate. As a result, young people feel an obligation to obey the directives of legal authorities and are willing and motivated to defer, comply, and cooperate with them. When legal authorities
do not act according to a script with which young people are familiar, they
create confusion and undermine trust and confidence leading to expressions of resistance and defiance.

CHAPTER 7

✦

Legal Socialization in the Family

Central to nearly all models of legal socialization is the primacy of the family and early experiences in life (Tapp & Levine, 1974; Trinkner & Cohn, 2014). The attitudes and values learned at this early stage are the bedrock upon which individuals define their relationship with the various rule systems they will encounter throughout their lives. Psychologists have demonstrated that people understand their later experiences through the lens of their early values and attitudes, so everything that happens later in life is understood through the framework of priors. Further, when they encounter discordant information people have a strong belief perseverance motivation and resist changing, so it is more difficult to change values and attitudes than it is to create them in the first place.

Expectations about how authority should wield power and interact with people flow from these early notions about rules and authorities. Judgments concerning the legitimacy of the law later in life are dependent on the degree to which they meet these expectations. Given the potentially long-term effects of early experiences on legal socialization, it is important to first examine the ways in which parents interact with their children and how these different styles can facilitate or hinder a general acceptance of consensual authority by fostering perceptions of legitimacy in parental authority.

This concern directs our attention to the issue of child-rearing. Psychologists suggest that children have propensities toward making and acting upon moral judgments beginning at an early age (Bloom, 2013; Olson & Spelke, 2008). These propensities are then influenced and shaped by the environment. In particular, families and parents are central features of the environment that serve to develop or undermine those attitudes and values that are most important to the legal socialization that leads to consensual models of authority. Of special importance are the ways in which parents wield their power and authority when they establish rules of conduct in the home, handle conflict among family members, and manage discipline when rules are violated. Generally, these critical interactions are a primary avenue through which children become acclimated to functioning in everyday social life and in social interactions (Vandeleur, Perrez, & Schoebi, 2007).

In regards to the legal socialization process, they serve as a means to communicate to children the purpose of rules and authority and in so doing shape the basis for their understanding of the legal system later in life. They stimulate the development of a framework, or working model, of authority and rules for its exercise. As we have discussed previously, this framework is dependent on three basic dimensions concerning issues of treatment, decision-making, and boundaries. This framework gives meaning to future interactions with authority and provides the basis for fostering legitimacy and securing voluntary compliance.

In addition, the importance of early socialization is not just in terms of imparting values, forming attitudes, and developing an understanding of rules. Families and parents have a direct and powerful influence on law-related behavior concurrently, and this influence extends later into life (Hirschi, 1969; Laub & Sampson, 2003; Sampson & Laub, 1993). For example, a recent meta-analysis suggests that parenting explains approximately 11% of the variance in delinquency (Hoeve et al., 2009). As such, considerations of early socialization in general, and legal socialization in particular, are also important in terms of efforts to prevent later socially undesirable behavior.

PARENTAL AUTHORITY AS A VEHICLE FOR VALUE ACQUISITION

The parent–child bond represents the first authority relationship that a child encounters. Because of its primacy and the dependence of the child on adults, this bond is crucial in forming the first blueprint of the appropriate role of authority in the child's life. As we will discuss, parents play a vital role in shaping the three dimensions of values upon which children will define their relationship with the legal system as adults. They supply the first life experiences that will shape expectations about how authorities should treat people, make decisions, and whether they will respect the limits of their appropriate authority.

Our focus is on how parents' behavior facilitates the acquisition of values within their children concerning the way in which authorities should and will wield power. However, importantly, not all forms of parenting are equal. They differ in terms of their goals, purposes, and methods concerning how they control their children and manage conflict. Variations in parenting inevitably impart different values in regards to power and authority. Such differences serve to create distinct reactions to attempts at control from authorities. As we will show, some patterns of parenting lead to voluntary deference and cooperation based on legitimacy, while other patterns of parenting can lead to rejection and mistrust where compliance must be enforced and maintained through coercive means.

THE COERCIVE MODEL: COMPLIANCE THROUGH POWER

The model of parenting via coercion is rooted in tendencies toward autocratic control. Here, obedience is a value in and of itself; one that is more important to instill in children than other values. This approach does not focus on issues of how power is wielded or how the exercise of authority influences the child's values. Instead, the relationship with authority is viewed in instrumental terms as a one-way affair. Put simply, a successful parent is one who secures obedience in children. A parent sets a rule and a child must follow it. If the child does not, then he or she must be punished. A good child is one who obeys; whether that obedience comes from voluntary consent or from fear of sanctions matters little. Again, only obedience matters and imparting that understanding to the child is of utmost importance.

Parents who try to instill obedience itself as a value tend to use physical discipline, such as spanking, to manage rule-breaking behavior. In large part this is a result of the reliance on instrumental control in order to promote rule-following behavior. Because the parent is not focused on instilling values that promote voluntary deference, they must utilize their superior power and status to exert control over their children. Ironically, however, this style of discipline has actually been shown to have no effect on value development. Psychological research linking child-rearing practices to subsequent behavior has consistently shown that physical discipline has very little benefit in terms of promoting internal controls and thereby decreasing later rule-breaking behavior (Gershoff, 2002).

In fact, rather than promoting rule-following behavior, coercive discipline actually serves to destabilize such behavior. It does not foster cooperation and rule-following by internalizing obedience as a value. It typically leads to the rejection of authority as untrustworthy and promotes noncompliance (Trinkner, Cohn, Rebellon, & Van Gundy, 2012). For example, autocratic parenting has been linked to increased rule violations within the home (Straus, 1991; Straus & Donnelly, 2001) and increased engagement in risky behavior such as alcohol and drug use outside of it (Newman, Harrison, Dashiff, & Davies, 2008). Other research has linked physical discipline directly to aggressive behavior in childhood and adolescence (Fine, Trentacosta, Izard, Mastow, & Campbell, 2004; Simons, Simons, Burt, Brody, & Cutrona, 2005). Gershoff and Bitensky (2007, p. 235) conclude that "if parents' goals are to increase children's moral internalization and to decrease their aggressive and antisocial behavior, there is little evidence that corporal punishment is effective in achieving these goals."

Physical punishment has been shown to cause antisocial behaviors like aggression, to be ineffective in producing long-term compliance with the law, and to have no influence in the internalization of desirable values (Fraser, 1996; Patterson & Yoerger, 1993; Earls, 1994). On the contrary, it can encourage anti-social behavior, as well as alienation and cynicism. For example, in a nationally representative study of over three thousand kids and six thousand couples, Straus (1991) linked the experience of physical discipline to increased violence both inside and outside of the home. In particular, those children that reported the highest levels of corporal punishment were also more likely to be arrested by law enforcement. Later work also connected the experience of physical discipline as children to later criminal behavior during adulthood (Straus & Donnelly, 2001). Although viewed as a relatively mild form of discipline to many parents, Straus argues that it is a powerful precursor to much of the violence we see in society.

Overall, this work highlights two consequences of using a coercive approach to parenting as it pertains to legal socialization. First, coercion defines individuals' understanding of their relationship with authority figures in terms of surveillance to detect and the use of force to punish rule transgressions. Rather than internalizing law-related values that serve to create a positive and healthy relationship with authorities, an exclusive focus on instrumentality creates a relationship characterized by distrust and apprehension where sheer obedience is the only thing of value. Such a stance leads to the view that authorities are distant and uncaring.

Second, despite its use as a means to control behavior, coercion actually increases a variety of different rule-breaking behaviors over time. These range from bullying in school to adolescent gang membership and later criminal behavior (Gershoff, 2002). Thus not only does it have severe ramifications for individuals' conceptions of authority, but it also does not actually attain the outcomes that it seeks. Given this, one wonders if the costs associated this this approach are worth the seemingly minor benefits of immediate compliance in the presence of authorities have sufficient utility to justify this model.

One part of the calculation needs to be that when properly deployed coercion can shape behavior. This is true with parents, in schools, and in the legal system. If the system can credibly deploy resources to create a risk of swift and certain justice, then people respond to the risk of punishment. This is certainly true of children. In the presence of their parents and threatened with superior physical power, children tend to obey their parents. And there may be times when immediate compliance is a necessary goal.

Isolating the influence of corporal punishment on the development of prosocial norms and values is difficult because there usually are strong intercorrelations among a number of parenting behaviors and variables (Morris & Gibson, 2011). In large part this exemplifies the tendency for corporal punishment to be connected to a number of parenting factors that revolve around issues of discipline. Complicating matters further is that styles of authority may operate within a cultural context. For example, Lansford and colleagues (2005) studied mother–child dyads across cultures and found that physical discipline is more likely to be associated with negative outcomes when it is *not* perceived to be normative. Those countries in which physical discipline was less common showed the strongest association between the use of physical discipline and children's behavior problems. They suggest that the key is whether the use of an approach leads children to think that their parents are good and caring parents. On the other hand, in all cultures the use of physical discipline led to higher levels of interpersonal aggression on the part of children. If parents use power to control their children, they are teaching their children to use power to control others in their own lives.

However, research generally points to two important factors that appear to be precursors to the use of physical punishment in discipline and precursors of later delinquency. The first is the use of inconsistent discipline practices, which in itself is an indicator of a larger conglomeration of parenting practices. The concern is with the way parents exercise their authority when disciplining their children. Are parents disciplining their children in a fair manner, for example by explaining decisions, allowing and maintaining open dialogue, and applying rules in a transparent and consistent manner? Studies show that the impact of sanctions varies depending upon the degree to which the sanction is perceived to be fairly enacted (Piquero, Gomez-Smith, & Langton, 2004). Moreover, the negative consequences of the use of unfair sanctioning procedures are well established and widespread. In terms of parents, different patterns of parenting generally have differential impacts depending upon whether parents are viewed as legitimate and fair authority figures (Keijsers & Laird, 2014).

Second, studies consistently point to the presence or absence of a relationship (i.e., social-emotional bonds) as important in the acquisition of social norms and values. The inability to link to others emotionally and to develop significant emotional attachments with one's parents has been linked to antisocial and delinquent behavior (Sullivan, 2008; Wasserman et al., 2003). Similarly, maternal hostility, which influences family attachment bonds, is linked to delinquency (Moffitt & Caspi, 2001). As Laub, Sampson, and Sweeten (2008) suggest, "the theoretically-predicted relationship between social bonds to family and school and delinquent behavior is supported by a great deal of research" (p. 318). For example, Kempf (1993) reviewed seventy-one studies and found that poor attachment to parents increased delinquency.

Laub and Sampson (2003) suggest that those who persist in criminal careers have an "inability to forge close attachments or make any connection to anybody or anything. One can view the men as possessing a distorted sense of autonomy without any commitment or concern for others" (p. 194). Similarly, Simons, Johnson, Conger, and Elder (1998) found that children with a history of childhood antisocial behavioral tendencies, but who developed stronger social bonds during adolescence, showed decreases in later delinquency. Parenting practices that communicate disrespect, humiliation, or other signs of viewing a child as of low value, as well as inconsistent and nontransparent actions that children cannot understand and which undermine inferences of benevolence and trustworthiness make the development of social bonds difficult. Rather they create relationships characterized by anger and hostility, defiance and rebellion.

ALTERNATIVE APPROACHES: CONSENT THROUGH RESPECT AND FAIRNESS

It is a core presumption of the value socialization literature that consensual social order requires that children take upon themselves values that will promote the responsibility to follow social rules. In an ideal society people would be generally less inclined to break rules because everyone would be socialized to hold supportive attitudes and there would be consistency between societal values and the actions of social institutions. As a result, people would be internally motivated to be compliant and engage in good citizenship behaviors. Ultimately, this would lead to a legal system with less need to control society through surveillance and sanctioning, allowing governments to shift precious resources to other areas of need like economic and social development in local communities.

We just showed that parenting that focuses on physical discipline and obedience is insufficient in terms of creating children that feel responsible for following rules. Further, parents need not focus on coercion in order to secure compliance from their children. Rather than exclusively focusing on obedience as a value and the instrumental control of punishments and rewards, other strategies focus on instilling values that lead to beneficial and supportive relationships with authority and rule-systems (Baumrind, 1971; Darling & Steinberg, 1993; Fondacaro, Dunkle, & Pathak, 1998; Freud, 1930; Smetana, 2002). These approaches not only emphasize motivating children to follow rules, but are also cognizant of the dialogue between parents and children. Invariably they emphasize the ongoing give-and-take in the parent–child bond and how that process shapes children's understanding of authority and engagement in behavior.

When parents exert their power in fair and equitable ways, children are more open to their attempts to socialize them (Darling & Steinberg, 1993). As a result, these strategies facilitate the acquisition of values and feelings of responsibility to maintain social order. Instead of leading to the rejection of parent's legitimacy, they promote the legitimacy of parental authority (Trinkner et al., 2012). In doing so, they gain deference through consent and voluntary cooperation rather than compliance in response to force and domination. We next turn our attention to examining different parenting strategies that emphasize the family as a socializing unit and the child-rearing strategies that promote the acquisition of values central to the legal socialization process.

FAMILY SOCIALIZATION

Freud (1930) framed the issue of value acquisition as a key concern of family socialization. As we have noted, his work led to the argument that there are two mechanisms that are potentially important in shaping value acquisition. One is internalization. Through a child-rearing style of reasoning (induction) and general cognitive development, children adopt values as their own because they come to see having those values as appropriate for the maintenance of social order. As a result, those values are considered functionally autonomous in that they have become ingrained in one's identity and motivate voluntary behavior. This mechanism is driven by the development of reasoning skills that are further accelerated through dialogue and conversing with children about rules and appropriate behavior (Blasi, 1980). Children must see the purpose of rules, recognize that they are being applied in neutral and fact-based ways, and understand that they are consistent and have explainable reasons (Grusec & Goodnow, 1994). Such conversations advance children's attainment of more advanced and sophisticated values and those values then assume a role in guiding their behavior.

A second mechanism is identification. Social bonds between children and their parents are central to the child's ability to meet basic psychological and material needs. Hence, children are focused upon behaving in ways that preserve those bonds. Parents can use a variety of strategies like "contingent affection" or "love withdrawal" that essentially link the maintenance of these attachments to engaging in appropriate conduct. As a result, children behave in desired ways in order to maintain social bonds (Hoffman, 2000; Tangney & Dearing, 2002). Over time, it is expected that the values needed to preserve relationships with significant others are taken on as one's own. Essentially, the values that define appropriate conduct in terms of the maintenance of social bonds then become part of a child's own identity. At that point, those values are now reflective of how the child sees him or herself as a person. As a result, they will behave in accordance with those values regardless of whether or the not such conduct is still linked to particular social ties.

A wide range of developmental psychological research points to the effectiveness of these two types of child-rearing strategies: inductive reasoning (internalization) and contingent affection (identification). The inductive reasoning approach to value socialization involves the development of the reasoning skills of children and adolescents through dialogue and discussion so that their values become more advanced and more actively engaged in guiding their law-related behavior (Blasi, 1980). Existing evidence suggests that strategies of socialization that encourage the development of cognitive reasoning skills are linked to law-abiding behavior among adolescents and adults (Bear, 1989; Eron, 1987; Galen & Underwood, 1997; Guerra, Nucci, & Huesmann, 1994; Harvey, Fletcher, & French, 2001; Huesmann & Guerra, 1997; Jurkovic, 1980; Kowalski & Wilke, 2001; Laible, Eye, & Carlo, 2008; Perry, Perry, & Kennedy, 1992; Tisak, Tisak, & Goldstein, 2006; Turiel, 1987). For example, Stams and colleagues (2006, p. 697) report in their meta-analysis of fifty studies that juvenile delinquents generally have a lower level of moral reasoning. They report that "developmentally delayed moral judgment is strongly associated with juvenile delinquency, even after controlling for socioeconomic status, gender, age and intelligence." This suggestion has obvious parallels to our prior discussion of the development of reasoning in children, a theme emphasized by Tapp, Cohn, and others.

Studies also consistently point to the importance of creating a significant initial attachment with parents, as well as later establishing and maintaining social bonds to others (Thompson, 2008). Such bonds and attachments signify the emotional links that are at the heart of the identification mechanism in parenting strategies. More importantly, a host of research has shown that they are associated with diminishing antisocial and delinquent behavior (Kempf, 1993; Laub, Sampson, & Sweeten, 2008; Sullivan, 2008; Wasserman et al., 2003). Conversely, when family attachment bonds are weak as a result of parental hostility or ambivalence, children are more likely to engage in delinquent behavior (Hirschi, 1969; Moffitt & Caspi, 2001). These findings indicate that when parents act in ways that interfere with a child's ability to develop an emotional bond with them, they hinder value acquisition. This includes acting in inconsistent, rejecting, emotionally cold, and punitive ways or undermining trust by engaging in behaviors that the child can see are not motivated by the desire to deal with the child's needs and concerns.

Furthermore, although the development of cognitive reasoning plateaus at adult levels during early adolescence (Steinberg, 2009), attachment and social bonds continue to develop throughout childhood and adolescence. Such emotional connections are of immense importance throughout life, especially in desistance from criminal activity. Laub and Sampson (2003, p. 194) suggest that those who persist in criminal careers throughout their lives have an "inability to forge close attachments or make any connection to anybody or anything. One can view the men as possessing a distorted sense of autonomy without any commitment or concern for others." Even later in life, the introduction of attachments and social bonds reduces rule violations. For example, children with a history of childhood antisocial behavioral tendencies are less at risk for long-term delinquency if they develop stronger social bonds during adolescence (Simons, Johnson, Conger, & Elder, 1998).

The strategies of internalization and identification articulated in the classic work on value acquisition are based on the goal of developing internal motivational forces to encourage desirable behavior in childhood and adolescence, forces which are then assumed to carry into adulthood. This foundation is starkly opposed to relying upon the instrumental approach of punishing and rewarding that plays a central role in the strategies that use physical discipline.

Furthermore, this classic work speaks to the potential effectiveness of efforts to prevent or correct misbehavior by facilitating the internalization of values through the development of reasoning and establishment and maintenance of social bonds. As we have shown, these strategies are associated with lower rates of offending for juveniles and increased law-abiding behavior among adults. This work supports our central argument concerning legal socialization: that the control and regulation of inappropriate behavior is best secured through imparting values leading to consent, rather than forcing obedience through coercion.

PARENTING STYLES

The initial models of parenting proposed in the classic work on value acquisition eventually gave way to new theoretical models of parenting. One of the most highly celebrated and supported theories of parenting strategies is the model of Baumrind (1966, 1967, 1971, 1978, 1991). Baumrind argued that there are different approaches parents use to control their children: permissive, authoritarian, and authoritative. These have important and far reaching implications both on the way children conceptualize authority and on their ability to regulate their behavior.

Permissive parents generally behave in a nonpunitive manner. The authority component of the parent–child relationship is largely nonexistent or unrecognized. They tend to accept and accede to their children's impulses and desires. They rarely establish any rules or standards of appropriate behavior. If rules are established, they are usually not enforced. Instead children are allowed to regulate their own behavior as much as possible. Although permissive parents may use reasoning to shape their child's behavior, they will rarely engage in direct and overt control.

Authoritarian parents are the exact opposite of permissive parents. Here the authority portion of the relationship is pivotal and viewed in unidirectional terms with parents dictating to children and children listening. Authoritarian parents do not defer to their children's wishes and desires. Instead, they go to great lengths to shape and control their children's behavior. Behavioral standards are absolute and clearly elaborated. Obedience to parental authority is prized over self-regulation. Authoritarian parents typically use forceful harsh punishment to control their children and preserve the order of a traditional hierarchical structure of authority. This style is synonymous with the coercive parenting approach presented earlier.

Finally, authoritative parents are responsive to their children's needs and desires. At the same time, they also direct children's behavior by establishing behavioral standards that they expect will be followed. Unlike authoritarian parents, these standards are not rigidly imposed, but are explained. The authority relationship between the parent and child is recognized and encouraged to be bidirectional and cooperative. Authoritative parents encourage verbal give and take where they explain the reasoning behind their rules and solicit their children for feedback. If the rules are broken, children are punished, but not in an overbearing or harsh manner. Parents display warmth and caring, even while enforcing rules. Authoritative parents promote independence and the self-regulation of behavior.

Later work (Maccoby & Martin, 1983) distilled Baumrind's classic parenting typology into two orthogonal dimensions that could be used to classify different parenting styles. The first dimension is "warmth," which represents the extent to which parents are responsive to their children's needs and concerns. This dimension includes parental support for children's wants and desires, consistency in providing treatment and support, and the use of rational discussion. This approach maximizes the degree to which parents are willing to allow their children freedom to grow and develop as individuals. To do this they have to communicate respect for their children, concern about their needs, and a belief that they are of worth as people. It is particularly important that parents support the belief that children will master the many problems associated with learning how to navigate the complex world of social rules. Parents need to communicate reassurance that children can and will emerge from socialization as people that can be and will be valued and respected by others.

The second dimension is "control," and represents the degree and ways in which parents try to regulate their children. This includes the behavioral standards parents place upon children and the degree to which they demand conformity to these standards. This dimension also includes the ways in which parents create and enforce rules, as well as how they supervise or monitor children and their willingness to confront those who break the rules.

Baumrind's original parenting typology can now be reclassified using these two dimensions. Permissive parenting is high in warmth but low in control, while authoritarian parents are low in warmth but high in control. Authoritative parenting incorporates aspects of both styles. This approach is high in control in that parents clearly delineate and enforce behavioral standards, and is also high in warmth in that parents are receptive to their children's needs while also encouraging their desire for autonomy.

Finally, an additional style not present in the original typology emerges using this approach. Neglectful parenting is neither warm nor controlling.

These parents largely shirk their responsibilities as parents by not providing any direction or structure for their children or meeting their needs. Children from neglectful parents largely see authorities as distant and uncaring. After all, even authoritarian parents care about preserving order and maintaining discipline and permissive parents are highly cognizant of showing their children warmth and love. Neglectful parents care for neither.

Generally speaking, authoritative parenting has been linked to a variety of positive outcomes for children (for reviews see Baumrind, 1991; Hoeve et al., 2008; Hoeve et al., 2009). Highly demanding and highly responsive patterns of child-rearing typically produce well-adjusted children who are willful, independent, and psychologically healthy. For example, Mowen (2010) linked authoritative parenting to high levels of self-esteem, self-reliance, and academic achievement, as well as a heightened sense of maturity and a positive self-image.

More importantly for the present discussion, authoritative parenting affects later law-related behavior, producing children that are able to control their actions without the need for sanctions or external control from an authority figure. Research has linked authoritative parenting to decreased delinquent behavior over time (Simons et al., 2005), later alcohol use (Ary, 1999), and later drug abuse (Peterson, Hawkins, Abbott, & Catalano, 1994). Consider a specific example. Trinkner and colleagues (2012) measured parenting style, perceptions of parental legitimacy, and delinquent behavior at three points in time in a sample of nearly six hundred children aged eleven to sixteen. The participants reported on the degree to which their parents used authoritarian, permissive, and authoritative styles. The results suggested that parenting style (time one) shaped delinquent behavior (time three), primarily through its impact on parental legitimacy (time two).

On the other hand, the other three parenting styles have been linked to a variety of negative outcomes for children (Baumrind, 1991; Hoeve et al., 2008, 2009; Maccoby & Martin, 1983). Rather than creating well-adjusted children that are capable of self-regulation, these parenting styles lead to children that are indifferent or hostile toward authority figures (Trinkner et al., 2012). Moreover, they are unable to control their own behavior as evidenced by their increased likelihood to engage in delinquency, substance abuse (smoking, drinking, drugs; see Piko & Balazs, 2012), and bullying (Newman et al., 2008).

Authoritative parents develop strong social and emotional bonds with their children by showing warmth, treating them with respect, making fair decisions, and encouraging discussions about the boundaries of parent authority. Children begin to understand that authorities can treat people well and be benevolent while still maintaining standards of appropriate behavior. Over time, this serves to legitimize parental authority and power in the eyes of children (Trinkner et al., 2012). The other parenting styles have an opposite effect. Children come to understand that authorities are likely to be unresponsive or domineering. Rather than creating an atmosphere in which children will see authority as benevolent and caring, authorities are viewed as unresponsive, harsh, or controlling. These types of parenting lead to antiauthority attitudes (Trinkner et al., 2012).

Parenting styles influence children by affecting their openness to their parent's attempts to socialize them (Darling & Steinberg, 1993). In essence, they create an atmosphere within which children can understand their parents' attempts to control them and interpret their exercise of parental authority. This not only influences the way they conceptualize their relationship with their parents, but it also has important ramifications for how they will interface with authorities later on in life. They play an important role in the legal socialization process by influencing the internalization of law-related values, particularly those that help to define and clarify the relationship between children and parental authorities. As a result, children internalize values that characterize different authority styles. Later, these values will form the basis by which individuals judge the appropriateness of legal authority. For example, young adults are more likely to view the police as legitimate authorities and be less involved in later of criminal behavior when they experience authoritative parenting during adolescence (Trinkner, 2015).

PROCEDURAL JUSTICE

Another perspective on parental practices that facilitate the acquisition of values that support voluntary consent toward authority can be found in the work on procedural justice in families (Brubacher, Fondacaro, Brank, Brown, & Miller, 2009; Fondacaro et al., 1998; Fondacaro, Jackson, & Lüscher, 2002; Jackson & Fondacaro, 1999). One of the noteworthy aspects of studies of coercive parenting styles that feature physical discipline is that children are not just sensitive to the magnitude of coercion being used, but also focus on the fairness through which that coercion is applied (Larzelere, Klein, Schumm, & Alibrando, 1989). Parents practicing such punishment not only undermine social bonds with their children through the application of force; they also tend to make little effort to explain rules and are inconsistent in their discipline practices, both of which detract from the development of internal conceptions of rules

(Dadds, Maujean, & Fraser, 2003). Further, their style of treatment is often cold, distant, humiliating, and dismissive, all elements of treatment that communicate to children that the authority views them as being of low social value and little importance, leading to low self-esteem and diminished feelings of self-worth (Laible & Carlo, 2004). These characteristics are consistent with the general literature on procedural justice and decision-making (see Tyler, 2011), suggesting that children, like adults, are strongly influenced by the degree to which parents use fair and neutral procedures when exerting their authority and treat them with dignity and respect.

Judgments about procedural fairness are vitally important to the relationships that people have with authority figures (Lind & Tyler, 1988). Part of learning about rule systems is developing a perspective on how rules should be created, implemented, and enforced. Unsurprisingly, this perspective first begins to emerge within the family context and is driven by the distinct style of managing conflict and making decisions inherent in any family. These initial encounters have an immense influence early on in life in terms of how children interface with parental authority.

Furthermore, through early experiences children develop a normative sense about the right and wrong way for them to interact with authorities and institutions more generally. This includes their own entitlement to be heard, to have decisions explained and to be treated respectfully, but it also includes their responsibility to accord the same treatment to others with whom they are dealing. It is this normative sense that forms the basis for how their future interactions with school, legal, and governmental authorities.

Human beings are born with at least a rudimentary understanding of right and wrong (Bloom, 2013). Even young infants have been shown to reliably distinguish between moral and immoral transgressions. These initial understandings of moral behavior are then honed and developed through interactions with the outside world, ultimately informing one's understanding of justice. Of particular importance in this case are instances of when rules are violated and how the subsequent conflicts are handled. Young children are highly sensitive to rule violations and motivated to address such infractions through restitution or retaliation (Fehr, Berhnard, & Rockenbach, 2008; Gummerun, Keller, Takezawa, & Mata, 2008; Moore, 2009; Nucci & Nucci, 1982a, 1982b; Schmidt & Tomasello, 2012).

What is especially striking is that even at a very early age children already incorporate procedural justice into their notions of fair play. For example, Thorkildsen and White-McNulty (2002) found that children as young as six recognized procedural fairness and could distinguish it from the fairness of outcomes. Studies testing procedural justice theories in children and youth have demonstrated that children value fairness in procedures and react negatively when they feel that the process is unfair (Weisz, Wingrove, & Faith-Slaker, 2007/2008). Gold, Darley, Hilton, and Zanna (1984) presented seven-year-old children with hypothetical cases of wrongdoing by a child for which they were punished by their mother. They showed that "children found punishment administered without due regard for procedural justice to be unfair" (p. 1758). Similarly, Shaw and Olson (2014) found that five-year-old children more willingly accepted inequitable payment if it was arrived at through a fair procedure.

Not only do children recognize procedural justice at an early age; their experience of fair procedures at the hands of their parents is incredibly important to the internal dynamics of the family. This is most apparent within the context of family conflicts, especially those involving the regulation of behavior. Such conflicts increasingly become more common as children exert their autonomy with age. When parents use procedurally fair means to resolve conflicts they encourage a healthy and supportive climate within the home where there is mutual understanding and respect between parent and child; however, resolving conflict in procedurally unfair ways creates a climate of toxicity and mistrust (Fondacaro et al., 1998, 2002). Parents who resolve family conflicts in procedurally fair ways also have children that are less deviant and more inclined to follow rules (Brubacher et al., 2009; Jackson & Fondacaro, 1999).

It is interesting how well the literature on parenting styles maps onto conceptions of procedural justice. The dimensions of control and warmth posited by Maccoby and Martin (1983) are similar to arguments by Blader and Tyler (2003a, 2003b) that among adults, procedural justice is based on two distinct issues: quality of decision-making procedures and quality of treatment. Decision making exudes the same characteristics highlighted during discussions of control and demandingness. Both refer to issues concerning how parents establish and communicate their behavioral standards to their children. For example, the procedural justice literature highlights the opportunity to be heard (i.e., voice; Thibaut & Walker, 1975), and the parenting style literature highlights give-and-take discussion (i.e., bilateral communication; Darling & Steinberg, 1993). On the other hand, quality of treatment is synonymous with the dimension of warmth and responsiveness. Both literatures highlight the importance of respectful treatment through which parents show their children that they understand, care about, and are responsive to their needs (Tyler, 2006a; Baumrind, 1971).

Additionally, like parenting styles which induce children to be more open to socialization efforts (Darling & Steinberg, 1993), procedural justice is also a means by which parents can instill legal values into children

(Trinkner & Cohn, 2014). In particular, it facilitates the internalization of those values that are paramount to the legal socialization process, in particular legitimacy. Legitimacy is linked to both treatment and decision-making. For example, in their study of almost two thousand sixth through eighth grade students, Brubacher and colleagues (2009) found that when parents used fair procedures, their children were much more likely to endorse the need to engage and communicate with people in ways that signified respect, acceptance, and fairness.

The fact that at an early age children can distinguish between a fair outcome and a fair procedure for exercising authority suggests an ability to recognize that there is more to authority relations and behavioral regulation than enacting rules that must be followed. Indeed this understanding becomes increasingly pronounced as children age and begin to reject parental authority and rules that are viewed as unfair. These legal socialization experiences drive their assessments of law and legal authority later in life, and, coupled with the behavior of such authorities, lead to judgments of legitimacy (Trinkner & Cohn, 2014). As Jackson and Fondacaro (1999) demonstrated, the criteria people use to judge the fairness of parents is nearly identical to the criteria used by adults to judge the fairness of the law and legal authority. Moreover, regardless of whether discussing parental or legal authority, power wielded in unfair ways only serves to promote illegitimacy and cynicism while creating little motivation to comply with directives or rules (Trinkner & Cohn, 2014). In fact, it may achieve the opposite and motivate defiance.

DOMAINS OF PARENTAL AUTHORITY

Many of the parenting approaches discussed above emphasize the importance of fairness in interpersonal treatment and decision-making in influencing the development of children's conceptions of authority. However, a third important dimension of legal values concerns the development of the concept of boundaries. Individuals do not acquiesce to authority in all cases, but instead demarcate certain boundaries or limits to the power of authority. Rather than viewing all behaviors and situations as equal, individuals make important distinctions between them. While the right of authority to control behavior may be recognized in some domains, that same authority will be rejected in others. The roots of this understanding can be traced back to early childhood. Even as young children, individuals are able to distinguish between different types of behaviors. Depending on the domain in question, children will either accept or reject their parents' attempts to make rules and control behavior within each domain.

Broadly speaking, individuals distinguish between three domains of behavior: the moral domain, the conventional domain, and the personal domain (Nucci & Turiel, 1978; Smetana, 1995b, 2002). Each domain is conceptually distinct. The moral domain focuses on behaviors and actions that will influence the rights and welfare of others. For example, aggressing against another person would be considered a behavior within the moral domain because it would cause harm to another individual, thereby damaging that person's welfare. The conventional domain is similar to the concept of social norms in that it encompasses shared uniformities within society that serve to facilitate and coordinate social interactions. This domain includes things such as how to speak to people, modes of greetings, and so on.

The personal domain includes behaviors and issues that are viewed as only pertaining to the individual themselves. Thus they do not influence the rights and welfare of others, nor are they viewed to have a particularly profound influence on coordinating social interactions at the societal level. Behaviors in this domain would be considered lifestyle choices, such as what people to associate with or what books to read. Whereas moral and conventional actions are seen to be within the boundaries of authority control, actions in the person domain are viewed as beyond the concerns of such regulation.

These distinctions are important because they are intricately tied to the way in which children begin to understand the limits of parental authority. Children recognize that parental authority does not have a right to control *all* of their behaviors and choices. Just as they distinguish between different domains of behavior, they also distinguish between different domains of parental authority as well (Tisak, 1986). They will acquiesce to authority in some domains, but not in others.

Typically, children accede to parental authority to regulate their behavior and make rules in moral and conventional domains, but not within the personal domain. This finding has been shown by a host of research both in the United States (Smetana, 1995b; Smetana & Asquith, 1994; Smetana & Daddis, 2002) and outside of it (Darling, Cumsille, & Martinez, 2007, 2008; Milnitsky-Sapiro, Turiel, & Nucci, 2006; Smetana, 2002; Yau & Smetana, 2003). For example, in a sample of fifth through twelfth grade students, Smetana (1988) showed that children agreed that their parents had legitimate authority to regulate a variety of moral and conventional behaviors approximately 90% of the time. However, in terms of behaviors in the personal domain, children viewed their parents as legitimate authority figures less than 30% of the time.

In addition, parents and children largely agree on these demarcations of regulatory responsibility between them. This is especially true for the moral and conventional domains. In Smetana's (1988) analysis, the parents of her participants also agreed approximately 90% of the time that they had a legitimate right to make rules and regulate behaviors in the moral and conventional domains. This agreement though becomes particularly more complicated when discussing the personal domain. Although both parents and children agree that the personal domain *itself* is not within the boundaries of parental authority (hence the name "personal"), disagreements arise in regards to what exact *behaviors* fall into this personal domain. As noted, Smetana found that children ceded their parents' authority less than 30% of the time in this domain; however, parents believed they had legitimate authority over 50% of the personal behaviors they were asked about.

The differences between parents and children in the personal domain highlight an important aspect concerning children's developing notions of authority. Children learn that there will inevitably be conflicts between themselves and authorities, especially when it comes to the limits or boundaries of authority power. While these conflicts typically are infrequent and begin very early in childhood, they become more pervasive and intense as children age (Smetana, 1995b). The vast majority of these conflicts arise out of arguments in the personal domain, driven by children's tendency to put an increasing amount of behaviors into this domain as they begin to exert their autonomy and establish their independence. Naturally, parents will resist to some degree their children's attempts to define more behavior as outside the scope of parental authority and regulation. Conflicts over the limits of parental regulation begin to increase rapidly with the onset of puberty and come to a head in early to mid-adolescence. After this period, conflicts over parental boundaries begin to decrease as teenagers and parents have largely worked through their differences and come to some type of resolution.

The development of boundaries through authority conflict has important ramifications for how children come to understand and conceptualize their relationship with parental authority, and authority more generally. First, children come to learn that power is not absolute or limitless. Instead, the power of authorities to regulate their behavior and choices is restrained to some degree. They learn that authorities cannot and should not control every facet of their lives. As a result, youth begin to understand that there are inappropriate ways to exert authority and that such exertions do not require obedience. For example, Darling and colleagues (2007) showed that when adolescents believed parents were trying to create and enforce rules within domains that they believed their parents had no right to control, they viewed them as less legitimate. In later work, Darling and colleagues (2008) showed that when adolescents viewed parental control as illegitimate they were also less likely to feel obligated to follow their rules within that domain.

How parents handle the conflicts over the boundaries of parental authority is also important to adolescent conceptions of authority. Once again, the style with which parents use to discipline and control their children is especially salient as they contribute to the nature of these conflicts and how they are resolved (Baumrind, 1991; Darling & Steinberg, 1993; Smetana, 1995a). Authoritarian parents are more likely to see more behaviors and domains as under their jurisdiction, while permissive parents see far less and authoritative parents are somewhere in between. Perhaps not surprisingly, parents using an authoritarian style are more likely than any other style to come into conflict with their children over the appropriate boundaries of their authority. These conflicts are also much more likely to be intense and damaging, given authoritarians tendency to wield power and resolve conflicts in a coercive fashion.

Authoritative parents on the other hand have fewer conflicts and arguments with their children over boundaries (Smetana, 1995a). When conflicts do occur, they are also less intense. While authoritarian parents actually detract from their children's sense of identity, authoritative parents stimulate personal and emotional autonomy in their children. Moreover, the way in which they go about managing these conflicts, especially their reliance on bidirectional communication and inductive reasoning, serves to promote a better understanding of where the boundary between appropriate authority control and personal autonomy lies. "By articulating clearly the societal or welfare concerns that complex issues raise, authoritative parents may facilitate adolescents' understanding of the limits or boundaries of their personal jurisdiction" (Smetana, 1995a, p. 313). This better defined understanding has a direct influence on how adolescents view their relationship with the legal system as they get older. For example, authoritative parenting during adolescence has been linked to more supportive legal attitudes and police legitimacy during adulthood (Trinkner, 2015).

"Defining those boundaries either too permissively or too rigidly may deprive adolescents and parents of the opportunity to negotiate appropriate boundaries, which in turn, may be detrimental to adolescent development" (Smetana, 1995a, p. 313). Part of developing as an adolescent is experimenting with boundaries and learning through experiences which work and which do not work. Making mistakes and learning from those mistakes is not only part of development it is a mechanism through which development occurs. While a child who simply obeys may generally follow rules (and of course in reality as we have outlined many times they do not), they have not developed any capacity to think about those rules, why they exist, when they are important, and how to use discretion in approaching them. These are the attributes of a consent-based orientation and they allow an adolescent or an adult to both obey rules when appropriate and to apply discretion to the application of those same rules when that is desirable.

THE CURRENT CLIMATE OF PARENTING

Throughout this volume we have argued that legal value acquisition is a vital process to successful legal socialization and the development of a supportive orientation toward the law and legal authority. So far in this chapter, we have shown that the acquisition of law-related values begins early in life and is greatly accelerated when children experience forms of parental authority that seek their consensual deference rather than impose coercive obedience, especially through the use of physical discipline. Given the amount of data suggesting the importance of this approach to parenting, it is worth examining the state of society's attitudes toward parenting. What is the current climate of parenting in the modern era?

One question is the importance placed upon obedience as a value. In general, a substantial minority of adult Americans place high value on obedience. For example, data from the World Value Survey (www.worldvaluessurvey.org)[1] indicates that between 1981 and 1984, 26% of Americans agreed that obedience is an important child quality that should be taught within the home. Although this belief increased in the 1990s (32%–39%), it has returned to its previous levels of 28% from 2005–2014.

Data from the General Social Survey (GSS, www.norc.org) comes to similar conclusions about American attitudes toward obedience. This survey asks respondents to choose from a variety of different values. Between 1973 and 1983 they asked if it was "important that children obey their parents." In 1973, 13.3% of American selected this as their top priority. Ten years later, in 1983, that number had risen to 16.0%. In 1986, the question was changed so that respondents were asked about the values "children need to prepare him or her self for life." In 1986, 39% placed "to obey" as one of their two top values; however, that dropped to 24% by 2014. Furthermore, in 2012, 26% of the respondents indicated that obedience was the most important value children should learn.[2] Taken together, this work indicates that a minority of the American population believes that obedience should be a primary goal during childhood socialization.

A second question is the degree to which parents support using physical discipline as a child-rearing strategy. As we noted earlier, such a strategy hinders legal socialization. Data from multiple sources all indicate that such practices are a common way of dealing with rule-breaking among American families. In a recent US sample of parents of one- to two-year-olds, 63% reported using physical discipline (Regalado et al., 2004). In another nationally representative study involving over 21,000 children, 80% of kids reported being corporally punished by their parents by the time they reached fifth grade (Gershoff & Bitensky, 2007). Finally, in his interviews with families and children from all of the U.S., Straus (1991; Straus & Donnelly, 2001) found that many parents continued using physical discipline during adolescence.

Perhaps unsurprisingly, the importance placed upon obedience as a value has been directly tied to the adoption of coercive parenting practices. The 2012 GSS found that 71% of respondents supported the use of spanking to discipline children, and 26% thought that obedience was one of the top two values children should learn while growing up. These two judgments were positively correlated as well. Those individuals who were in favor of spanking were almost twice as likely to report that obedience was an important virtue that must be imparted to children than those who did not favor spanking (17% vs. 9%).

Another important question in regards to the current climate of parenting is whether values concerning the importance of obedience in child-rearing are changing. The results in this case are not consistent. For example, Starks and Robinson (2005) used GSS data to compare people's support for learning "to think for oneself" relative to learning "to obey." They found near stability in support for these two values over a sixteen-year period from 1986 to 2002. This work is similar to the World Values Survey cited earlier in showing little movement in regards to American's support for the value of obedience.

On the other hand, other studies suggest that Americans are increasing their support of imparting the value of obedience onto children. Earlier we noted that the number of Americans who selected obedience as a top value rose from 13.3% in 1973 to 16.0% in 1983. Additionally, other GSS data show that the number of people reporting that it is important to "obey laws without exception" rose from 43% in 1985 to 53% in 2006.[3]

However, others have suggested that support for values of obedience has been decreasing. Alwin (2001, p. 122) argues that "there is considerable evidence that a major historic trend has been occurring in the child-rearing values of parents—from values stressing obedience to those giving more emphasis on autonomy." This is also consistent with GSS data showing that support for simple obedience dropped between 1986 and 2006 from 39% to 34%.

An issue within this work is that, given the nature of the questions asked, it is hard to determine whether parents are endorsing blind obedience (characteristic of a coercive approach) or encouraging thoughtful questioning of authority prior to obedience (characteristic of a consensual approach). The question is how to understand what people mean when they say that children should learn to obey. In particular, the underlying assumption might be that children should learn to obey legitimate authorities, which implies that authorities are not simply entitled to obedience.

The question now becomes what framework is being instilled in children to help them make judgments about the legitimate authority of others. Recent work on the millennial generation provides a possible answer. This generation has been shown to be generally more separated from loyalty to traditional institutions when compared to older generations (Pew Research Center, 2014b). However, this is not because young people are less obedient per se, but rather because they are more focused on issues of trust and process when it comes to their inter-relationships with institutions. As Shore (2011) argues, millennials demand fairness, transparency, clear and consistent rules, and the opportunity to have their voice heard. These expectations come from having family democracies in which children and parents discuss authority and negotiate over rules. Millennial children are more accustomed to discussing decisions in their families.

This set of findings about recent child-rearing approaches suggests that the child-rearing values of parents have moved from values stressing obedience via an authoritarian relationship to ones stressing obedience through consent. In other words, children in the modern age appear to be increasingly taught to reason through the question of obedience not only in terms of how they should behave, but also in terms of how the institutions around them behave. Such cognitive machinations lead to an internalization of the commitment to follow rules where the decision to obey is motivated by a consensual connection to the rules. Although data is inconsistent, it appears that parents and adults are beginning to learn that they can obtain obedience from their children through fair interactions that produce mutual benefits for all involved, rather by fiat.

In this respect children reflect the general view of prior Americans who have long placed value on disobeying any authority, legal or political, who does not reflect the values of the US democratic and Constitutional system (for example, King, 1963; Paine, 1997; Thoreau, 1993). While legal and political authorities enjoy strong support and a presumption of legitimacy and deference, that presumption is based upon their acting in ways that reflect the values of democratic governance, the rule of law, and justice. When political leaders have gone outside this framework (such as Lyndon Johnson and the war in Vietnam) or when they have stepped over the boundaries of the rule of law (Richard Nixon and Watergate, Ronald Reagan and Iran Contra, Bill Clinton and perjury, the post-9/11 surveillance state) they have found considerable willingness to question their authority and raise issues about whether to either trust the leaders involved or obey their directives.

LAW-RELATED ATTITUDES

In addition to acquiring legal values, childhood is also an important time for the development of the positive and negative attitudes that will eventually grow to shape evaluations of the law and legal authority during adulthood. There is a large intellectual tradition that links the smooth functioning of society to the existence of supportive attitudes among members of the general population (Easton, 1965, 1975; Krislov, Boyum, Clark, Shaefer, & White, 1966; Melton, 1985; Parsons, 1937; Tapp and Levine, 1977). The roots of these attitudes can be traced back to early childhood. In terms of legal socialization, these attitudes also provide meaning to people's experiences with the law by shaping the way they interpret and react to the creation, maintenance, and enforcement of the law among members of society (Cohn & White, 1990).

Early in life children's general orientations toward formal institutions, including the legal system, are fairly simplistic. Children's legal senses at this point are mostly motivated by instrumental concerns, so they view the law as an institution that rewards good behavior and punishes bad behavior (Tapp & Levine, 1974). In so doing, the legal system is understood as something that protects children from bad things and bad people. Unsurprisingly, these institutions are viewed mostly in positive terms (Hess & Torney, 1967; Rigby, Schofield, & Slee, 1987; Tapp & Levine, 1974).

This generally positive orientation toward the law can be seen in the way children view authorities. Children often idealize formal authority figures. For example, young children are likely to believe that leaders are benevolently motivated and there to help everyone (Hess & Torney, 1967; Torney, 1971). As a result, they tend to be more trusting and willing to personalize government and the law (Easton & Dennis, 1969). When asked about the abstract authorities of government, they usually refer to police officers or the President and describe how they envision they would interact with them. Unsurprisingly, these interactions are generally viewed in favorable terms (Hess & Torney, 1967). For example, young children believe that if they write a letter to the president he will read it and care about what they say. Additionally, a police officer is viewed as someone who will always help out if needed. As a result, young children generally have more of an unquestioning and obedient orientation toward formal authority figures. For most, they have difficulty conceiving of reasons to disobey an adult authority such as a police officer (Greenstein, 1960).

However, as children age their views about the law and legal authority become more nuanced and differentiated as their cognitive capacities and social relationships expand and become more complex (Tapp & Levine, 1974). In particular, their views about the purposes of the law shift. Whereas early on they think of the law in terms of its restrictive and punitive aspects, they increasingly come to view the law as having benefits for themselves and their community (Adelson, Green, & O'Neil, 1969; Tapp, 1991). In essence, they begin to better grasp the social importance of having a system of laws that maintains social harmony. As a result, they begin to more willingly embrace the idea of voluntary adherence to rules without the need of coercion or instrumental control of rewards and punishments (Furnham & Stacey, 1991).

Children's views about the creation and enforcement of rules also begin to shift in a number of ways as well. First, attitudes supportive of democratic norms emerge. As children come to see the law as a social endeavor, they come to understand that it is also a social creation that provides mutual advantages for all (Tapp, 1991). They better realize the usefulness of processes where everyone has a voice and participates and to value laws that are meant to benefit everyone. Increasingly, they care about how laws are implemented and whether they are fairly enforced (Gold, Darley, Hilton, & Zanna, 1984). Such features become prerequisites for developing supportive attitudes of the law and the perception that the legal system is entitled to obedience (Fagan & Tyler, 2005; Trinkner & Cohn, 2014).

Second, as children's internal controls emerge, their attitudes about specific rules and rule-violating behavior also change. Early conceptions of rule violation are centered on rewards and punishments (Cohn & White, 1990; Tapp, 1991). So long as children do not get caught and punished, then violating rules is not necessarily a bad thing. Hence, children's attitudes toward upholding rules themselves are largely inconsequential. With the realization that the legal system is a vehicle for maintaining social harmony, children also begin to see the importance of rule-following outside of instrumental concerns. As a result, normative notions about the utility of violating and upholding laws begin to emerge (Cohn & White, 1990). For example, Cohn and colleagues (2010, 2012) have shown that as adolescents are better able to grasp the social nature of the law, they are also less likely to approve of breaking both formal and informal rules. At the same time, they also are more supportive of punishing those who violate the law.

Finally, although the relationship to parents is usually discussed in terms of value acquisition within legal socialization, the exercise of parental authority is also important in terms of the formation of positive and supportive attitudes toward the law. As we noted earlier, children are sensitive to the way in which parents exert their power. When parents behave in a fair and impartial manner, youth come to see them as legitimate authorities (Trinkner & Cohn, 2014; Trinkner et al., 2012). Parental legitimacy is associated with less approval of rule-violating behavior (Cohn et al., 2012).

Over the long term, early experiences bolster the sense that rules and regulatory institutions are just enterprises and therefore should be obeyed (Tapp & Levine, 1974). This effect can be seen in two ways. First, it has long been known that attitudes toward formal authority and informal authority are interrelated (Rigby & Rump, 1981; Rigby, Schofield, & Slee, 1987; Trinkner, 2012). Given that individuals encounter parental authority before any other, it is likely that experiences with parents and their use of power shape later legal attitudes. Indeed, research bears this out. For example, in their study of ten- to sixteen-year-old children, Fagan and Tyler (2005) found that children were more likely to view the police as legitimate authorities when they had parents that provided adequate supervision. More recently, Trinkner (2015) showed when adolescents experience authoritative parenting practices as children, they are more likely to view the police as legitimate and be less supportive of criminal behavior when they reach adulthood.

Second, parenting also shapes children's cynicism toward the law. In this respect, legal cynicism is reflective of a general sense of malaise or anomie concerning the regulatory structures in society (Srole, 1956). A legally cynical individual is someone who feels that laws and rules in society are not normatively binding (Sampson & Bartusch, 1998). In essence, cynical individuals reject the notion that laws apply to them in their day-to-day lives (Piquero, Fagan, Mulvey, Steinberg, & Odgers, 2005). Traditionally, legal cynicism has been viewed as a result of interactions with the law (Kirk & Matsuda, 2011; Kirk & Papachristos, 2011). However, cynical attitudes have their roots in the family context as well (Trinkner & Cohn, 2014). In particular, when individuals experience unfair parental authority, they not only come to be cynical about the rules in their home, but also about the rules governing society.

THE FAMILY CONTEXT AND LAW-RELATED BEHAVIOR

The development of internal controls—that is, acquisition of legal values and the formation of supportive attitudes—promotes law-abiding behavior among the population (Furnham & Stacey, 1991). We have demonstrated throughout this chapter that the family context is essential to this aspect of the legal socialization process. As a result, it is not surprising that the family context has long been identified as an important driver of deviance and criminal behavior. This is supported by a range of classic studies (Glueck & Glueck, 1950; McCord, 1979; Robins & Ratcliff, 1978) to literature reviews (Farrington, 2005) and meta-analyses (Loeber & Loeber-Stouthamer, 1986). Indeed, as the Gluecks highlighted in their tome on juvenile delinquency, in many cases family factors are significantly more noteworthy in the production of deviance than other well-established factors such as poverty, exposure to popular culture, and neighborhood level variables.

Echoing earlier social scientists (Durkheim, 1973; Hirshi, 1969), Laub and Sampson (2003, p. 6) argue that "crime and deviance are more likely to occur when individual's bond to society is weak or broken." Social bonds represent a buy-in of sorts to the social order. When people feel they are tied socially to the world around them, they are motivated to uphold societal rules concerning appropriate behavior. This includes formal regulations like laws. However, when people are not tied to the world, when they feel like they have nothing at stake, it is much easier to disregard the law and behave with impunity. The family acts as the initial—and in many ways most powerful—unit of society that creates and strengthens these social ties (Hirschi, 1983, Sampson & Laub, 1993). As we have already noted, identification is linked to social bonds and is one of two primary mechanisms through which values are accepted by people as reflecting their identity and sense of self.

What is it about the family context that is so vitally important? There have literally been hundreds if not thousands of studies over the years linking various family characteristics to antisocial, aggressive, deviant, and criminal behavior. Central to many of these studies is the primacy of the parent–child relationship, especially in regards to how parents exert their authority in disciplining and maintaining behavioral standards within the home (Loeber & Loeber-Stouthamer, 1986). Indeed, parenting practices have a drastic influence on children's acquisition of the internal controls that will eventually lead to the self-regulation of behavior. As we noted above, coercive discipline-heavy parenting hinders this acquisition, while consensual, authoritative, and fair parenting accelerates it.

It is no wonder that across a wide variety of research, parental discipline and authority has been linked to delinquent behavior in adolescence. This includes poor parental supervision, overly harsh or punitive discipline, detached or unresponsive attitudes, and erratic or inconsistent punishment (Farrington, 2005; Loeber & Loeber-Stouthamer, 1986; Rothbaum & Weisz, 1994; Shaw & Scott, 1991; Simons et al., 2005; Trinkner et al., 2012; Trinkner & Cohn, 2014; West & Farrington, 1973). Furthermore, these parental experiences serve as a precursor to later legal experiences and behavior. Those who become juvenile offenders and move into adult criminality "have a difficult time with all types of authority, rules, and structure" (Laub & Sampson, 2003, p. 182). Such resistance has been noted by a number of researchers as an "attractive" feature of criminal behavior for young individuals (Katz, 1988; Laub & Sampson, 2003; Sherman, 1993). The beginnings of this resistance can be seen in the work linking perceptions of parental legitimacy to increased rule-violating behavior over time (Darling et al., 2008; Trinkner et al., 2012).

SUMMARY

Acquiring values, attitudes, and capacities that lead to a supportive relationship with the law is central to the legal socialization process. Our review of the parenting and family socialization literature identifies childhood as an essential period that provides the foundation for this process. The attitudes and values that are acquired during this time clearly shape rule-following behaviors of varying types and can be directly tied to people's legal behavior and experiences with legal authority later in life. Hence, the extent to which children develop supportive attitudes and values during this time matters.

One of the most important features of this review in regards to legal socialization is the idea of child-rearing practices, specifically in terms of parents' establishment and maintenance of behavioral standards within the home. The way parents exert their authority when interacting with children establishes a framework for their understanding of rules and the relationship between them and authority figures. This is particularly important because this initial blueprint concerning rules and authority acquired in childhood shape orientations toward subsequent authorities encountered later in life (e.g., teachers, school resource officers, law enforcement, judges). In this way, family dynamics during childhood ultimately influences the proclivity to obey and engage with authorities during adolescence and adulthood.

In particular, we have identified three key issues concerning family dynamics:

(1) The establishment of social bonds between parents and children and the enactment of parenting behaviors that demonstrate caring, concern, and responsivity. This is connected to the importance of treatment that communicates respect and benevolence.

(2) The manner in which parents apply rules and regulate violations of those rules, including their attempts to actively engage their children and their application of fair and neutral standards. Here the issue is fair decision-making.

(3) Reactions to children's attempts at asserting autonomy and the degree to which parents recognize and negotiate the boundaries of their authority.

Two contrasting models of parenting were outlined in regards to these issues. One strategy emphasizes a coercive relationship between parents and children and the management of behavior via the manipulation of rewards and costs. This strategy is characterized by strict obedience and force-based discipline where parents dominate children with physical punishment and coercion, with little concern about whether they are viewed as fair, as consistent, or as attentive to their children's well-being. Children raised in this way adopt an instrumental approach to rules and authorities and come to define their relationship with authority figures in negative and coercive terms. As a result, they are less willing or able to keep their behavior within the framework of formal rules and more likely to believe that interpersonal expressions of force are acceptable as a mechanism for achieving their social goals. They have been socialized to understand the authority relationship in terms of dominance-submission, coercion, and power. As such, they learn that behaving in such ways is an acceptable and appropriate way to obtain goals. Not surprisingly, such children break rules when they can benefit and feel unlikely to be detected and regard achieving their goals by threatening or using force as appropriate. It is, after all, what they have learned by watching their own parents.

An alternative strategy emphasizes a consensual relationship with parents where children are socialized in ways that lead them to adopt supportive civic attitudes and legal values. Here, parents are responsive to their children's needs. Their aim is to not only provide a safe and secure environment for their children, but to also teach them responsibilities and appropriate behavior while also stimulating their personal autonomy and self-reliance. Moreover, parents are not just concerned with enforcing behavioral standards, but they are also cognizant of how those standards are enacted. These parents value the consistent and rule-based application of rules, encourage discussions with their children, and are careful to provide adequate explanations to their children concerning their authority. Children raised this way define their relationship to rules and authority in personally compelling ways. Acquiescence and deference to authority and rules is not driven by rewards and punishments, but rather by the incorporation of rules into a child's sense of self.

CHAPTER 8

Ⓐ

Legal Socialization in the School

Our discussion of legal socialization will next examine the school context. School presents growing children with the challenge of dealing with adults of whom they have no family ties. This is likely the first time that children will have to build and form a relationship with an authority figure that is initially a complete stranger, has only limited contact with them constrained to a particular situation, and oversees many other children. At this point, authority experiences begin to be more impersonal in nature and guided by formalized rules. Additionally, the school environment represents the first time that children have to deal with multiple authorities who will likely have different authority styles and exercise their position and role in different ways. Any of these factors may potentially pose challenging problems. Indeed, it is during this time that it may become apparent to children that not only will different authorities interact with them in different ways, but that the same authority may also interact with other children differently than they do with them. These varying experiences serve to further refine and develop their values concerning fair treatment, decision-making, boundaries, and rules.

As was the case in the previous chapter, our goal is to examine how legal socialization pressures within the educational context influence the development of civic values, legal attitudes, and reasoning capacities that underlie a consensual model of law and the maintenance of social order. Again, our focus will be on the creation and enforcement of rules by teachers and other administrative authorities. We will highlight the detrimental effects of a school regulatory climate rooted in coercive models of authority compared to more consensually-oriented models. At the same time, the discussion will be expanded to include civic education and the transmission of legal knowledge through formal and informal curriculums. However, we begin by asking a more general question concerning the overall purpose of education.

THE PURPOSE OF EDUCATION

What is the purpose of formal K–12 education? In recent years discussions about education have emphasized the goal of skill acquisition, often equating the value of school with the ability to give students adult jobs that provide a career and a high level of income. This equates education with learning skills like reading, writing, and arithmetic. The most important outcomes in this respect are largely performance-based (e.g., test scores). Taking it a step further, some even argue that schools are designed to mirror and hence help students become effective at working in environments like the modern work office (Bowles & Gintis, 1976).

It is worth noting, however, that other alternative views place just as much focus on developing moral qualities and social and civic skills as they do on acquiring job skills. As Arum (2003, p. 3) argues, "problems of moral authority strike at the core of public education, because primary and secondary schooling is as much about the socialization of youth as it is about teaching rudimentary cognitive skills." Moreover, "while policy makers widely recognize the fact that education serves as an engine for economic growth through the accumulation of human capital, education is also strongly associated with boosting levels of social capital. Indeed, an important justification for the large expenditures on education within many democratic nations is its social, and not just economic impact—the benefits an educated electorate brings to civil society" (Campbell, 2006, p. 25).

In other words, schooling is also important because it is a means to provide children with civic education and knowledge about how society and its institutions are supposed to work. Such education is linked to many attributes associated with good citizenship. For example, Campbell (2006, p. 28) recently noted that the 1999 International Association for the Evaluation of Educational Achievement (IEA) Civic Education Study found significant relations between many aspects of education and civic and social engagement across twenty-eight different nations. "One [finding] in particular that stands out is the openness of the classroom climate, or the degree to which students are able to discuss political and social issues in class. Classroom climate has positive impact on every dimension of engagement included in the analysis: knowledge, skills, intention of being an informed voter, intention of being civically engaged, intention of being politically engaged, institutional trust, and tolerance."

A positive ideal of public education as civic instruction has a long intellectual history, going back at least to the writings of the famous educational reformer John Dewey (1916). Dewey emphasized the importance of ensuring that democratic deliberation was based upon informed public opinion through the education of children. His model of education emphasized building the school curriculum around student interests to encourage active involvement in learning, with teachers acting as guides and motivators. Dewey also believed that real world experience should be an important part of childhood education.

A key contribution of Dewey's writing was the argument that schools themselves must be laboratories of democracy, with children learning about the democratic process through experiencing it as students who were encouraged to ask questions, discuss issues, and generally become active and willing learners by following their own interests. If schools are laboratories of democracy where children learn about democratic process, then by definition they are going to learn or be socialized into the values that society uses to define the appropriate relationship between the individual and legal authorities. Moreover, their interactions with teachers during this time is going to be an ideal testing ground to assess the validity (i.e., legitimacy) of such systems in terms of whether they are meeting these ideals.

Similarly, Durkheim (1973) emphasized that school authority represents the moral authority of society and in this way serves to internalize societal norms of appropriate behavior and facilitate the development of self-control. When schools are successful in this task they do not need to focus on the enforcement of rules or the use of punishments, because students accept the rules and feel responsible for obeying them. Sanctions, when used, are primarily messages of disapproval for rule violations which reinforce the importance of following rules. This approach leads to a focus on fairness because perceptions of fairness are central to the legitimacy of authorities and the rules they enforce. When students think teachers are unfair, they are more like to break rules (Hollingsworth, Lufler, & Clune, 1984). This connection of fairness in the exercise of authority to behavior is something we have already noted in our discussions of parenting, and it is central to discussions of schools and teachers.

The key issue here is that the educational experience is not (and should not) be simply about skill acquisition, nor should it be evaluated only in terms of cognitive skills children acquire or the amount of money they make once they become adults. Rather schooling, especially public schooling, can and often does play an important role in providing students with a set of common values that are important to the successful functioning of a democratic society. In particular, those values comprise the way individuals understand their role within a democratic society as it relates to the operation of the law and legal authorities.

For example, in discussing whether students should have hearings in school disciplinary cases, the Supreme Court has argued that "the school room is the first opportunity most citizens have to experience the power of government. Through it passes every citizen and public official, from schoolteachers to policemen and prison guards. The values they learn there they take with them in life" (*New Jersey v. T.L.O. 469 US 325*, 1985, p. 385). It follows in a later case that "the process of educating our youth for citizenship in public schools is not confined to books, the curriculum, and the civics class; schools must teach by example the shared values of a civilized social order. Consciously or otherwise, teachers—and indeed the older students—demonstrate the appropriate form of civil discourse and political expression by their conduct and deportment in and out of class. Inescapably, like parents, they are role models" (*Bethel School District v. Fraser*, 478 US 675, 1986, p. 683).

MODELS OF SCHOOL SOCIALIZATION

In our discussion of the dynamics of families we contrasted parenting approaches that do and do not facilitate the development of a consensual orientation toward authority. A similar distinction emerges in schools with respect to their approach at transforming students into good citizens. In some cases, schools focus on inculcating habits of obedience toward authority. Learning to sit still when so instructed and follow directions and school rules are central to this model. But this approach does not necessarily promote values or a more complex understanding of rules. A second approach is to exercise authority in ways associated with building legitimacy via approaches to learning that involve discussion and compromise through the use of deliberative procedures for reaching consensus. Learning such skills mirrors what adults ideally do later as citizens in a democratic society: discuss, consider alternative views, compromise, and respect the rights of everyone.

EDUCATING THROUGH DISCIPLINE AND FORCE

One popular model of school authority is coercive in nature. Many critics of schools favor severe punishment and rigid and strict disciplinary practices as the way to train children to obey rules. The idea animating these individuals that schools have become too lax and supine with regards to maintaining control in schools. The obvious answer in their minds is a greater focus on discipline. As Arum (2003, p. 163) notes, "according to the deterrence model, the appropriate solution to address increasing student disorder is simple: setting stricter rules and punishments will reverse the problem and bring most misbehaving students into line. Students who continue to misbehave may have to be 'incapacitated' or otherwise sacrificed for the good of the school." There are many variations of such "get tough" or "zero-tolerance" policies for maintaining social order in schools. For example, suspension rates in US public schools have doubled since the 1970s (Losen, 2011). A recent report from the Department of Education (2016) notes that in the 2013–2014 academic year, 2.8 million students grades K–12 received an out-of-school suspension.

The problem with such approaches however is that they are not effective ways of developing values or teaching supportive civic attitudes. Ironically, as we will show, such approaches actually undermine the very thing that such critics seemingly want to stimulate: obedience and acceptance of school authority. Moreover, as we have argued throughout this volume, instrumental control of rewards and punishments do not effectively motivate individuals to self-regulate their behavior. Second, and highly related to the first point, such approaches are not consistent with those values dictating the appropriate relationship between individuals and authorities held in democratic society. When authorities adopt such a style of behavioral control individuals recognize that the authorities are being inappropriate and reject the authority's claims of legitimacy and demands for compliance. This perspective is supported by Arum (2003, p. 163), who argues that "increasing school rules and implementing harsher punishment will not necessarily address the nature of school disorder and could potentially make the situation worse, as students often resist authoritarian disciplinary policies that are perceived as unfair and illegitimate."

Policies of exclusionary discipline in school have been found to create a climate which undermines achievement among all students, not just those excluded (Perry & Morris, 2014). Similarly, these practices undermine trust for formal authority among all students, not just those potentially personally influenced (Kirk & Matsuda, 2011). More broadly, schools prepare children for participation in democratic society. School suspensions are found to undermine voting and civic participation indicating the potential for long-term social costs of punitive disciplinary policies (Kupchik & Catlaw, 2014). Perhaps most insidiously, a coercive focus on obedience and control has increased the likelihood that school infractions will lead to criminal consequences and sanctions, drawing youth into the juvenile justice system which is itself associated with greater criminal conduct (as we will describe in the next chapter). Such a path has been coined the "school-to-prison pipeline" to emphasize how problematic school behavior that has traditionally been considered the purview of school officials can now lead to the incarceration of youth in the juvenile justice system (Morris, 2012).

A second development in education is the increasing tendency to define student misbehavior through a criminal justice prism that uses crime control strategies to inform policies of student discipline and management (Hirschfield, 2008). This feature of the modern educational environment is most glaring with the widespread proliferation of school resource officers (SROs) that either are or act like police officers. As an example, 68% of secondary school students report law enforcement officers in their schools (Cox, Sughrue, & Alexander, 2012). Whereas sworn officers officially assigned to police school environments were almost unheard of prior to the 1980s, today nearly one quarter (24%) of all elementary schools and almost half (42%) of all high schools contain such officers (Department of Education, 2016). Police officers are also more prevalent (51%) in schools with large Black and Latino populations.

In many cases, SROs rely on the same strategies used to control crime on the streets, such as the use of metal detectors, video surveillance, and an in-school version of stop-question-frisk where students' bodies, lockers, and backpacks are searched with little warning. These policies increase the likelihood of suspension, expulsion, or enrollment in alternative schools (Morris, 2012; Skiba, 2000), or, more problematically, being swept into the juvenile justice system by being arrested, adjudicated, or detained within a juvenile facility (Hirschfield, 2008; Mukherjee, 2007). As Ufer (2012, p. 1374) notes, "every day . . . students are stopped, searched, summonsed, or arrested by poorly trained and inadequately supervised police personnel." Further, "low-income and minority students are much more likely to experience intense security conditions in their schools than other students, even after taking into account factors such as neighborhood crime, school crime, and school disorder" (Nance, 2014, p. 79). This might be one reason why Black K–12 students are almost four times as likely to receive an out-of-school suspension as White students (Department of Education, 2016).

Although having police officers in schools is a response to issues of student safety (Kupchik & Ward, 2014), the linkage of officer presence to safety is unclear (James & McCallion, 2013). Studies suggest no clear relationship between having this type of security and student safety (Arum, 2003; Curran, 2016; Kupchik, 2010). Further, it is important to ask how this change in school climate influences students. One argument is that SROs build respect for the police and promote rule-following; the other is that they criminalize student behavior and move problematic students into the criminal justice system. The suggestion that SRO presence builds police legitimacy receives mixed support (Jackson, 2002). Other studies indicate that high school security can alienate students (Bracy, 2011; Mukherjee, 2007), undermine the academic environment (Perry & Morris, 2014), and potentially lead to greater student misbehavior (Mayer & Leone, 1999).[1]

From the procedural justice perspective, it is striking how often officers treat students in ways that do not reflect procedural justice by yelling and cursing at students and subjecting them to indignities such as body pat downs by opposite sex officers and being forced to lean against walls (Arum, 2003; Mukherjee, 2007; Rios, 2011). Such behavior is not unusual and mirrors behavior they are likely to experience dealing with police officers on the street (Carr, Napolitano, & Keating, 2007; Fagan & Tyler, 2005; Tyler, Fagan, & Geller, 2014). Most striking is the general tone of hostility and threat that students report in those interactions (Mukherjee, 2007). In general, findings suggest that the presence of officers undermines the legitimacy of nonpolice school authorities, making it harder for them to act to maintain order (Hyman & Perone, 1998).

DEMOCRATIC MODELS OF EDUCATION

An alternative model of teacher and school authority features the use of democratic ideals and procedures to manage student behavior. As we have noted, a similar perspective flows from the writing of John Dewey (1916, p. 87), who suggested that "since a democratic society repudiates the principle of external authority, it must find a substitute in voluntary disposition and interest." The idea of internal development is consistent with the work of Piaget (1932) and Kohlberg (1980, p. 35), who argued that school should provide "the adolescent with direct power and responsibility for governance in a society that is small and personal, like the family, but that is complex, rule-governed, and democratic." As would be expected and consistent with this argument, a longitudinal study of adolescents indicates that participation in an open classroom environment promotes political trust (Claes, Hooghe, & Marien, 2012). Such democratic approaches have become more common in recent years with classrooms "increasingly structured for teachers to be facilitators rather than authority figures" (Twenge, 2006, p. 29).

SCHOOL AS AN EXTENSION OF FAMILY

Of course, children come into school with already preexisting conceptions about rules and authorities. The work of Mark Fondacaro and his colleagues demonstrates that adolescents who report low levels of procedural justice in the manner in which conflicts are resolved in their families (i.e., less dignity and respect, less neutrality, and less trust in the motives of their parents) are more likely to be involved in a variety of forms of deviant behavior once they are in schools (Fondacaro et al., 2006; Fondacaro, Dunkle, & Pathak, 1998). In particular, they are more likely to become involved in deviant peer groups (Stuart, Fondacaro, Miller, Brown, & Brank, 2008).

One of our central arguments here is that the experiences children have with their families will form a blueprint of sorts that lays out how they expect authorities to treat them, make decisions, and control their behavior. That blueprint will have a powerful influence on the way they interact with teachers, especially concerning the way in which they respond to teachers' exercise of authority and power. When teachers behave in ways that are inconsistent with their values determining the appropriate use of authority, children will reject them and see them as illegitimate (Chory-Assad, 2002; Gregory & Ripski, 2008; Trinkner & Cohn, 2014).

It is also possible that children develop different "codes" for defining situations in which they should enact varying types of behavior toward authorities (Anderson, 1999). The key issue in that case is the cues that trigger coercive and consensual models. Children may be aware that they should obey some authorities but that they can talk to others. This is consistent with the common narrative that there are some authorities within a school that the students feel understand them and that they go to when they need someone to speak for them to other authorities or to understand their problems and needs.

PEERS AS AUTHORITIES

For any given child it is important to ask: who is a legitimate authority to that child? Teachers and school administrators are one set of authorities who promulgate a particular type of rules. However, during school hours children join peer groups and develop complex peer networks as they interact with other students. In some cases those peer groups can parallel formal authority (e.g., sports teams, school clubs) and support positive social development, and provide an important protective factor with regards to the development of antisocial behavior (Eccles, Barber, Stone, & Hunt, 2003, Mahoney, Larson, & Eccles, 2005). In other cases, students can attach themselves to deviant peer groups that present alternative sources of authority and rules that can encourage risky and delinquent behavior (Rios, 2011). The central example of an alternative group is a gang.

Students who are less likely to be accepted by school authorities or feel they are not popular in their school are more likely to become involved in deviant peer groups (Stuart et al., 2008). Membership in a gang can provide a means to be respected and valued within an alternative status system, even while being a marginal or suspended or expelled student in school. And those in deviant peer groups are less likely to cooperate with authorities by reporting students who bring weapons to school (Brank et al., 2007). Consistent with this research, Younts (2008) argues that deviance itself may be the result of the high legitimacy of alternative peer groups that feature deviant behavioral norms in contrast to other more traditional school authorities. Other studies further suggest that lack of trust in school authorities influences the likelihood of students becoming involved in deviant groups and displaying defiant behavior toward school administrators and teachers (Gregory & Ripski, 2008; Gregory & Weinstein, 2008).

Emler and Reicher (1995, p. 147) suggest that children can have two types of relationship with authorities. They can view rules as "a relation of constraint; the individual is required to abide by regulations, to observe formally defined proscriptions and prescriptions and to obey the instructions and directives of those who are formally authorized to issue them." The other relationship is one of protection and promotion in which the system offers students "protection of their rights, their person and their property, and provides them with a means of redress when those are violated." They argue that when students experience a formal system based on constraint, they seek noninstitutional solutions to their problems and become loyal to informal and personalized networks such as gangs.

The attraction of gangs is considered in detail by Rios (2011). He suggests that adolescents join gangs for protection, something that they feel other authority figures do not provide. Rios (p. xiv) argues for the existence of a youth control complex in which traditional authorities treat adolescents as "deviant, threatening, risky, and criminal," with punitive social control requiring constant surveillance, intrusion and punishment. He highlights how youth "[strive] for dignity, demanding to be treated as fellow citizens who are innocent until proven guilty. Working for dignity has to do more with a sense of humanity than a sense of power" (p. 39). The problem is that in many cases school becomes a place where they are "systematically denied the universal human need to be perceived by others in a positive light, with consideration instead of degradation" (p. 58).

Finally, Rios argues that the constant efforts to constrain and control young people leads them to define themselves in relationship to external control, so that they become unable to act based upon internalized values when they are in a situation that lacks formal authorities. In his interviews with delinquent teenagers he noted that "often, the boys did follow strict orders of the probation officer, but only in the direct presence of the officer. Probation officers' punitive approach failed to teach young people how to desist on their own, through self-control instead of through external threat. This threat often developed resentment in the boys and led to resistance, which was sometimes articulated through deviance and criminality" (p. 87).

One reason that children may prefer gangs, in addition to feeling accepted and respected within deviant groups, is that the way that authority is exercised may be familiar to them from their families. Authority within gangs is characterized by dominance, instrumentality, and using force to achieve desired ends. While discussions of gangs and of bullying emphasize the unacceptability of the approaches to exercising authority they reflect, it is also important to note that some patterns of family socialization make it hard for children to understand authority that involves discussion and consideration of other points of view. They may find physical aggression as a mechanism for managing others consistent with their earlier understanding of the normal dynamics of authority.

LINKING FAIR SCHOOLS WITH THE DEVELOPMENT OF AUTHORITY ATTITUDES

The attitudes toward authority that children bring with them to school are shaped by family dynamics. Similarly, the amount of justice experienced in schools continues to refine those attitudes that either promote or disrupt obedience toward authority (Paulsel, 2005). Many of the same themes found with the research on family dynamics, parent authority, and procedural justice resonate within the educational context. Poor student–teacher relationships characterized by ill-defined rules, inconsistent or biased rule enforcement, unidirectional communication, harsh discipline, hostile demeanor, and a lack of respect for student autonomy are all elements often present in schools that undermine the development of conceptions of legitimate authority and thereby promote delinquent behavior (Arum, 2003; Slobogin & Fondacaro, 2011; Payne, 2008; Jenkins, 1997).

Research findings particularly point to procedural fairness as a key criteria for evaluating teachers and schools (Berti, Molinari, & Speltini, 2010).[2] For example, Gouveia-Pereira, Vala, Palmonari, and Rubini (2003) studied over four hundred students aged fifteen to eighteen years old and found that their evaluations of the quality of treatment inside schools led to the legitimation of teacher authority and more positive evaluations of legal authorities more generally. Their results indicated that "the bestowal of legitimacy on teachers and their proposals is influenced more by relational and procedural justice than by distributive aspects" (p. 318). In essence, students' acceptance of school authority was driven more by how they were treated than by whether teachers' gave them good grades. More importantly, students reported engaging in less disruptive behavior to the extent that they felt heard and understood by their teachers.

The results of Gouveia-Pereira and colleagues are not an isolated occurrence either. Studies from elementary school to high school to college have shown that experiences of injustice within the educational environment have a profound effect on student behavior, especially with regards to aggression on school grounds and delinquency outside of it (Chory-Assad, 2002; Chory, Horan, Carton, & Houser, 2014; Chory-Assad & Paulsel, 2004a, 2004b; Estevez, Murgui, Moreno, & Musitu, 2007; Estevez, Murgui, Musitu, & Moreno, 2008; Gottfredson & Gottfredson, 1985; Gottfredson, Gottfredson, & Gottfredson, 2005; Hollingsworth, Luffler, & Clune, 1984; Herrero, Estevez, & Musitu, 2006; Horan & Myers, 2009; Horan, Chory, & Goodboy, 2010; James, Bunch, & Clay-Warner, 2015; Liska & Reed, 1985; Musitu, Estevez, & Emler, 2007; Paulsel, 2005; Welsh, 2001, 2003; Wu, Pink, Crain, & Moles, 1982). As James and colleagues (2015, p. 169) concluded: "Students who perceive unfair treatment from teachers are more likely to bring a weapon to school and fight at school than are students who believe that their teachers are fair. Students who perceive that rules are unfair are more likely to bring a weapon to school than are students who believe rules are fair." And, consistent with our argument, these behavioral effects reflect the fact that unfairness undermines the legitimacy of teachers and formal authority more generally (Gouveia-Pereira et al., 2003).

Such effects are not limited to the individual interactions between students and teachers either. Together, those many interactions among students and teachers on any given day shape the overall disciplinary climate within schools. Fairness at this more macro level is also important to positive student outcomes. For example, Cornell, Shukla, and Konold (2016) asked nearly one hundred thousand middle school (grades 7 and 8) and high school students (grades 9 through 12) in Virginia about their experience of an authoritative school climate. This included the perception that school rules were "strict but fairly enforced," and that school staff members both treated students "with respect" and wanted "them to be successful" (p. 5). They hypothesized that such a climate fosters the sense that faculty and staff care about students, who in turn feel comfortable seeking help from them. Their results largely supported their expectations showing that schools with a more authoritative climate were more likely to have students with better grades, higher aspirations, and more engaged in school programs. These findings are consistent with a number of other studies linking fair school rules and positive relationships with staff to lower levels of violence (Johnson, 2009), lower problem behavior (Henrich, Brookmeyer, & Shahar, 2005), and higher academic achievement (Gregory & Weinstein, 2004).

Interestingly, Cornell and colleagues (2016) note that the imposition of strict rules in and of itself is not associated with negative outcomes; rather, its effects are dependent on the extent to which students believe they are fairly administered. They distinguish this type of school climate from one that is punitive, suggesting that "school authorities can be strict and fair in their discipline without being harsh or castigatory" (p. 13). The question is not one of whether students have rules or do not have rules; rules and consequences are clearly needed. The question is more concerned with what those rules are and how they are enforced. Students respond to attempts at regulatory control when they are given opportunities to explain their behavior when accused of wrongdoing and are punished in a fair and respectful manner when they deserve it. This model is nearly identical to the notion of authoritative parenting described in the previous chapter. As was the case then, schools with authoritative climates are better able to manage their student populations more effectively than those with authoritarian climates (Pellerin, 2005).

These effects are not constrained to the school environment either. As we noted earlier, experiences in school have long been thought to prepare students for later engagement with law and government. If this is true, then such experiences should be associated with students' perceptions and expectations about legal and state institutions and agents. We already noted this to be the case with the Gouveia-Pereira et al. (2003) study showing that teacher fairness was associated with more positive attitudes toward legal agents outside of the school context. Additional evidence is provided by Jennings and Niemi (1974) in their study of twelfth-graders' views about teacher and administrator fairness. They found that students' judgments shape their trust in the government. Interestingly, the effect was dependent on students' family climate. Perceptions of school fairness had an especially strong positive effect on political trust among students whose parents were low in trust for the political process. The school environment, in other words, produced more change in political trust among those preadults who had politically cynical parents. However, the authors' emphasized that the impact of school upon political attitudes and later participation, while detectable, was weak.

Differences in school fairness and teacher authority are especially pronounced among minority group members. We already noted that minority students are more likely to be subjected to punitive sanctioning and schools with higher populations of minority students are more likely to rely on police officers to manage their students. Perhaps unsurprisingly, minority students are more likely to report that they experience a negative school climate and unfair treatment, which contribute to feelings of marginality within the school community and hinder their integration into school activities (Bruch & Soss, 2016). These perceptions serve to undermine later civic participation, including voting and trust in government. As Bruch and Soss (p. 48) argued, "few institutions rival schools as repositories for egalitarian hopes and schemes. . . . Yet a vast empirical literature suggests that the American education system does not conform to this image." From their perspective, schools convert "social subordination into civic and political marginalization" (p. 49), as adolescents learn alienation and disengagement from the school community and later the larger polity.

Fairness throughout the educational context is clearly important in terms of developing attitudes toward institutions and authorities. However, what exactly constitutes fairness in teaching? In many respects, fairness in teaching is composed of the same elements as fairness in parenting or policing for that matter. One element is caring and showing interest in students (Wu et al., 1982). Fair teachers are those that show they care about students by respecting them and communicating praise when earned (Dornbusch, Erickson, Laird, & Wong, 2001). A second element of fair teaching is the application of clear and transparent rules in consistent ways, explanation of decisions, discussion of potential rule-violating before making grading or punishment decisions, and inclusion of opportunities to voice one's concerns and issues (Gottfredson et al., 2005). Simply put, a fair teacher is one who is "competent, caring and respectful" (Way, 2011, p. 366). This largely overlaps with our discussion of the general procedural justice literature.

In discussing procedural justice we have noted the distinction between quality of decision-making and quality of treatment. This distinction is rooted in the idea of relational authority (Tyler & Lind, 1992). Authorities both make decisions to enforce rules and they communicate important social messages about inclusion and status. If a child is within the social boundaries of the group they are entitled to courtesy, respect, and concern from group authorities. Further, the degree to which they receive them reflects their status and standing within the group. Hence, an authority who treats a child or an adult with humiliation or disdain is giving them the message that society does not respect and value them, see their needs and concerns as important, or have their interests at heart. These messages are relational because they talk about the valence of the social bond. Even if an authority is neutral, allows opportunities for voice, and explains decisions, they can still communicate negative social messages, and vice versa. Irrespective of what decisions are made and how they are made, people can be treated with respect, courtesy, and dignity.

The distinction between treatment and decision-making concerns emerges in the literature on school authority as well. For example, in his study on the role of school climate in shaping school disorder among 4,640 students aged eleven to seventeen, Welsh (2001) distinguishes between decision-making rules (e.g., fairness and clarity of rules) and how students feel they are treated (e.g., respectful school climate). He finds that both criminal offending and noncriminal school misconduct are equally linked to rule fairness, rule clarity, and respect for students.

SCHOOL AS CIVIC EDUCATION

Experiences of justice or injustice in school transmit ideas about the nature of society and its institutions more generally (Resh & Sabbagh, 2014a, 2014b). Students learn the knowledge, skills, attitudes, and values needed to be engaged in society as participating citizens. In democratic societies especially, schools are responsible for communicating an understanding of democratic structures and processes and developing a commitment to democratic attitudes and values (Nie, Junn, & Stehlik-Barry, 1996).

A key focus is upon institutional trust. Trust is a precondition for creating networks and institutions that create solidarity and advance civic engagement (Sullivan & Transue, 1999). Institutional trust is particularly important to law and school is a central socializer of civic identity and attitudes. School is the first institution in which children experience institutional authorities and the fairness of the experiences that children have in school shapes their broader views about society. In particular, teachers and other school authorities communicate information to students about their status as people and standing in society (Emler & Reicher, 2005). Fairness tells students that they belong and are a valued part of the school community, increasing their trust in the institutional capabilities of the school.

Resh and Sabbagh (2014a, 2014b) argue that it is not the formal curriculum that shapes attitudes and values. Instead, they suggest that it is the sense of being treated justly by others. They find that schools characterized by a climate of fairness encourage a democratic liberal orientation that includes respect for the rights of minority groups. They find that students are influenced by whether they feel procedures at their school are fair, whether they receive fair treatment from authorities, and whether grades are given in an equitable manner. Just as people on trial believe that the verdict should reflect the evidence about their true behavior, students believe that fair grades should reflect an impartial and factual evaluation of the amount and quality of their work.

The theme of school as civic education has been an important one. One general argument is that more education advances attitudes and values that support democracy. As Converse (1972, p. 324) argued, "whether one is dealing with cognitive matters such as level of factual information about politics or conceptual sophistication in its assessment; or such motivation matters as degree of attention paid to politics and emotional involvement in political affairs; or questions of actual behavior, such as engagement in any of a variety of political activities from party work to vote turnout itself: education is everywhere the universal solvent, and the relationship is always in the same direction. The higher the education, the greater the 'good' values of the variable. The educated citizen is attentive, knowledgeable, and participatory and the uneducated citizen is not." Similarly, Marsh and Kaase (1979, p. 186) argued that "education is one of the most important predictors—usually, in fact, the most important predictor—of many forms of social participation—from voting to associational membership . . . Education, in short, is an extremely powerful predictor of civic engagement."

Consistent with the suggestion that schooling is today talked about in terms of skills acquisition, scholars suggest that there have also been "decades of neglect" to the topic of formal education about law and government (Galston, 2001; Tapp, 1976), with the consequence that despite huge increases in the formal educational level of Americans, knowledge about politics has not increased over the last fifty years. Niemi and Junn (1998) also note the "near-abandonment" of research on political socialization, arguments echoed by others who have noted the state of disarray in political socialization research (Conover & Searing, 2000).

From currently available research it is clear that education about civics in schools can raise political knowledge and attitudes. This has not always been the view about formal education. Early research suggested that civics classes have little influence on children's political knowledge and behavior

(Langton & Jennings, 1968). However, more recent studies dispute this pessimistic conclusion and show influences of the formal curriculum (Denver & Hands, 1990; John & Morris, 2004; Westholm, Lindquist, & Niemi, 1990). For example, curriculums explicitly focused on voting and elections have been shown to increase students' willingness to vote in a number of countries (Torney-Purta, 2002). These findings support the general suggestion that political knowledge shapes adult political behavior, in particular adult engagement in the political system (Jennings & Stoker, 2004).

An example of the importance of civic education to the development of democratic values comes from the 1999 IEA Civic Education Study, which studied ninety thousand fourteen-year-olds across twenty-eight countries (Campbell, 2006; Torney-Purta, 2002). This study found that the degree to which students experienced an open classroom climate where they were able to discuss political and social issues in class was associated with more civic knowledge and skills and greater citizen empowerment. These students were more likely to report wanting to be civically and politically engaged, and were more trusting of their political institutions and the legal system and police. The primary influence of education upon institutional trust was linked to attitudes about conventional citizenship obligations. Children who have a conventional citizenship orientation engage in conventional political activities and follow rules. And, as has been noted, a person's understanding of appropriate authority relations impacts their views of law and government. Someone who believes that their role is to obey law is also likely to believe that their role in government is to defer to political leaders without questioning them.

In a later analysis of the IEA data, Torney-Purta and Wilkenfeld (2008) found that experiences with democracy in school led to more knowledge about human rights and greater propensity for tolerance. Further, more open class and school climates lead to stronger student norms supporting immigrants' rights. They concluded that "there is strong corroboration that for all students the everyday experience of democracy is important in shaping attitudes. In other words, being in a classroom where students are free to discuss opinions and in a school where students feel that they can participate in a productive way are both positive for young people's human rights support" (p. 875).

Instead of treating civic education as an abstract idea, it is also possible to consider the content. Studies that do so find an emphasis upon citizen rights to the relative exclusion of the idea of citizen obligations (Gonzales et al., 2004). Not surprisingly, studies of high school students suggest that students are more likely to endorse rights than obligations (Bos,

Williamson, Sullivan, Gonzales, & Avery, 2007). To the degree that students have perceived obligations, they are more likely to participate in political and civic activities, and the influence of obligations is stronger than that of perceived rights. This suggests the limits of rights-based individualism and points to the need to develop obligations as part of the political socialization process. One important way to do that is to shift the coverage of high school civics textbooks, since "students may be less encouraged to be politically active when they are reminded only of the rights they possess, and not of the civic and political obligations upon which they should act" (p. 1278).

In their early examination of the civics curriculum in high schools, Jennings and Niemi (1974) found that less than half of the students in their sample took courses in American government (43%) or American problems (27%), although almost all (98%) had taken a course in American history. Interestingly, they found that African American students were the most influenced by civics education. For example, Jennings and Niemi noted that their political efficacy increases when exposed to civics education, a finding attributed to the tendency of civics curriculum to emphasize "the legitimacy, desirability, and feasibility of citizen participation and control" (p. 196). What is unclear, the authors note is how much this leads to later disappointment as poor and minority students confront the reality of actually living in a low efficacy world.

One possible example of this is the finding that minority youth become less politically trusting at a faster rate than Whites, perhaps reflecting experience with political realities. When preadult views about the good citizen are divided into two groups—those emphasizing participation and those emphasizing loyalty—61% of African American and 41% of Whites emphasize loyalty. Taking civics classes increases the importance of loyalty among minorities by 24%, but it lowers the percentage among Whites by 7%. Jennings and Niemi concluded that civics "appears to inculcate in blacks the role expectation that a good citizen is above all a loyal citizen rather than an active one" (p. 202). The authors argue that this reflects a realistic appraisal of actual opportunities for participation among preadult African Americans.

THE DEVELOPMENT OF LEGAL REASONING

A key aspect of legal development is an increasing sophistication regarding ones understanding of the law and legal issues. This growing sophistication continues as children enter school. To some extent, formal education accelerates this development with its emphasis on cognitive skills (Tapp,

1976). However, increasing maturity and neurological development are also important, as reflected in our earlier discussions in chapters 5 and 6. Furthermore, reasoning about rules and authorities is a product of interaction with peers, as well as deviant subcultures, who may present alternative conceptualizations of the law that challenge the ideals taught in civics courses (Anderson, 1999).

Studies of adolescent reasoning suggest that views about rules change in several important ways. One is that law loses its absolutistic meaning (Tapp & Levine, 1974). As we have mentioned, young children typically seek adult intervention to resolve conflict and young children's conceptions of legal procedures involve giving power to an adult. Such views are not absent in adults, but adults typically also recognize the concepts of individual autonomy and freedom and seek to limit authority against autonomy (Milnitsky-Sapiro, Turiel, & Nucci, 2006) and evaluate it in terms of how it is exercised (Adelson & Beall, 1970; Adelson, Green, & O'Neil, 1969; Adelson & O'Neil, 1966). Although this is largely a function of natural maturation, experiences with school authorities have been argued to augment this trajectory (Tapp & Kohlberg, 1971; Levine & Tapp, 1977).

As laws and rules lose their absolutistic meaning, youths come to understand that some rules regulating behavior only apply under certain conditions. We already noted in the previous chapter that children resist parents' attempts at control within domains of behaviors that they believe are off limits to parental authority. A similar dynamic emerges in school. For example, Yariv (2009) conducted semi-structured interviews with over two hundred Israeli elementary and middle school students about their normative conceptions of teacher authority and obedience. He found that many students had well-developed and articulable understandings concerning the limits of teacher authority. Students were least likely to recognize and accept teachers' authority if they tried to intervene in personal matters, violated school norms, made demands beyond the students' ability, put students in a situation that went against their personal morals, or violated their civil rights. Within each of these domains, less than half of the students felt any great need to follow the directives of their teachers.

In addition to recognizing limits within behavioral domains, youth also come to understand that some rules and authorities can only regulate behavior within certain contexts. This is especially poignant in school, where children come to recognize that teachers have little authority outside of school grounds (Laupa, 1991; Laupa & Turiel, 1986). In a small sample of K–6 grade students, Laupa and Turiel (1993) asked participants if they would obey their principal's directives across three contexts: a different school, a public park, and the child's home. In large part, students rejected the principal's authority outside the jurisdiction of the school, except in immediate situations involving harm (e.g., stopping a fight in a public park). This finding is echoed in Yariv's (2009) interviews with students explicitly noting that teachers have little authority (if any) once they are no longer on school property. As children grow, they increasingly understand that the legitimacy of an authority (and their subsequent obligations to obey them) is not only dependent on the behavior in question, but also on the social context within which it is happening. Schools provide an environment that facilitates learning this distinction.

As adolescent reasoning develops it influences attitudes about both law and government. As conceptions of authority evolve, children increasingly come to recognize the idea of democratic and participatory processes (Helwig, 1998; Helwig, Arnold, Tan, & Boyd, 2007), the possibility that laws can be bad and should be disobeyed (Helwig & Jasiobedzka, 2001), and the idea of individual rights (Sherrod, 2008). This speaks to the third element of legitimacy: recognizing that there are boundaries. A person is not an authority over all aspects of life, and people need not obey within some spheres. Further, they can question whether authority is properly exercised and resist unjust orders in terms of how decisions were made. As they develop, children increasingly believe that an illegally obtained order does not have to be obeyed.

THE EDUCATIONAL CONTEXT AND LAW-RELATED BEHAVIOR

A key purpose of inculcating supportive civic attitudes and values during educational experiences is to increase the likelihood that children will obey rules and accept the authority of the law to regulate their behavior. Schools, especially their overall disciplinary climate and the way teachers wield power affect the degree to which youth engage in criminal and deviant behavior both within and outside of school. Although many times these behaviors have their roots in the parenting dynamics we highlighted in the previous chapter, administrators can exacerbate such externalizing behavior depending on the ways in which they try to manage it within the school environment.

The linkages between the educational climate and student misconduct can be seen in the literature on bullying and physical aggression toward other children (Brubacher, Fondacaro, Brank, Brown, & Miller, 2009). Bullying has quickly become a highly visible national issue, encompassing interpersonal experiences (Wang, Iannotti, & Nansel, 2009) and cyberbullying (Kowalski, Giumetti, Schroeder, & Lattanner, 2014). Although bullying behavior can occur anywhere, state and federal governments have increasingly focused on its occurrence inside schools (Stuart-Cassel, Bell, & Springer, 2011). This includes physical acts of aggression, social exclusion by rumor spreading or leaving children out of activities, verbal bullying such as name-calling, and cyberbullying (Brank, Hoetger, & Hazen, 2012). Bullying behavior is important in and of itself, but has become more visible to criminologists and legal scholars given its association with later interpersonal violence, drug use and arrests (Farrington & Ttofi, 2011).

Perhaps unsurprisingly, bullying has been shown to be more prevalent among individuals who lack family emotional bonds or experience harsh and coercive parenting styles (Bayraktar, 2014; Cook, Williams, Guerra, Kim, & Sadek, 2010; Dishion & Tipsord, 2011; Espelage, Low, Rao, Hong, & Little, 2014). Similar associations emerge within educational research. A recent meta-analysis involving 172 independent studies found that a positive and supportive school climate was associated both with lower levels of bully perpetration and victimization (Cook et al., 2010). For example, Gendron, Williams, and Guerra (2011) followed over seven thousand students in fifth, eighth, and eleventh grade for one year. They found that the school's disciplinary climate was associated with lower bullying concurrently and over time. Importantly, a positive noncoercive school climate was most important for those students who were especially vulnerable (i.e., had low self-esteem). Their results indicate that schools can increase students' propensity to follow rules and refrain from engaging in aggressive or disruptive behavior by ensuring a fair and supportive climate.

Similar findings emerge with regards to school violence more generally. Schools with a warm positive climate where students feel safe from harm and humiliation are associated with lower violent offending (Wilson, 2004). Despite these links, many school administrators seek to address the issue of school violence using quick-fix solutions rooted in deterrence-based crime control strategies, such as suspension or expulsion of potentially disruptive students, enhancing school surveillance, making it more difficult to enter the school, or increasing police presence (Arum, 2003; Greene, 2005; Limber & Small, 2003). Not only are these types of solutions limited in their effectiveness (as has been a central argument throughout this volume), they also are reactive strategies only being implemented after the behavior has taken place. This is in stark contrast to the proactive strategies espoused by psychologists and other educational researchers that focus on improving the school climate with regards to equitable rule enforcement and respectful treatment (Gendron et al., 2011; Sherer &

Nickerson, 2010) as a means of preventing the behavior from occurring in the first place.

Although bullying and aggression are problematic in their own right, they are not necessarily instances of *illegal* behavior. If our contention that legal socialization is connected to the educational environment, then teacher authority should not only be linked to youth's development of legal attitudes, values, and reasoning, but also to their engagement (or lack thereof) in explicitly illegal behavior. In this regard, the literature on educational authority is consistent with our argument, indicating that the way school authorities discipline and manage student populations has a direct impact on delinquency.

In his study of the attitudes and behaviors of over ten thousand high school students from the National Education Longitudinal Study, Arum (2003) found that strictness in the enforcement of rules was unrelated to students' willingness to disobey rules when enforcement was fair, but when it was unfair students became more likely to engage in delinquent behavior. The same pattern emerged when he examined fighting on school grounds. Importantly for our discussion here, discipline strictness was actually found to be associated with lower arrest rates only when students thought it was imposed in a fair and respectful manner.

Using the same data, Way (2011, p. 346) found that "more school rules and higher perceived strictness predicts more, not less, disruptive behavior." A key issue to emerge in her findings was that the legitimacy of school authority lessened disruption. She notes that "when students believe it is okay to disobey teachers and rules, they are more likely to do so" (p. 363). Moreover, beliefs about the appropriateness of disobeying teachers were rooted in student perceptions that teachers were unfair.

This supports arguments we have made here and elsewhere (Fagan & Tyler, 2005; Tyler & Fagan, 2008) that it is not inherent that exercising authority inevitably undermines legitimacy and promotes offending, but rather *how* that authority is exercised that truly matters. Indeed, our overall argument about the superiority of building consensual orientations toward the law versus coercive orientations is largely based on process over outcome.

A fair process is crucial because it builds legitimacy both within and outside the school context (Gouveia-Pereira et al., 2003). As Arum (2003, pp. 182–183) notes, "school authority that is not perceived as legitimate often produced student's resistance and was counterproductive . . . authority exercised without legitimacy will usually be counterproductive." He argues that the efficacy of school discipline depends on whether students internalize rules as fair and just. Schools that are able to enact discipline in ways that students perceive as fair—even if they think rules are strict—are more likely to have students that think it is unacceptable to disobey the law. In this way, schools can serve to promote both educational achievement and the legal socialization of youth. When school discipline is consistent with students internalized values concerning fair and just authority, students judge that authority to be legitimate and are motivated to behave in appropriate ways.

FORMAL VERSUS INFORMAL EDUCATION
ABOUT THE LAW

Another way children can develop civic values and attitudes toward law and legal authorities is through formal training in civics (Justice & Meares, 2014; Tapp, 1976). This training teaches a positive—and, we will argue, idealized—version of law and government. It presents the proper and appropriate role of the legal system within the community as dictated by the values underlying the legal system. It presents American law in its structural form. For example, it describes trials as an important forum for resolving judicial questions. And it conveys an image of law as a public good that works to the universal benefit of people in society. However, in many instances the formal civics education that students receive in school bears little resemblance to what they experience in reality.

For some students the idealized version of the law has substantial validity. Particularly for those who come from economically well-off backgrounds, it is likely that they will find similarities between what they learn in their formal curriculum and their own experience with law. However, even for this group contact with the system will highlight divergences between idealized versions of societal legal values and the imperfect criminal system realities. For example, while the trial is an iconic representation of American justice, it is virtually nonexistent in the realities of our system (Goode, 2012). Adolescents, imagining that there will be a neutral forum in which a judicial authority will determine their guilt, enter a reality of charge stacking, plea bargaining, and pretrial detention if they are drawn into the legal system. Similarly, those who initially view the police as benevolent and concerned often find the reality of their interactions with the police jarring. For example, contact with the police has been shown in some studies to have the biggest influence on legal attitudes for those individuals that have the least exposure to police (Rusinko, Johnson, & Hornung, 1978). In both of these instances, individuals come to learn that in many ways the realities of the legal system are not in concordance with the values upon which the system is supposed to be founded.

This discordance is especially pronounced for students from minority and poor backgrounds. For these students there is a substantial divergence between images of the law and the realities of the legal system (Justice & Meares, 2014). The system provides an image of justice but also functions as a system of social control. This includes efforts to dominate and control adolescents considered potentially at risk of criminal conduct. And studies suggest it too frequently involves intimidation, harassment, and humiliation (Carr, Napolitano & Keating, 2007; Fagan & Tyler, 2005; Mukerjee, 2007). In other words, while these individuals are legally socialized to want and expect the same things out of the legal system as everyone else, all too often they come up against a legal actor that systematically behaves in ways that go against the very values that are embodied within the system they are supposed to be upholding. In light of this, it is no wonder that an enormous amount of research shows that minority and poor communities are more likely to view the police as illegitimate and not representative of appropriate legal values (Trinkner & Goff, 2016).

LEGAL MOBILIZATION

The law is not only a regulatory force through which people deal with the police and courts because they have or are suspected to have broken laws. It is also a set of ideals and procedures providing a forum for the redress of grievances. Authors such as Breyer (2010) suggest that the viability of communities depends upon people believing that there are places they can go to have disputes resolved in a fair manner and their rights enforced. Hence, the law is not simply a set of rules that people need to follow. It is also an ideal linked to providing justice. However, in order for the law to maintain such ideals, it is dependent on citizens being mobilized to engage the legal system in order to pursue grievances against others and seek remedies like injunctions and damage awards.

In her study of legal consciousness among fourteen-year-old students, Silbey (1991) found that youth felt that the law was empowering, giving them a voice and means to ensure they were being heard. However, those studied were primarily middle-upper-class students and their views reflect a positive view of law and rights. This is a perfect example of the benefits of having consistency between societal values concerning the appropriate legal system–citizen relationship and the actual behavior of the legal system when interacting with citizens. This group of students did not experience conflict between their idealized view of law and their personal experience with law.

An example of such positive experiences is provided by mock courts of the type students experience in school (Nessel, 1998). In such situations "teen juries" allow young people to participate in criminal trials and even make sentencing decisions (some even allow teen courts to determine innocence or guilt) with regards to their peers (usually first-time offenders). Many teen courts also have young people take on other important roles within the courtroom (e.g., prosecutor or bailiff). The goal here is to involve youth in legal procedures that most directly reflect American legal values and ideas as a means to transmit those ideals to young people and foster good citizenship, while at the same time providing an important diversion program that reduces offender exposure to the juvenile justice system. Despite these good intentions, research examining potential benefits has been mixed (Bright, Young, Bessaha, & Falls, 2015; Harrison, Maupin, & Mays, 2001, Stickle, Connell, Wilson, & Gottfredson, 2008). It seems that whether teen courts prepare youth for future citizenship is dependent on the particulars of each individual program, of which there are many (see Nessel, 1998).

However, students do not have to experience formal court procedures at school in order to learn about the ideals underlying those procedures. Many disciplinary hearings within the school environment functionally act as proxies to the formal juvenile justice system. The problem, at least from a legal socialization perspective, is that many students actively avoid becoming involved in such hearings, even if they are victims. Morrill and colleagues (2010) studied students' experiences with issues of discrimination, harassment, freedom of expression and assembly, and due process in disciplinary hearings in a large sample (5,461) of high school students aged fifteen to seventeen. They found that adolescents generally sought extralegal ways to resolve problems, including confronting the person verbally or physically, avoiding them, and talking to family or peers (76.3%), although some tried quasi-legal approaches such as using school complaint procedures or mediation and peer counseling (21.4%).

Subsequent interviews with students suggest great reluctance to take action against perceived rights violations among minority students because "law was strongly woven into this sense of vulnerability that placed [minority students] one step away from having their lives disrupted, if not destroyed, by unwanted and unpredictable legal incursions" (p. 681). In line with the argument made earlier about the ideal versus the reality of law, this study found that minority students were aware of gaps between the ideal concept of rights and the realities of everyday law. The findings highlighted "the unfairness and resignation with which African American youth regarded how their schools handle rights violations and discipline"

(p. 683). While all students are socialized to idealized values associated with law, minority students often do not see those values played out in their experiences in everyday law, leading them to view the legal system as illegitimate. They experience illegal, demeaning, and harassing actions from legal authorities. But, not always and it is important to emphasize that fairness can and does build legitimacy among minority communities as well (Tyler, Fagan, & Geller, 2014).

SUMMARY

In this chapter we turned our attention to the educational context to examine how experiences within the school environment shape the legal socialization process. Here, children learn to deal with rules and authorities who are more distant and formal. Although the primary initial contact for children is a teacher who shares some qualities with their parents (e.g., informal, long-term contact), students increasingly interact with a greater variety of teachers from year to year and eventually throughout any given day. As a result, they must learn how to deal with a more impersonal style of authority that may be wildly different from teacher to teacher. This process of learning is not only constrained to individual interactions with teachers, but also permeates the entire school climate. Indeed, the overall disciplinary climate in schools had just as much of an impact on students as their contact with school authorities and administrators.

Despite these differences, the message of the literature on schools is similar to that from research on families. It is possible to manage schools using strict discipline and harsh punishment, but these strategies are not found to be effective in promoting rule-following (voluntary or not). On the contrary, like harsh parenting techniques, they promote rule-breaking not only within the school but also outside within the community.

On the other hand, supportive attitudes and values are found to promote rule-following both for adolescents in the school environment and in relationship to deviant peer groups and law-related behavior. If students view their teachers and administrators as legitimate—that is, if they feel obligated to accept their authority and they trust them as authorities—then rule-following behavior ensues. Students are less likely to join gangs or bring weapons to school, are more likely to follow rules and regulations, and they are less likely to engage in aggressive interpersonal behavior such as bullying.

The most striking finding of studies on the school environment is the centrality of the fairness of rules in terms of how they are created, implemented, and enforced. Studies suggest first that the impact of school rules is very much related to their perceived fairness both along decision-making and treatment dimensions. They further point to the perceived fairness of teachers in shaping a variety of student outcomes, ranging from academic achievement to rule-following. These findings concur with those of the literature on families which also suggest that the fairness of the family climate of discipline shapes children's reactions to parental rules and decisions.

Finally, as was the case in the parenting context, there are contrasting visions about what is the most effective form of school authority. On the one hand there are signs of increasing interest in educating children about democratic values and having open and fair classrooms. This seems to fit with emerging features of younger people, who expect more participatory procedures. However, more problematically, there are definite signs of support for coercive approaches to managing and regulating student behavior. Increasingly schools seem to be becoming more inflexible, harsh, and criminal-justice minded in handling their students. This can be seen in the proliferation of zero-tolerance policies, rigid rules, and the willingness to make school behavior criminal, something facilitated by the increasing presence of law enforcement officers in schools. It seems that although schools recognize the importance of teaching their students the values the law is supposed to embody, some are reluctant to ensure that they are personifying those values on a daily basis.

CHAPTER 9

⚜

Legal Socialization in the Juvenile Justice System

In the final chapter of this section we will focus on the juvenile justice system with a particular emphasis on adolescence. This period represents an important time in the legal socialization process because it is when individuals are most likely to come into initial contact with the legal system and its authorities. Although teenagers will have likely had contact with police previously (e.g., "Officer Friendly" visits to their school), contact during adolescence usually comes within the context of behavioral regulation (i.e., an individual has been or is suspected of violating a law). Unlike their previous experiences with parents and teachers, these interactions require adolescents to manage interactions with strangers with whom they have no personal or long-term connection and whose authority arises solely from their role as a representative of an institution.

To some extent loyalty toward law and government requires an abstract sense of institutions as impersonal entities entitled to loyalty, and to some extent it involves reasoning about appropriate attributes of legitimacy. Although young people have been learning about these concepts through their experiences in the family and school, they now are in a position to see how they are expressed within the practical realities of everyday life. The experiences they have in the legal realm will further develop the abstract concepts at the core of the formal legal system. At the same time, the tenor of their interactions with legal authority will promote or hinder an emotional attachment between them and the law. Individuals want to feel attached to their social world; they want to feel a part of the society around them (Lind & Tyler, 1988). Moreover, the legal system is a symbol of a shared sense of normative values among society members (Jackson, Bradford, et al., 2013). When individuals are emotionally attached to the system, they feel a deep sense of connection to society as a whole. Many times it is the attitudinal feelings of attachment to the law that stimulates loyalty and cooperation, rather than an abstract sense of legal principles and appropriate authority (Deigh, 1999).

Legal institutions themselves are remote, so their authority is primarily experienced through interactions with particular representatives. For example, the law and the courts are experienced through interaction with one judge. That authority represents the courts and speaks for the law, but is one person. Irrespective of how they are experienced by the children or adolescents who are directly encountering legal authorities, these initial encounters present young people with the challenge of dealing with people they do not know and with whom they have no personal history, but nonetheless have authority over them based upon the person's status as a judge or officer. The first time someone in a uniform deals with a young person they are presenting them with a different form of authority than they experience with their parents or teachers.

Our discussion of the juvenile justice system is framed by several research findings. First, for many people in our society their largest point of contact with the criminal justice system occurs during adolescence and young adulthood. National crime statistics show offending rates increase dramatically from ages fourteen to eighteen and then gradually decline until they level off in the mid-twenties (Steffensmeier & Ulmer, 2002). This frequently brings young people into contact with the juvenile justice system. Although many adolescents commit minor crimes, almost all of those who do so subsequently mature into law-abiding adults, given time to develop cognitively and socially (Moffitt, 1993, 2007). Second, contact with juvenile justice authorities has been shown to, on average, increase the likelihood that an adolescent will engage in further crimes later in their lives with more extensive contact, leading to an even greater likelihood of future criminal conduct (Aizer & Doyle, 2015; Bartollas & Schmalleger, 2011; Petrosino, Turpin-Petrosino, & Guckenburg, 2010). Given that most adolescents will naturally mature out of crime, this means that contact with the system has counterdevelopmental consequences and interferes with a natural maturation process that overwhelmingly yields desirable outcomes.

The juvenile justice system increasingly impacts the lives of many adolescents and based upon the nature of that contact can powerfully shape their views about legitimacy as well as future law-related conduct. Our argument is that while contact with the juvenile justice system may currently be negative in its impact, this need not be the case. There is evidence that when authorities act in ways that the people they deal with view as fair, supportive attitudes are created, and trust is not undermined. Further, the likelihood of future criminal behavior is not increased; instead, it goes down (Tyler, Fagan, & Geller, 2014).

Trust can be built when adolescents experience fairness from the police, the courts, and the law. This has been found both in the case of young people (Tyler et al., 2014) and with adults (Tyler & Fagan, 2008). Contacts can build trust, even if people are receiving sanctions (Tyler & Jackson, 2014). To build legitimacy legal authorities need to exercise their authority in ways that the people they are dealing with experience as being fair. Like adults, adolescents are found to react strongly to whether or not they experience contacts with legal authorities as being fair (Fagan & Tyler, 2005; Tyler & Huo, 2002). Such judgments influence whether young people defer to authority, and also whether they develop favorable views about law and legal authority (Tyler, Casper, & Fisher, 1989; Tyler et al., 2014).

Because of research documenting the criminogenic consequences of contact with the juvenile justice system there has been considerable recent policy discussion about diversion, with an emphasis upon shifting young people away from the criminal justice system at any possible point (e.g., National Center for Mental Health and Juvenile Justice, 2013). This includes encouraging the police to warn rather than cite or arrest and when teenagers are arrested trying to keep them from going into juvenile detention or other forms of incarceration.

Contacts can also build legitimacy if they are managed correctly. When policies and practices are being established, young people need to participate in decisions about how their community is policed. In the case of adolescents this may involve simply allowing them to express their concerns and showing evidence of taking those concerns seriously. As those policies and practices are implemented in the community, the legal authorities doing so need to make decisions fairly and treat the people they deal with respectfully. Studies show that adolescents react separately to fairness in rule creation and in rule implementation and that both distinctly shape legitimacy (Tyler et al., 2014).

ADOLESCENCE AS A SPECIAL PERIOD
OF LEGAL SOCIALIZATION

The period of adolescence is a transition period between childhood and adulthood. As children, people are not expected to have the capacity to reason and act as adults. As adults, people are held responsible for their law-related behavior and considered to have the capacity to shape their conduct to laws. The problem is that developmentally speaking, adolescence is qualitatively different than either childhood or adulthood (Steinberg, 2014). Unlike children, adolescents have the pure cognitive capabilities of adults to distinguish right from wrong and act accordingly; however, unlike adults they are not especially proficient in using those capabilities and tend to be highly impulsive. In fact, developing an understanding of rules and laws and their importance requires adolescents to experiment with different behaviors, some of which include taking excessive and ill-considered risks (Casey, 2015). Sometimes a person needs to know how much is too much before they can understand how much is enough, and children have to find these boundaries through experimentation in addition to instruction. Making mistakes is inevitable and in fact necessary.

ADOLESCENCE AS A LEGAL CATEGORY

Historically, the legal system has not accounted for an adolescent period that is distinct from childhood and adulthood (Scott & Steinberg, 2010). It has focused on the simple issue of whether individuals are legally categorized as adults or minors, although whether this distinction is applied varies depending upon the circumstances. Traditionally both police officers and other juvenile authorities have recognized this to various degrees and used their discretion to avoid bringing many adolescents into the formal system to be charged and incarcerated. However, more recently formal processing has become more frequent, as can be seen in the gradual propensity to try juveniles as adults when they commit especially heinous crimes (Redding, 2010). There is an increasingly blurred standard between the adjudicative adult court and the therapeutic juvenile court, the latter being managed with the idea that the legal authority involved is looking out for the welfare of the child. As we will discuss, when these inherently gray areas lead to formal processing within the juvenile justice system, it can be counterproductive.

To date, the legal system still does not consider adolescence to be a qualitatively distinct category separate from childhood, and there is variability from state to state in terms of when adulthood begins. Research on neuroscience gives guidelines because it directly speaks to the question of the ability of juveniles to reason and to use their socioemotional skills. As we noted in chapter 6, several facts emerge from that literature. First, the process of development is a continual one characterized by immense changes until the mid-twenties. From this perspective, it is arbitrary to divide development into childhood, adolescence, and adulthood. Second, development continues into the mid-twenties, meaning adolescents are not like adults in their ability to function until that time. Third, different types of development have distinct trajectories. For example, abstract reasoning skills are adult-like at age sixteen, while socioemotional regulation continues to develop until the mid-twenties.

The complex and multiple trajectories of neurological, biological, and social-emotional development make clear that judgments about what adolescents are capable of are complex. One striking finding, for example, is that while adolescents calculate risk at a level similar to adults, they put greater weight on immediate rewards and are less sensitive to costs, particularly to long-term costs (Bonnie & Scott, 2013). This directly impacts the influence of sanction threats on behavior. Conversely, adolescents are more susceptible to peer pressure than adults, which potentially undermines the role of personal attitudes and values in shaping behavior. The particulars of research findings aside, it is clear that adolescents cannot be treated as simply smaller adults.

ADOLESCENTS' PROPENSITY TO OFFEND

As already noted, adolescents commit a large number of the crimes that occur. Fortunately these are mostly of a minor nature—things such as recreational drug use, underage drinking, or trespassing. Many of these young "criminals" are arrested and drawn into the juvenile justice system, at least in comparison to the proportion of the people of older ages who are arrested. For example, Brame and colleagues (2012) estimate that between 15.9% and 26.8% of juveniles have been arrested by age eighteen. This reflects that fact that "the rates for both prevalence and incidence of offending appear highest during adolescence; they peak sharply about age seventeen and drop precipitously in young adulthood" (Moffitt, 1993, p. 675).

Further, offending may be even more frequent than is reflected in official arrest rates. Earls (1994), for example, reports that 21% of adolescents say they have engaged in at least one violent incident by age eighteen, and "only a fraction" are apprehended (p. 6). Slobogin and Fondacaro (2011) argue that by age seventeen well over 20% of youths (and well over 40% of male youths) have engaged in at least one serious assault, drug crime, or theft. And as Moffitt (1993, 2007) discusses, self-report studies of delinquency suggest that as many as 80 to 90% of teenage boys report engaging in behaviors for which they could have been arrested.

The propensity for committing crime diminishes sharply as people age, and by age twenty-five only a small proportion of people are still committing crimes. Moffitt (1993) suggests that this group is approximately 5% of the adult population, a group that is "life course persistent" and which accounts for approximately 50% of all crimes. The larger group of adolescents, who are termed "adolescent-limited offenders," move on with their lives and complete school, get married, develop careers, have children, and generally move forward with the tasks of being an adult. As Scott and Steinberg (2008, p. 24) note, "many adults look back on their risky adventures or mishaps as teenagers with chagrin and amazement—and often with gratitude that they emerged relatively unscathed."

Other criminologists disagree about the exact age distribution of criminal conduct, although there seems to be broad agreement about the argument that most adolescent criminals cease or at least diminish their criminal activity as they mature into adulthood (see Laub & Sampson, 2003; Sampson & Laub, 1993). For example, Sampson and Laub suggest that "criminal offending begins in preadolescence, peaks sharply during adolescence, and rapidly declines in the transition to young adulthood" (p. 16). Furthermore, they argue for continuity across these ages with those who engage in criminal conduct early in life being more likely to continue into and through adulthood.

CONTACT WITH THE LEGAL SYSTEM

Given their higher likelihood of engaging in criminal or otherwise deviant behavior, adolescence is a period where individuals are especially likely to come into contact with the legal system, particularly within regulatory contexts where the legal system is using its power in an attempt to curtail or control their behavior. This is another reason why adolescence is an especially salient time for legal socialization. A crucial question for their developmental trajectory into law-abiding and productive adults is what happens when they have personal and indirect contact with the formal criminal justice system. Young people are the targets of the police in many neighborhoods, so they are likely to have personal contact or at least be aware of the experiences of neighbors and friends (Carr et al., 2007; May, Gyateng, & Hough, 2010). It is usual for juveniles, particularly those from poor areas, to have knowledge about police behavior in their community.

And that knowledge about what is going on in the community can be even more influential than personal experience (Tyler et al., 2014).

The police are given great discretion concerning how they handle minor juvenile offenses (Parker & Sarre, 2008), and there are different policies and practices within different departments. As noted, the widespread use of stop-and-frisk approaches leads many more young people into contact with the police in some cities (Fagan, Geller, Davies, & West, 2010; Tyler et al., 2014). This pattern of contact with the legal system, initiated by arrests for minor crimes, has recently been described in detail by Kohler-Hausmann (2013, 2014). Those drawn into the court system typically experience repeated court appearances often ending in no formal adjudication of their case.

In exercising their discretion the police frequently focus on the immediate situation and issues of legality and risk, rather than thinking about how the interaction is a "teachable moment" through which a young person develops their understanding of and trust or lack of trust in law and legal authorities (Tyler et al., 2014). From a legal socialization perspective, three facts are particularly relevant. First, almost all of the people who have dealt with the police are not committing any crime at the time of the contact, even when they are being stopped by the police. In street stops in New York City, for example, less than one in one hundred young people are found to be committing a crime when the police stop them (Fagan et al., 2010). Second, almost all young people who are committing crimes as young people grow up to be normal law-abiding adults (Moffitt, 2007). If left alone, almost all adolescents will mature out of crime and become law-abiding adults. Finally, the general influence of contact with the criminal justice system is to increase the likelihood of future criminal conduct (Aizer & Doyle, 2015). Consequently, programs that divert young people or minimize their contact with the police, juvenile courts, and juvenile detention increase the likelihood that adolescents will transition out of this period of their life by becoming law-abiding members of the community.

What happens in the aftermath of arrest when a young person deals with their charge in the court system can also have enormous impact upon the later lives of the young people. Drawing people into the system involves arrest, beginning a ceremony of degradation that changes a "free person into a criminal defendant, with all the attendant social meanings, physical discomforts, and civil burdens" (Kohler-Hausmann, 2013, p. 374). Instead of being within the law-abiding community and condemning socially marginal "deviants," a larger group of residents find themselves being excluded from the category of "decent people" and socially marginalized by the police and courts. This occurs through repeated contacts with the courts, all linked to an initial charge by the police. These continuous contacts are enforced by the promise of eventual dismissal following some series of court appearances (i.e., adjournment in contemplation of dismissal). A goal of these repeated interactions is to determine if the youth in question can and will follow rules; in other words, to test whether they still have criminal proclivities. For example, charges may be dismissed after some period of time without further infractions because the person has shown an ability to adhere to the law. Finally, these minor-crime arrests provide law enforcement with information about people by marking their files with a history that follows them through life and influences their later experiences with law enforcement.

At the same time that the system is focused upon making risk predictions, the legal socialization experience for the adolescent is twofold. First, they are labeled as a deviant person who has a problematic nature and criminogenic personality. Labeling youth as delinquent has been shown to actually increase future offending (Paternoster & Iovanni, 1989). Second, they become a person whose life is controlled by a system that bears little relationship to the ideals of the justice system. Young people are unlikely to come in contact with sympathetic or even caring authorities, and they are unlikely to have experiences in which they see decisions about their future as being made in procedurally just ways (Carr et al., 2007; Gau & Brunson, 2010; Humes, 1997; May et al., 2010). In fact, the system never gives most defendants any opportunity to talk about the merits of the initial charge or to hear a clear explanation from a judge of how their case is being decided. They are trapped in a bureaucracy in which they appear repeatedly without ever facing a trial and eventually are let go without any explanation. They do not expect and typically do not find that they will deal with anyone who is concerned about them and their welfare or who focuses on their views about the legal system.

Increasing and continuous contacts with the criminal justice system results in many people experiencing "procedural hassle," with the risk of a criminal record for petty crimes (Gerstein & Prescott, 2015; Kohler-Hausmann, 2013). As an example, many young people have been arrested for marijuana possession during police stops and ended up with criminal records. The key point is that "experiences in adolescence and adulthood can redirect criminal trajectories in either a more positive or a more negative matter" (Laub & Sampson, 2003, p. 6). A record of a minor conviction, or even of an arrest later dropped, can influence getting or keeping a job, getting public housing, being able to attend school, or receive financial aid for college.

DEVELOPING ATTITUDES TOWARD LEGAL AUTHORITY

Contact with the legal system has a powerful effect on adolescents' continuing development of legal attitudes, particularly those toward legal authority figures. A central theme running through most (if not all) legal socialization models is that the acquisition of supportive attitudes and values decreases the likelihood that young people will violate the law and increases their acceptance of the law as a regulatory force within society (Fagan & Tyler, 2005; Tapp & Levine, 1974; Trinkner & Cohn, 2014). Studies support this argument. In a now classic study of students from grades 7 through 12, Brown (1974a, 1974b) asked students about their attitudes toward the police using items such as "Police spend most of their time helping people" and "Policemen are often not fair." He found that more positive responses were strongly linked to the frequency of compliance with laws among these adolescents.

Similarly, in her studies of middle school, high school, and college students, Cohn (Cohn & White, 1990; Cohn, Bucolo, Rebellon, & Van Gundy, 2010; Cohn, Trinkner, Rebellon, Van Gundy, & Cole, 2012) consistently finds that more positive attitudes about the police, laws and rules, and the legal system as a whole are associated with decreased deviancy concurrently and over time. In their study of a large sample of twelve- to sixteen-year-olds in England, Emler and Reicher (1995) found that positive attitudes toward the law, in particular institutional authority, predicted their engagement in delinquent behavior. Interestingly, even though the favorability of such attitudes declined with age, positive attitudes continued to predict self-reported delinquency in the future.

Clearly, the development of legal attitudes is an important factor that influences youths' engagement in delinquency and other forms of deviant behavior (see also chapter 4). This leads to the question of where such attitudes come from. To some extent, these attitudes are formed by interactions with nonlegal authorities (Trinkner & Cohn, 2014), consistent with our argument that attitudes toward teacher authority have their roots in experiences with parental authority (see chapter 8). Take for instance a study by Amorso and Ware (1983) of over 1,500 students aged eleven through seventeen. They found that attitudes about teacher authority was one of the strongest predictors of attitudes toward police officers, even more so than experiences with parents. They argued that "[nonlegal authority] experiences and reactions to them provide the frame of reference for [youth's] later attitudes to other social systems" (p. 193).

However, unsurprisingly one of (if not the) biggest determinant of legal attitudes are young people's contact with agents of the legal system. For example, in the Emler and Reicher (1995) study, children were especially concerned with the behavior of police officers. They found that "young people differ sharply in the degree to which they believe that police officers are honest, that they are not unnecessarily brutal, that they are impartial in the protection they provide and so on" (p. 153). This is similar to the suggestion of Gau and Brunson (2010) that young men are highly sensitive to whether they receive respect from law enforcement and whether they believe that police officers are themselves sources of victimization in that they represent an institutional system that unduly persecutes their social group. Indeed, Carr and colleagues' (2007) qualitative interviews with youth in Philadelphia clearly indicate that negative contact with the law fosters animosity and mistrust.

FOSTERING THE LEGITIMACY OF THE LAW

As we have noted throughout this volume, the perception that the law is a legitimate authority and entitled to obedience is a central element of any properly working legal system and the legitimation of legal authority is a key dynamic in the legal socialization process (Fagan & Tyler, 2005; Flanagan & Sherrod, 1998). Legitimacy has been tied to greater compliance and cooperation across a variety of countries and populations (see Tyler & Jackson, 2013 for review). Research on legitimacy and the law is premised upon the assumption that legitimacy views arise in large part out of social interactions and experiences with legal actors (Tyler, 2006a, 2006b). Every interaction an individual has with legal authorities, particularly youth, is an opportunity for the law to foster or hinder its status as an appropriate source of formal social control (Tyler et al., 2014). And consensual approaches rooted in fair and respectful treatment and decision-making better promote legitimacy and trust than coercive strategies rooted in force and dominance.

Two studies by Jeffrey Fagan and Tom Tyler provide cogent support for this argument. In a 2005 study, they examined attitudes about the law and legal system in a relatively small (n = 215) community sample of ten-through sixteen-year-old children in two racially and socioeconomically contrasting neighborhoods in New York City. In particular, they focused on three domains of legal attitudes strongly tied to legitimacy: legal cynicism, which reflects the acceptance and endorsement of acting outside the law and community norms (Srole, 1956; Sampson & Bartusch, 1998); moral disengagement, which reflects the separation of conduct from the internal controls transmitted via the moral standards of society (Bandura, 1996);

and the felt obligation to obey legal directives even when one disagrees (Tyler, 2006a; Sunshine & Tyler, 2003a).

Their results showed that legal cynicism increased and felt obligation decreased as adolescents got older, echoing other research findings with similarly aged youth (Emler & Reicher, 1995; Fine & Cauffman, 2015). However, outside of this natural tendency for authority attitudes to become less positive (see Darling, Cumsille, & Martinez, 2007, 2008 for a similar pattern within parental authority), their results also demonstrated that the personal experiences adolescents had with police officers and the courts also had a tremendous impact. To the degree that teenagers believed their interactions with legal authorities (e.g., police officers, school security personnel, retail store officers) were procedurally fair, they were more likely to feel obligated to obey the law and were less cynical, even after controlling for a variety of other psychological (e.g., impulsivity) and social (e.g., deviant peers) factors. Furthermore, the perception of the law as legitimate was strongly and negative associated with self-reported criminal behavior.

Why would legal cynicism increase? When adolescents compare the actual behavior of legal actors to their expectations based upon the values they learn in school and through other sources of civic education concerning democratic authority, they often find that their experience presents a different, and more coercive model of authority. Because their own or their observed experiences is that the police harass, demean, or threaten adolescents via the use of force, their evolving image of legal authority is unlikely to conform to a favorable model of legal authority. Instead this image undermines legitimacy and enhances cynicism. In other words, it is not necessarily the legal values underlying the democratic attitudes that change, but rather children increasingly come into contact with the reality of legal authority that many times does not correspond to those values. Overall, the Fagan and Tyler study illustrates the general framework for successful legal socialization articulated in this volume: that the acquisition of supportive attitudes and values that shape law-related behavior are driven by the fairness of interactions with legal authorities. Fair interactions reinforce the ideals of the legal system and connect with values. They also build favorable attitudes toward existing legal authorities.

In a later study, Fagan and Piquero (2007) extended the model presented in the 2005 study to a population of offenders. They interviewed 1,355 serious offenders, ages fourteen to eighteen, at six-month intervals over two years after they had been adjudicated delinquent by a juvenile justice court. Even among these individuals, they found that perceptions of legitimacy and cynicism toward the law were associated with lower levels of self-reported aggressive offending (e.g., assault) and income offending (e.g., theft), as well as overall offending. More importantly for our arguments here, perceptions of legitimacy were strongly influenced by the degree to which young people believed the police and courts treated them in a procedurally fair manner during the adjudicatory process, although it should be noted that court authorities had no influence on cynicism. These findings emerged even after controlling for a number of other factors espoused by deterrence and rational choice perspectives, such as the perceived risk of punishment, personal or social rewards, and punishment and social costs of engaging in illegal activity.

The authors note that these findings are especially relevant because their study focuses upon juveniles already involved with the court system; that is, those youth that commit the majority of adolescent crime. They conclude that "beginning in adolescence, legitimacy is an important value shaping law-related behavior" (p. 740), and that views about legitimacy are primarily linked to evaluations of the procedures used by the police and courts. Combined with the results of the 2005 study, this work indicates that legitimacy is not an invariant property of authorities, but rather is strongly shaped by what authorities do and how they wield their power. Regardless of whether we are discussing adolescent offenders or nonoffenders, the actions of legal authorities can enhance or diminish their legitimacy and the legitimacy of the institutions they represent (Tyler et al., 2014).

More recently, the centrality of procedural justice, legitimacy, and law-related behavior within the context of legal interactions with adolescents has been confirmed across a number of studies (Gau & Brunson, 2010; Hinds, 2007; Piquero, Fagan, Mulvey, Steinberg, & Odgers, 2005; Slocum, Wiley, & Esbensen, 2013; Trinkner & Cohn, 2014). For example, Kassa, Malloy, and Cauffman (2008) found that among a sample of incarcerated juvenile offenders procedural justice judgments were linked to self-reported offending. Harvell (2008) demonstrated that among a sample of detained adolescent offenders procedural fairness predicted more positive attitudes toward legal authority. More recently, Murphy (2015) directly compared the influence of procedural justice on cooperation with the police among adults and adolescents and showed that procedural justice was especially influential among adolescents, relative to its influence among adults. This supports the argument of Tyler and Huo (2002) that issues of interpersonal respect, in particular, are central to the way that adolescents evaluate their experiences with the police and the courts.

PRIMACY OF LAW ENFORCEMENT CONTACT

Up to this point we have shown that first contact with the legal system in a regulatory context is likely to happen during adolescence and the tenor of these contacts has a dramatic impact on the development of legal attitudes in youth, particularly their views about the status of the legal system as a regulatory agent and their acceptance of its power. However, we would be remiss to not spend some time discussing the influence of policing and law enforcement specifically. Police officers are the essential authority within the legal socialization process. Although most legal institutions are distant from the everyday realities of life, officers are tasked with patrolling communities and in many ways serve as the most tangible piece of the law that most people will ever face (Skogan & Frydl, 2004). In this respect officers serve as both the face of the legal system more than any other legal actor, and are the gateway into the system given that whether an individual will be formally processed by the legal system is largely at their discretion. Because of this position, both social scientists (Tyler et al., 2014) and legal scholars (Meares, 2009) have argued that any hope at improving the public trust deficits in the law highlighted in Part II of this volume must start with a focus on police.

Research on police contact with juveniles suggests that they react to the fairness or unfairness of the treatment they experience (Fagan & Tyler, 2005) or that they hear about from others (Flexon, Lurigio, & Greenleaf, 2009). As Hinds (2007, p. 195) notes, "Young people's attitudes toward police legitimacy are positively linked to police use of procedural justice." These reactions include changes in their attitudes about the police (Norman, 2009), in views about police legitimacy (Hinds, 2007), and in compliance with the law and willingness to cooperate with the police (Fagan & Piquero, 2007; Hinds, 2009; Reisig & Lloyd, 2009; Reisig, Tankebe, & Mesko, 2013).

In evaluating contact with the police, it is important to distinguish the messages that adolescents receive. One concerns lawfulness. Are police actions lawful, and do police officers follow lawful procedures and practices? More broadly, the issue is one of fair decision-making. Are rules applied consistently, impartially, and appropriately? Here the issue is whether experiences with legal authorities lead to a reinforcement of police legitimacy or contribute to legal cynicism.

A second element of fairness involves the quality of treatment received. Examinations of the content of police interactions with young people reveal an amazing number of examples of insulting, harassing, and demeaning behavior by the police. In fact, when young people are interviewed about the police it is such behavior that is frequently the focus of complaints (Fratello, Rengifo, & Trone, 2013; Stoudt, Fine, & Fox, 2011–2012).

The issue for policing is whether the message communicated by the police is one of reassurance or fear. Many young people initially learn that the police are the people they go to if they are in trouble or for help. They are told to expect fair treatment and fair decision-making from the police. In particular, the image of the police as benevolent and caring is often socialized, especially in White middle-class communities. But how do they experience their interactions with the police? Are those experiences of reassurance and safety or involving threat and fear? Do those interactions reinforce societal values concerning the way police are supposed to confront and resolve conflict or do they undermine those values?

The police become associated with fear when they are viewed as the agents of sanctioning (Stoudt et al., 2011–2012). This is because individuals do not initially define their relationship with the police in terms of rewards or costs; hence when the police behave this way, they are engaging in behavior that is counter to the values and ideals upon which the legal system stands. Rather than being viewed as people who understand, acknowledge, and address people's everyday concerns, thereby communicating reassurance, the police punish and are authorities who can come to be feared and avoided (Fratello et al., 2013). In particular, the widespread use of arrest to address minor crimes associates the police with demeaning experiences and the risk of being drawn into the criminal justice system for misdemeanors or minor lifestyle misconduct.

By dealing with the public through a framework of suspicion and sanctioning, the police undermine their legitimacy (Tyler et al., 2014). This is precisely because society does not view the police through an instrumental framework. Thus when they judge a system using tactics that are in stark contrast to the principles they believe that the police are supposed to represent and reflect, individuals see them as inappropriate and ineffectual legal authorities. These negative effects are not counterbalanced by a favorable impact upon legitimacy based upon declines in disorder and fear of crime, because disorder and fear of crime are not major factors that shape legitimacy (Tyler, 2006a, 2006b, 2009).

Why are factors such as disorder and fear of crime not the key drivers of legitimacy? They are not central concerns, because people define their relationship with the police and the courts in terms of values about how they are supposed to use their power (Jackson, Bradford, et al., 2013). A key issue to the public is their belief that they share a normative framework about authority with the police and courts ("normative alignment"; Tyler & Jackson, 2014). That framework includes the belief that the police are concerned about the community and the well-being of the people within it, and further, that they will make an effort to help those in need. Finally, people expect that the police will respect people when they deal with them, so it makes sense to bring community problems to the police. It is also expected that they will make decisions in a fair and unbiased manner when they deal with the public. These are not instrumental concerns, but speak to the relationship between the public and legal authorities (Tyler & Sevier, 2013/2014).

In a recent study Tyler, Jackson, and Mentovich (2015) demonstrate that the legitimacy of the police flows directly from judgments about the social bond between the police and the policed. This includes whether people trust the motives of police officers, whether they feel proud of the police, and whether they feel respected by the police. These judgments are influenced by whether people feel that the police view them as included in the community of "good citizens" whose values and actions should be respected. In other words, do the police regard them as marginal and problematic community members who should be the object of suspicion and scrutiny, or are they decent and upstanding members of the community? Such social messages resonate powerfully in adults, but particularly in adolescents whose identities and sense of self and self-worth are more fragile, developing, and easily influenced by outside information (from peers or authority figures).

Discussions of experiences with the police confirm that the public, particularly young men, experiences suspicion and indignity during encounters with the police. For example, in their in-depth interviews with forty-five young men aged thirteen to seventeen, Gau and Brunson (2010, p. 266) found that "respondents felt that their neighborhoods had been besieged by police and ... that law enforcement efforts on their streets consisted primarily of widespread stop-and-frisks." They noted that these individuals came to associate the police as overly aggressive characterized by demeaning and involuntary contact. In other words, these actions are frequently physically invasive and psychologically distressing. Research in New York City and elsewhere suggests that young men are often handcuffed, thrown to the ground, or slammed against walls while their bodies and belongings are searched (Brunson & Weitzer, 2009; Fratello et al., 2013; Rios, 2011; Ruderman, 2012a). Force is significantly more likely to be used against minority suspects in street stop encounters than Whites (Fagan et al., 2010).

Stops also frequently involve assaults on dignity by including a dimension of racial targeting (Carr et al., 2007; Fagan et al., 2010; Tyler et al., 2014). In interviews, both young men and women report that street stops are laced with violence, threats, hypermasculine and homophobic invective, and degrading and racially tinged language (Brunson & Weitzer, 2009; Gau & Brunson, 2010; Rios, 2011). Participants in the study by Carr and colleagues (2007), regardless of their race, reported that police officers were often more aggressive and disrespectful toward minority youth. Some young women stopped by the police report feelings of embarrassment and sexual intimidation when stopped, particularly when they are frisked by male officers (Ruderman, 2012b).

Similar messages come through arrests for minor crimes. When arrested, people are drawn into contact with the criminal justice system, which treats them as miscreants rather than as respected citizens (Ward et al., 2011). The demeaning procedures of arrest and detainment convey a message of social marginality and suspicious character (Jones, 2014). This both communicates mistrust and makes the social message of deviance and suspect character clear. As was suggested years ago, going through this process is a punishment in itself (Feeley, 1979). But it is also a social message, one of being viewed by societal authorities as a "criminal."

The core concern here is that given the potential for contact with law enforcement to be perceived as unfair and demeaning, a strategy to more aggressively pursue minor crimes can backfire in that it will promote illegitimacy among those targeted. As Sherman and Rogan (1995, p. 692) stated, "Most worrisome is the possibility that field interrogations could provoke more crime by making young men subjected to traffic stops more defiant toward conventional society . . . and thus commit more crimes." In this respect, there is potential for overly harsh criminal sanctions to actually *increase* crime among those groups that are subjected to it (see also Sherman, 1993 and Tyler, Fagan & Geller, 2014 for empirical support).

Studies show that adolescent judgments about police fairness shape law-related behavior (Wollard, Harvell, & Graham, 2008). Similarly, legitimacy shapes law-related behavior including substance abuse (Amonini & Donovan, 2006), drinking (Cook, 2013), and aggression (Arsenio, Preziosi, Silberstein, & Hamburger, 2012; Estevez, Murgui, Moreno, & Musitu, 2007; Levy, 2001; Musitu, Estevez, & Emler, 2007; Rigby, Mak, & Slee, 1989; Tarry & Emler, 2007). More generally, supportive attitudes shape law-related behavior (Brown, 1974a, 1974b; Butler, Leschied, & Fearon, 2007; Chow, 2011).

They also shape the willingness to cooperate (Brank et al., 2007; Clayman & Skinns, 2012; Eller, Abrams, Viki, Imara, & Peerbux, 2007; Viki, Culmer, Eller, & Abrams, 2006). For example, trust in the police can lead adolescents to provide the police with crime-related information (such as snitching; Clayman & Skinns, 2012). Similarly, Slocum, Tayler, Brick, and

Esbensen (2010) studied a large sample of 1,354 adolescents from across the United States. They found attitudes toward the police shaped the willingness to report crimes to the police, controlling for a variety of demographic and neighborhood contextual factors.

PUNITIVENESS IN JUVENILE JUSTICE

In the face of the fact that personal contact with the legal system undermines law-abidingness, two aspects of recent trends around policing are striking. One is the large increase in the number of total contacts that all adolescents have with the police. Through a series of policies designed to more proactively fight the problem of crime, the police have approached ever larger and broader groups of people and especially more minority adolescents on the street for identification, questioning, and searches (Fagan et al., 2010).

This approach began with the "broken windows" model of policing (Wilson & Kelling, 1982), which emphasizes arrest for lifestyle crimes; this led to zero-tolerance policies that require arrest for minor crimes, and ended up at the stop, question, and frisk method, which involves widespread stops but not necessarily arrests (Tyler, Goff, & MacCoun, 2015). As police tactics have developed, they have changed in several ways. First, though the policy built around broken windows was originally conceived of as targeting a small group of consensually defined deviants (squeegee people, prostitutes), its transformation into zero tolerance brought a larger group of people into the system with minor citations and brief incarceration. The further expansion of this policy into stop, question, and frisk relaxed the idea that those approached were actually committing a crime. Although the overt purpose of stop, question, and frisk tactics is finding guns and drugs, in reality almost none of the adolescents stopped have in fact been committing any crimes (Fagan et al., 2010). For many teenagers this policy has led to repeated stops in situations in which the person is never doing anything illegal at the time they encounter the police (Tyler et al., 2014). This type of contact with the police in cars or on the street has increased dramatically in recent decades.

There has also been a parallel development that we have already noted: the growth of school resource officers in high schools. Today, nearly half of all schools in the United States have a sworn police officer officially assigned to patrol school grounds (Department of Education, 2016), with many others having officers routinely at school or other security personnel that largely act as police officers (Arum, 2003). The goals and tactics of such officers vary greatly, but a general feature has been the increase in authorities with law-like features such as uniforms, guns, and tasers. And tactics have more frequently included bag searches, locker searches, personal searches, questioning in the hall, and metal detectors (Mukherjee, 2007). Along with this there have been increases in suspensions, expulsions, and other types of punitive response to rule violations (Department of Education, 2016). The older system of informal lectures by school administrators have been gradually replaced by formal sanctions by separate security personnel.

These developments reflect a new punitiveness in dealing with juveniles. After a long history of treating juveniles as distinct from adults and focusing upon the use of discretion in the direction of rehabilitation when dealing with juveniles, all of these developments push in the direction of drawing adolescents into more adult-like criminalized and punishment-focused interactions with the justice system (Slobogin & Fondacaro, 2011). These findings help to make sense out of the finding that contact with the legal system has the general consequence of increasing the likelihood of future criminal behavior.

The general effect of contact with the formal legal system is to increase the likelihood of a later criminal career (Aizer & Doyle, 2015; Petrosino, Turpin-Petrosino, Guckenburg, 2010; Redding, 2010). This does not mean that contact inevitably leads to undermining legal authority. It is clear that what matters is the type of contact. If adolescents experience fair treatment, their views about legitimacy go up. However, aggregate studies show that overall declines occur in response to contact, suggesting that fair treatment is not what is typically experienced (Tyler et al., 2014). Hence, whether people are drawn into the formal legal system is crucial to their later development.

It is particularly important to note that the many of the more punitive approaches developed as a response to perceived crises in juvenile offending have not been effective. As Scott and Steinberg (2008, p. 26) note, "studies have found that punitive reforms have little effect on youth crime ... little evidence supports the claim that adolescents are deterred from criminal activity by the threat of harsh sanctions, either generally or because their experience in prison 'taught them a lesson.'"

As an example of a widely touted sanctioning program for juveniles, consider "Scared Straight." This approach emerged in response to a widely viewed television documentary that aired with widespread fanfare in 1978.[1] Since then the documentary has been widely shown in the mass media and the program (or variants) has been replicated in over thirty jurisdictions. The core aspects of this program involve organized visits to prison facilities by juvenile offenders or by children that are identified in schools or in other ways as being at risk. During their visits the children are berated by the facility guards and inmates as a way to show them what will happen if they get caught committing a crime. Such programs fit well with the belief that more punishment (or at least the threat of it) is needed to combat juvenile crime, a belief that defines many popular programs against crime. For example, when then-Governor Rod Blagojevich signed the Illinois version of the program into law, he said it would "give some kids a chance to see what happens if they don't follow the rules, follow the law, and what's ahead for them if they don't do that" (Long & Chase, 2003).

Despite many people's intuitions, research suggests that "not only does [Scared Straight] fail to deter crime but it actually leads to more offending behavior" (Petrosino, Petrosino, & Buehler, 2004, p. 6), an argument that is consistent with the general findings about deterrence. After outlining evidence concerning this program, Petrosino and colleagues (2004, p. 37) note:

> We note the following irony: despite the gloomy findings reported here and elsewhere, "Scared Straight" and its derivatives continue in use, although a randomized trial has not been reported since 1992. As Finckenauer and Gavin (Finckenauer 1999) noted, when the negative results from the California SQUIRES study came out, the response was to end the evaluation—not the program. Today the SQUIRES program continues, evaluated by the testimonials of prisoners and participants alike. Despite evidence, beliefs in the program's efficacy continue. Middleton and his colleagues report on the extension of this strategy in one UK town to scare ordinary schoolchildren by using former correctional officers to set up a prison-type atmosphere in the public school system (Middleton 2001). In 1982, Finckenauer called this the "Panacea Phenomenon," describing how policy-makers, practitioners, media reporters and others sometimes latch onto quick, short-term and inexpensive cures to solve difficult social problems (Finckenauer 1982).

Regardless of the evidence such programs continue to capture the attention of the public and gain traction with politicians. The original *Scared Straight!* documentary has seen numerous sequels. In 2011, the A&E television network aired *Beyond Scared Straight*, a television series that presents a highly stylized version of the program. In marketing their new series they reiterated claims that the program works, saying that "over the years, both the prison program and the film have turned countless kids away from drugs, violence and crime, and kept them out of prison" (Vignati, 2011). This example illustrates the allure of severe sanctioning as a response to crime, despite research finding that not only is it ineffective policy, but can actually be counterproductive.

RESOCIALIZING ADOLESCENTS
THROUGH REHABILITATION

Should juveniles be managed differently than adult offenders? One aspect of this question is whether it is possible to resocialize juveniles. The lifespan literature suggests the idea of critical periods, but when are those critical periods for the development of supportive legal attitudes and values? Can we develop a type of contact with legal authority that enhances legitimacy? We have argued that it is not contact per se, but the social message conveyed by contact, that is important. It is possible that conveying a different social message would produce a different effect on legitimacy and later conduct. Doing so is especially possible with adolescents because they are in the process of developing their views and it is especially important to target this age group for this same reason, that is, their values and attitudes are being formed.

Studies show that the key to reducing reoffending lies in minimal system intervention and maximum diversion away from the criminal justice system (McAra & McVie, 2007). For example, Huizinga, Schumann, Ehret, and Elliott (2003) found that arrests and sanctions led either to the maintenance of or to increases in prior levels of offending. They also found that more severe sanctions were especially likely to lead to *increases* in offending. On the other hand, a substantial body of literature on community and institution-based juvenile treatment programs suggests that they can substantially reduce crime. The most promising programs reduce crime by 20 to 30% (Lipsey, 1999).

However, it is not feasible to simply divert all offenders into noncriminal programs. Some people will need to be confined or treated by the state. When this does need to occur the focus should be on rehabilitation, which has been shown to be especially effective for adolescent populations (see Curtis, Ronan, & Borduin, 2004; Eddy, Whaley, & Chamberlain, 2004; Fisher & Chamberlain, 2000; Frias-Armenta, Lopez-Escobar, & Silveira, 2016; Gordon, Graves, & Arbuthnot, 1995; Leve, Chamberlain, & Reid, 2005).[2] In fact, empirical studies often show that long-term crime prevention strategies based on rehabilitation are more successful than punishment-based ones.

Juvenile offenders are socialized when they have contact with the law through experiences with corrections—for example, by being held in jail or in a detention facility—and a key question is whether it is possible to build values in such an environment or afterward that can lower the rate of recidivism. In general the rate of criminal recidivism is high (Durose, Cooper, & Snyder, 2014), but it is widely argued that the possibilities for rehabilitation are greater for young people because they are still young and in the process of developing (Scott & Steinberg, 2010; Slobogin & Fondacaro, 2011). Indeed, the notion that youth are not fully formed and still able to be steered away from a life of crime was the primary motivation behind the establishment of a juvenile justice system in the first place at the turn of the twentieth century (Bonnie, Johnson, Chemers, & Schuck, 2013).

Restorative justice practices provide one example of a procedure found to be capable of effectively resocializing adolescents by facilitating the acquisition of supportive attitudes and values (Bradshaw, Roseborough, & Umbriet, 2006; Latimer, Dowden, & Muise, 2005). To help make the case, we contrast this approach with traditional punitive practices. Restorative justice involves conferences that include the offender, their family, the victim, and members of the community. At the conference all of those involved discuss the offender's behavior, offenders acknowledge responsibility for wrongdoing, and the group crafts an approach to restoring justice that incorporates atonement in some way.

The focus of restorative justice is on a "bad behavior, good person" approach that emphasizes that the behavior involved was bad, but the offender is a person of worth who is respected by family, friends, and others in the community. By this strategy those present seek to reconnect the offender to their preexisting supportive values, with the goal of motivating them to want to follow the law in the future. Braithwaite's (1989, 2002) model is based upon the connection of the motivation to follow rules to social ties with family, friends, and others in the community. As we noted in chapter 4, the desire for the approval of significant others has long been recognized as a strong motivation for engaging in socially desirable behavior, including rule-following.

The restorative justice approach seeks ways to heighten the future motivations of adolescents to engage psychologically and behaviorally in society. This engagement includes developing or becoming more committed to social values that promote self-regulation, and allowing for a consensual orientation toward law. That framework promotes adhering more closely to laws and social regulations in the future, leading to lower levels of recidivism and rearrest. In other words, one important goal is being able to create better community members and citizens as adolescents transition into adulthood. Building upon and fortifying their natural trajectory toward becoming a law-abiding adult is a clearly desirable way to achieve that goal.

Research results support the facilitative role of restorative justice conferences (Roberts & Stalans, 2004; Sherman, 1999). Studies suggest that at least with regard to the types of crime committed by juveniles, and among offenders who have social ties with family or others in the community, participating in a restorative justice conference leads to greater cooperation with the law in the future (Bradshaw, Roseborough, & Umbriet, 2006; Latimer, Dowden, & Muise, 2005; Nugent, Williams, & Umbreit, 2003; Poulson, 2003). Such conferences, it seems, do increase the motivation to accept the law and the decisions of legal authorities and to be a law-abiding citizen (Tyler, Sherman, Strang, Barnes, & Woods, 2007).

Latimer, Dowden, and Muise (2005) directly examined evidence concerning the impact of restorative justice on recidivism in adults. They concluded that in approximately two-thirds of the programs studied, restorative justice programs "yielded reductions in recidivism compared to nonrestorative approaches to criminal behavior" (p. 137), a difference which they found statistically significant. The authors emphasized using approaches consistent with an increased focus on values and a less singular focus on instrumental approaches. Other research suggests that strategies of socialization that encourage the development of social ties and interpersonal skills are linked to effectiveness in the treatment of juvenile offenders as well (Landenberger & Lipsey, 2005).

Individuals' perceptions of the legitimacy of the legal system are already forming by the time children reach early adolescence, making intervention into those perceptions at an early stage essential for establishing the legitimacy of the legal system. Fagan and Tyler (2005), for example, find that legal cynicism, legitimacy, and moral disengagement with the law can all be measured among children ages ten to eleven, but are also in the process of change throughout adolescence. Studies emphasize that rehabilitation is most successful among adolescents because as we have shown their values are still in the process of development (Lipsey & Cullen, 2007: McCord, Widom, & Crowell, 2001).

SUMMARY

In this chapter we examined the legal socialization process with regard to adolescents' experiences with the juvenile justice system and law more broadly. The research findings reported in this chapter continue to provide support for several key arguments that flow from prior chapters. First, it is possible for legal authorities to manage social order through the threat or use of force. However, supportive civic attitudes and values have a stronger influence upon law-related behavior. In particular, they are more powerful forces shaping empowerment, cooperation, and engagement. It is these types of behavior that are most desirable and which define superior forms of police–community relationships. Creating and maintaining favorable orientations toward law and legal authorities has important implications for the functioning of the legal system.

It is clear that adolescent orientations toward authority are responsive to both personal experiences with the police and courts and to perceptions about how legal authority is being exercised in the community. As has been the case within the other authority domains, adolescents are especially sensitive to whether legal institutions and officials utilize their power in fair and respectful ways. Such conduct has a demonstrable effect on the development of the attitudes and values that facilitate the acceptance of legal authority and the internalized responsibility to support and cooperate with the law. On the other hand, legal power used in coercive and instrumentally-focused ways tends to be counterproductive and associated with increased offending and rejection of the law.

Despite the clear implications of the research, once again there seems to be a clash of visions with respect to the purpose and optimal strategy of the juvenile justice system: the same clash that emerges within families and schools in regards to the best way to control behavior and produce law-abiding individuals. Although research supports the value of nonpunitive approaches and suggests that contact with legal authorities undermines perceived legitimacy and hence increases future lawbreaking, current policies lean in the direction of increasing punitive approaches and undermining consensually-based systems of law and social order. This includes increasing efforts to draw young people into contact with the police and the courts and heightened attention to treating minor infractions as crimes. However, the research shows that these approaches, while presented as crime reduction strategies, actually increase crime over time. Alternatively, prevention and rehabilitation efforts aimed at improving the relationship between youth and legal authorities build civic attitudes and lead to consensual orientations toward the law where children follow and cooperate legal directives because they want to, not because they are forced to.

PART IV

————————⌒⌒————————

Conclusions and Final Thoughts

Our core argument is that our democratic society benefits when its members are socialized in ways that *first* encourage them to develop a framework of values that can be the basis for a consensual approach to law and legal authorities and that *second* lead them to adopt the type of supportive values that motivate them to consent to appropriately exercised authority. We suggest that it is not automatic that young people develop in ways that lead them to have a framework of law-related values that foster the sense of the legitimacy of the legal system, nor is it necessarily the case that those values are incorporated into their motivational system and shape their adolescent and adult behavior. Further, when such values are a part of a developing motivational system it is not inevitable that the experiences of the young lead them to conclude that the legal authorities they encounter are legitimate and ought to be obeyed and the legal system more broadly should be supported. A variety of developmental trajectories are possible and the one any particular child takes depends upon their experiences in three phases of their lives: their family, their school, and their contact with criminal justice authorities.

From the perspective of the system, we suggest that the successful legal socialization of most of the members of any democratic society in ways that lead most people to hold supportive attitudes and values and to act upon them is central to the viability of that society. The viability of a democratic society depends upon widespread consent. To the degree that people hold civic values concerning the proper role of the legal system and the degree to which that system meets those expectations and garners support, people are more willing to voluntarily obey laws and accept the decisions of legal authorities. Ultimately this leads to a smaller legal footprint in society featuring a diminished police, court, and correctional presence, relying instead on the loyalty of the public to motivate law-abidingness.

Although it is unlikely that a society without any form of coercive authority would ever exist, the findings outlined suggest that there is the possibility of creating a system in which most people follow most rules most of the time because of their attitudes and values, not the fear of sanctions. Given this possibility, it is striking how little attention the issue of socializing civic attitudes and legal values has received in recent discussions about American society.

This book argues that legal scholarship should focus more heavily on the socialization of orientations toward law and legal authority during childhood and adolescence. Recent scholarship makes clear that the creation of such orientations, including the development of capacities for legal reasoning and the internalization of favorable legal attitudes and values are important factors shaping adults' law-related dispositions toward and behavior in relationship to law and the directives of legal authorities. Because such orientations are largely formed prior to adulthood, it is important to focus upon their development during childhood and adolescence.

Several developments have highlighted the importance of a focus on value creation. One is the increasing recognition that legal values are important to law-related behavior (Tyler, 2011). Studies that compare the role of deterrence mechanisms to that of values demonstrate that legal values are as or more important in shaping compliance with the law. Further, values are a key factor motivating cooperation with legal authorities. As the problems of deterrence and its limited effectiveness have become more salient, a focus upon values has become more important. Such a focus leads to concern with their origin in the legal socialization process. The alternative to a value-based orientation—an orientation based upon coercion—is less desirable, and effective socialization can create the values that promote the more desirable value-based framework. A key problem with instrumental frameworks is that they define people's relationship to law as being linked to rewards and punishments, not values. People with this oreintation follow and support the law to the extent that the legal system can reward and punish accordingly. However, because of the inherent nature of criminal behavior, due process, and the fact that law enforcement cannot be everywhere at all times, such an orientation is limited in motivating people to comply. If children and adolescents develop this orientation, then that is how they consider law as adults. Of course, there will always be a role for coercion in any system of law. The issue is balance.

The other development is the heightened awareness that Americans' attitudes about legal, political, and social authority have become more negative and less trusting over time. It is increasingly the case that the attitudes that exist within the general population about societal authorities are not favorable, leading to a variety of issues ranging from legal problems of noncompliance with laws and unwillingness to cooperate with legal authorities to larger issues of engagement in society. The need to address such trust deficits adds importance to efforts to understand how more favorable orientations toward law can be created and maintained. Society does not benefit from a willingness to defer to legitimate authorities if existing authorities are not viewed as legitimate.

As an example, consider the case of schools. In recent years there have been extensive discussions about education and American schools, public and private. And the government has developed and implemented a series of national reforms, including No Child Left Behind and, more recently, a national effort to create a uniform core curriculum. Whatever the merits of these efforts, and irrespective of the importance of children acquiring more job-related knowledge and skills, what we find striking about this national debate is what it does not discuss. Schools, in particular public schools—elementary, high school, and college—are not viewed as important because they are potential sources of civic education and legal value socialization.

This relative neglect of the issue of civic education contrasts with the efforts made in an earlier historical era to focus on public schools as an important framework through which to build children's loyalty to law and government (Justice & Meares, 2014). Schools were viewed as a key social institution for the socialization of both a value-based orientation and of the supportive attitudes needed for a viable democracy. And this failure to focus on civic education mirrors a general neglect of the field of legal socialization, an area that we argue needs to be central to discussions of what makes any democratic society successful.

Why is legal socialization important? This analysis contrasts two basic orientations toward legal authority. The first is a model of coercive authority. Coercive authorities direct the actions of others and motivate compliance through the threat or use of physical punishments or the promise of material rewards. A second model is consensual. When value socialization is successful, children and adolescents develop a framework for understanding legitimacy and supportive legal attitudes about existing authorities that leads to deference to law and legal authority.

While it is possible for children, adolescents, and adults to continue to relate to legal authority in coercive terms, the process of legal socialization leads most young people to develop both reasoning capacities and attitudes and values that define concepts of legitimate authority and develop the capacity to relate to law consensually. We suggest this is good because a legal system built upon consent is superior and more desirable to one based on coercion.

Supportive attitudes and values about the police, the courts, and the law shape a variety of important public behaviors. These include deference to police authority during personal encounters, everyday compliance with the law, cooperation with the police, acceptance of police authority, and diminishing support for public violence. As a consequence, there are clear costs associated with low levels of popular support.

While we discussed a variety of such costs, one clear finding is that lower levels of support are associated with higher levels of criminal behavior in adolescence and adulthood. Our argument, however, is broader. Supportive attitudes and values allow a framing of law and legal authority that is more generally cooperative and which is not based upon dominance and the use of force. Law becomes something that people accept and endorse because they are working with authorities to produce a form of social order that they view as legitimate.

It is also important to note that an important role of law is to provide a mechanism for the redress of injustice. If people do not believe that there are such mechanisms they are less likely to engage in society, taking the risks that make communities vibrant and productive. Similarly, if they are mistreated or are the victims of a crime people need to have some way to address those issues besides acts of private violence and revenge. All of these positive social goals require people to believe that if they deal with legal authorities their will receive just treatment and have their concerns listened to; considered and taken seriously. This is not about the ability of law to regulate conduct. It is about the importance of law as a facilitator of viable communities. But it is equally about legitimacy.

SOURCES OF LEGITIMACY

If legitimacy is desirable, how is it obtained? A large literature on attitude and value socialization demonstrates that the dynamics of the family are the first important source of the experience and information which shapes children's understanding of appropriate rules and authority. Three key issues emerge from this literature: the nature of the social relationship between parents and children, the manner in which parents manage rules and rule-following behavior, and the domains of behavior in which parents try to regulate behavior,

Research consistently suggests that warmth and caring create the type of emotional bonds that encourage the internalization of supportive attitudes and values in young children. In contrast, harsh and punitive parenting is associated with the failure to develop such attitudes and values. Hence, a beginning point of any discussion of legal socialization has to be a focus on the emotional dynamics of the family. This is linked to the issue of quality of treatment that is central at all stages of life. Children, adolescents, and adults all use the manner in which they are treated by authorities to assess their status, standing and self-worth. Cold and rejecting treatment, discourtesy, and humiliation all influence the person because they convey a social message that he or she is unwanted and not a valued member of the group. Unless that message is one of a caring and concerned authority who is trusted to take the needs of the person into account in their actions, it is unlikely that the subject of authority will view an authority as legitimate and consensually accept its directives.

The centrality of issues of quality of treatment resonates with the findings of the adult literature on the dynamics of authority. The relational model of authority (Tyler & Lind, 1992) suggests that the quality of the interpersonal treatment people experience when dealing with authorities is a primary cue through which people determine whether they are included within their community as respected and valued members. In particular, people focus on whether or not the authority is benevolent and sincere in their concern about their needs. This is something that people must infer with respect, politeness, and courtesy acting as important cues. It is also important that authorities show signs that they are attending to and responding to the ongoing situation in ways that reflect a concern for the people with whom they are dealing. These different aspects of treatment convey powerful messages of inclusion and status that shape people's identity. They can convey or undermine the search for respect and dignity, for a positive and valued identity.

The manner in which parents enforce rules is also important. One aspect of this issue is simply whether parents supervise their children, are aware of their ongoing behavior, and react when rule-breaking behavior occurs. Permissiveness is bad, as is inconsistent and nontransparent authority. Rule enforcement through fair procedures is the key. If parents consistently apply rules, explain their decisions, and allow children to talk with them about rules and discuss their reasons for their actions, children are more likely to internalize supportive legal values and attitudes, leading to a stronger commitment to authority. These elements of decision-making are closely linked to the cognitive development of reasoning skills, as young people develop a framework within which they understand the meaning and operation of rules.

In addition, the domains of which parents are considered to have rightful authority to regulate their children's behavior are also important. Early in children's lives they recognize that their parents' authority to control much of their behavior through the implementation of rules and behavioral standards. However, as children age and begin to exert their autonomy, two important things occur. First, they progressively gain a better understanding of a personal domain of behavior that is outside the regulatory capacity or their parents' authority. Second, they begin to include more behaviors within that personal domain. Having a clear and understandable framework for articulating the boundaries of authority is crucial to legitimacy, since no authority is entitled to exercise total control over someone else's behavior.[1]

Schools are a second important arena of legal socialization. Studies demonstrate that children in schools are influenced by the three elements already outlined with families. One is evidence of caring and concern. The second is the impartial and neutral application of rules of discipline and grading by teachers and administrators. The third is further refinement of the boundaries of behavioral domains over which teachers have authority. Again, the endorsement of civic attitudes and values is dependent on the extent to which youth experience these elements within their school disciplinary climate.

As with the family, experience in school does not automatically promote the development of supportive legal attitudes and values. Unfair experiences with teachers can promote legal cynicism and alienation from school authorities. Reicher and Emler (1985) describe how adolescents who feel disrespected by school authorities seek social standing and support for their problems outside of formal channels, for example by joining gangs. School experiences can either facilitate or undermine the attachment of youth to the social institutions that are sources of formal social control in society.

Finally, there are adolescent experiences with the juvenile justice system. Most of the experiences that people have with legal authorities, in particular the police, occur before they become adults. It is during the period of adolescence that many people commit minor crimes that may bring them into contact with law enforcement, the courts, and detention facilities. This is a third opportunity for society to teach adolescents about the appropriate role of the law and the legal system and to show them that legal institutions adhere to the values and norms that underlie them. As we have noted, studies suggest that the general impact of having contact with legal authorities is diminished support for the law. However, it does not appear that it is contact in and of itself that leads to a negative orientation toward the law, but rather the fact that in many cases contact with legal actors is tinged with hostility, bias, and disrespect. This suggests either that legal authorities do not view the legal socialization of supportive attitudes and values as part of their job, or that they do not know how to do it.

Contact with juveniles generally undermines support for the law. Studies indicate that the factor that is especially important in this result is the general finding that juveniles evaluate their contact with the police and the rest of the legal system as reflecting unfair treatment. Legal authorities are not acting as effective agents of legal socialization, instilling respect for and support of law and legal authority. More often, they are perceived as agents of dominance and forceful control.

In reality the police, the courts, and the law convey a second and less publically articulated message about law: fear of the police. Parents of minority children teach their children to avoid the police who they fear do not act in ways that represent the values of the rule of law. And when juveniles deal with the police, they experience disrespect and humiliation. This communicates a message about law—but not one of reassurance. Instead, it associates legal authorities with discourtesy and sanctioning, rather than an expectation of fair and benevolent treatment. Rather than being something that is sought out to help diffuse social conflict within the community, the legal system becomes something to be avoided, precisely because it creates more conflict than it alleviates.

This message from the police has two important implications. One is that the law is not something to be respected and supported. Legal cynicism is a product of unfair treatment. The other is that legal authorities are not people to go to for help. This leads to a culture in which there are campaigns against involving the police in local problems, such as not snitching on neighborhood deviants, resorting to carrying guns on the street for self-protection against others, joing gangs, and engaging in violent acts to resolve grievances. Or people may simply feel unable to use the law to protect themselves, as when illegal immigrants do not report robberies for fear of calling themselves to police attention.

Psychological studies suggest models concerning the ways that parents, teachers, and juvenile justice authorities should act to develop legitimacy in the young. Current policies and practices in families, schools, and the juvenile justice system, however, reflect a conflict between styles of exercising authority in ways that are coercive and do not build legitimacy or that are consent-building, and are shown to be connected to the development of legitimacy.

The key paradox outlined in this analysis is that at a time when research increasingly suggests the benefits of consent-based models of legal authority, there continues to be substantial support for coercive approaches to legal socialization during each of the three phases of socialization: family, schools, and through contact with criminal justice authorities. The degree to which strategies for building legitimacy will be enacted is unclear at a point in American history when the need for higher legitimacy is clearly emerging. That need reflects both the greater recognition of the role of legitimacy in the effective maintenance of social order, and increasing evidence that the framework of institutional trust that has sustained American society since the 1950s is declining.

WHAT LINKS PEOPLE TO RULES AND AUTHORITIES?

What creates loyalty to rules and authorities? The research outlined points to three primary factors. These factors are also found to dominate judgments about the fairness of the exercise of authority among adults (i.e., procedural justice).

The first issue is how authority is exercised. A variety of key concepts are articulated in different discussions of the nature of the procedures of decision-making used by authorities when applying rules. Do people have the chance to reason with decision-makers by stating their case, making their arguments, dialogue and discussion? Is the process transparent and when decisions are being explained can people see that rules are being consistently and impartially applied? Is it clear that appropriate information is being collected and used to make decisions? Are rules being consistently applied across people and situations? And finally, are there mechanisms to evaluate the fairness of the authority, such as opportunities to appeal and have an independent review of decisions?

The second aspect of the exercise of authority involves the quality of treatment and what it indicates about the intentions and character of the authority. People react to evidence about whether an authority cares about them and is motivated to do what is in their interest. This means that the person dealing with the issue tries to do what is best for the parties involved and sincerely wants to do what is right. They are benevolent and concerned about those over whom they exercise authority, rather than acting to favor their own interests or those of some small group in the community. These are issues that revolve around trust in the character and motivations of the authority. Do they care about the well-being of the people about whom they are making decisions?

The third aspect of the exercise of authority involves the scope of the regulation of behavior itself. It is about the boundaries of authority. While the first two aspects pertain to questions of how legal authority behaves once it comes into contact with the system, this third aspect is concerned with the nature of the things that bring people into contact with the system in the first place. This third aspect revolves around issues about what kinds of behaviors will be deemed to be under the jurisdiction of the legal system (i.e., what things are illegal or what things will the legal system try to control or regulate). Note that this aspect is not focused on the *way* behaviors are regulated, as that is the domain of the previous two aspects. Rather, this is focused on what things are or should be regulated and in what situations such regulation should occur.

There are at least two key concepts at play in terms of boundaries. The first is what kinds of behavior are appropriate or inappropriate for the police to regulate. While it is certainly clear that the majority of the public recognizes the right of police to regulate certain kinds of behavior (e.g., behavior that causes physical harm to other people or their property), it is also certainly clear that there are distinct boundaries concerning behaviors that police should not regulate. As an example, in recent years there has been a growing clash between the public and the police over the war on drugs. While there are many facets of this debate, undeniably one of the more prominent ones is the argument over when the police have the right to regulate what individuals can and cannot put into their body (so long as they are not hurting anyone else or their property).

The second concept concerns where police are allowed to regulate behavior and where they are not. For example, although there is an argument to be made concerning whether it is appropriate for the legal system to regulate what people put into their body, there is also something to be said about whether the police can regulate that behavior in some situations but not others. Indeed, although there are no restrictions concerning how much you can drink in the privacy of your own home, many cities have laws concerning public intoxication.

What unites these different concerns? They represent the values upon which a society, group, or community defines their relationship with the legal system. By extension, they are factors that shape whether people identify with a group, organization, neighborhood, community, or society. When people identify with a collectivity, they take on supportive attitudes and values. Further, they follow rules and they do so consensually. What is especially important from our perspective is that people both take on the responsibility to act on behalf of their group and do so more voluntarily. In particular, they engage in their society and behave in ways that they believe will help their society to succeed. So long as both the individuals and the legal system are acting in accordance with these values that stipulate this reciprocal relationship, both parties will promote social solidarity and cooperation.

As we have noted, the legal system can be a framework of order and reassurance that undergirds economic and social development. This happens when the legal system acts in accordance with community values concerning the appropriate ways in which it should provide that order and reassurance. People invest in communities when they think there are mechanisms for the just redress of grievances and when they trust the legal authorities to manage social order fairly. Rather than be an oppressive and occupying force, the police can communicate safety and security and encourage willing and active engagement in the community.

These possibilities are enhanced when the police and courts can operate in communities within which the people generally hold supportive attitudes. Such communities willingly cooperate with legal authorities. This reduces the number of hostile and combative interactions and gives legal authorities greater leeway to enact strategies for community development. Rather than being a controlling force, law can be an engine of community growth and viability.

POTENTIAL PROBLEMS WITHIN
A VALUE-BASED FRAMEWORK

What might be problems associated with a focus on creating and maintaining legal values through the process of legal socialization? One perspective is provided by Kahan (1999) in his article on the secret ambition of deterrence. Kahan argues that one reason that attention has been directed at deterrence is that it is a goal that is commonly accepted by people of all political orientations. He argues that "citizens conventionally defend their positions in deterrence terms only because the alternative is a highly contentious expressive idiom" (p. 414) involving a conflict over cultural styles and moral outlooks. A focus on this commonly accepted goal avoids conflicts over the appropriate values for public policy.

The Kahan argument is important because it incorporates the empirical finding that deterrence does not work very well by arguing that the effectiveness of deterrence was not the reason for adopting it as a model for criminal justice policy. He suggests that the "intensity of the debate" over criminal justice policies "cannot convincingly be explained in terms of their behavioral consequences, which are patently negligible in most cases and exceedingly ambiguous in the rest" (p. 417). Instead, he contends that they are battles to control the expressive capital of the criminal law.

He concludes that the disembodied idiom of costs and benefits cools such expressive disputes.

Is a call for a focus on the socialization of civic attitudes and values something that will lead to a rekindling of expressive value disputes? There is certainly room for conflict concerning facts and values associated with different issues in education. An example is the teaching of evolution in public schools. This is a perennial focus of conflict when the content of textbooks is being debated, and it reflects the way the distinction between facts and values can be blurred in such discussions.

However, our argument is that the key to an effort to socialize supportive legal attitudes is to focus on the content that is least likely to be controversial. In particular, we suggest focusing on how the legal system and its agents use their authority to regulate behavior. Although people will eternally disagree about what should and should not be legal, most everyone will agree that an appropriate legal system within any democratic society should be impartial and humane. Such behavior fosters democratic legitimacy which leads to both trust and confidence in the legal system and the obligation to obey the law. We suggest that these are generally held values that are likely to be supported by all of the members of our society irrespective of their ideological values.

Of course no model of legal socialization can create a society in which everyone develops supportive attitudes and values. And this is particularly true of a comparatively heterogeneous society like our own comprised of many ethnicities, races, and cultures. Hence it is important to recognize the idea of a pyramid of regulation (Ayres & Braithwaite, 1992). That model suggests that people first be approached with the idea that they can deal consensually with authorities. Only for a small group that proves unable to act in this way is a coercive system applied. This approach has the advantage of minimizing the extent of coercion that needs to be applied and maximizing the degree of self-regulation based upon supportive attitudes and values.

TOWARD A POSITIVE AND PROACTIVE CONCEPTION OF LEGAL AUTHORITY

Four models of legal authority are outlined in Table 2. Those models divide authority along two dimensions: reactive–proactive and coercive–consensual. The reactive–proactive dimension relates to whether legal authorities respond to crime after it occurs or try to prevent it. The coercive–consensual distinction relates to how authority is implemented: via instrumental mechanisms or by appeals to values.

Table 2. MODELS OF LEGAL AUTHORITY

	Reactive	Proactive
Negative	Catch and punish people who have committed crimes. Coercive.	Anticipate and prevent crimes by assessing future risks and intercepting people before they can commit crimes.
Positive	Focus on rehabilitation and restoration when dealing with criminals.	Create a value climate within which people view authorities as legitimate and consent to follow laws.

As it has traditionally been conceived, the legal system is negative and reactive in its orientation toward the people in the community. It is negative in the sense that it is coercive and motivates people through fear. While incentives can also be part of an instrumental approach, deterrence is largely about fear. And legal authority is reactive because it focuses on punishment after rules are broken (or the threat thereof) as a motivational tool to encourage law-abiding behavior. The system is focused upon postevent consequences, in particular punishment as a response to wrongdoing.

Since the 1960s there has been a major change in orientation in the legal system toward proactive efforts to stop crime. In policing this involves patrolling and dealing with people on the street in an effort to identify future criminal intention by finding guns, drugs, or other paraphernalia. More widely, it involves the use of future risk assessment tools to deny bail and release and to sentence longer those people who are likely to commit crimes in the future. Despite this change in goal, the system continues to rely on coercive approaches to implement proactive goals.

The model advocated here focuses upon a proactive approach. But it is positive, not negative. It is positive in that it is concerned with socialization that involves thoughtful and reasoned acceptance of the importance and value of rules and authorities. In other words, people are encouraged to willingly engage with law, legal authorities, and society more generally because they believe that authorities and institutions are legitimate. This lessens the need to impose credible threats backed by surveillance and sanctioning, because people take the responsibility to obey the law upon themselves willingly and via consent. A positive approach further encourages people to identify with society and societal institutions and to more generally work for the well-being of society. At all of these levels it is based upon a model in which people hold and act upon supportive attitudes and values.

This approach is proactive because it advocates building supportive attitudes and values during childhood socialization so that adults are motivated to voluntarily follow rules because they consent to the arrangements of legal authority. Instead of reacting when adults have inadequately positive attitudes and values to support engaging in law-abiding behavior, this approach focuses upon creating a system within which young people are socialized to have a framework for understanding legitimacy and for developing the supportive attitudes and values that encourage them to be law-abiding. The goal is to prevent crimes proactively by encouraging a focus on developing a supportive orientation toward law that motivates obedience.

In discussing these changes it must of course be acknowledged that they have a broader connection to society. Many adults may themselves be bullied or coerced by forces in society -- economic, political, social and legal. They might find the argument that they have consented to the conditions they live in a strange suggestion. An important direction for this line of argument in the future is the broader question of the overall nature of authority in American society.

FINAL THOUGHTS

An important development in American law in recent decades has been a focus on proactive responses to crime: that is, on preventing crimes in advance. However, that focus has been on making risk assessment that can identify potentially dangerous people, as well as engaging in surveillance approaches such as stop, question, and frisk that seek to prevent crimes by proactive police contact with possible future offenders. While these approaches are also proactive, they are not focused on building values. They seek to communicate the risk of apprehension and punishment and thereby to motivate people not to commit crimes, or to remove people judged to be likely to commit future crimes from society before they can act. They are based upon a coercive model of law.

When young people are not legally socialized in ways that allow consensual legal regulation, they are in a situation in which their behavior is shaped by fear of punishment and, if needed, by a reactive punishment approach in which their lawbreaking is punished. After people break the law, they are caught and potentially punished. This fits well with a model of policing, proactive or reactive, that shapes behavior through influencing estimates of risk and reward.

Once a positive and proactive approach is accepted as a model, a concern with value creation seems natural. Such a concern then leads to a desire to promote effective cognitive development and the acceptance of supportive attitudes and values. Against this backdrop it is striking that within each of the three phases of development examined—family, school, and juvenile justice—a struggle is occurring between policies and practices that are coercive and those that promote the development of legitimacy and through that development, facilitate the operation of consensual mechanisms of regulation.

Given the benefits of consensual regulation, the evidence presented argues strongly for the virtues of enhancing policies and practices that encourage the development of legitimacy during socialization. The review of research contained here indicates first that it is possible to socialize the young in ways that do both allow and promote a consensual framework. At the same time, a review of policies and practices indicates that within each phase whether the policies and practices supported by research will be enacted is a contentious issue. There are divided views about how to socialize, and many recent developments in the way young people are treated in our society are counter to the approaches that research suggests are most likely to be effective in socializing legitimacy in the young.

Addressing these issues about socialization are crucial to a future era of low legitimacy for legal, political, and social authorities. The benefits of consensual authority based upon supportive values and favorable attitudes are important but they will only be available in the future if these conflicts are resolved in ways that support value creation and attitude development during the childhood socialization process.

NOTES

1. When social scientists (e.g., Moffitt, 1993) write about adolescent vs. life-course criminals they typically suggest that only a small proportion of people (under 10%) continue to engage in criminal behavior over the course of adulthood.
2. While this is true of adults in general there is a smaller group of adults, typically poor and often minority, who continue to have interactions with the police over criminal involvement throughout life (Delisi, 2005). These life-course criminals are typically estimated to constitute 5 to10% of the adult population.
3. Ferguson, Missouri was the site of a police shooting of an unarmed Black teenager, which spurred nationwide protests. It was the first of many police-related shootings that brought trust in the police (and the legal system more generally) into national attention in 2014–2015.

CHAPTER 1

1. As we will elaborate later, it is important to distinguish these declines in trust from the possibility that people may also be increasingly likely to have an instrumental orientation toward authority. They may be acting out of self-interest rather than based upon attitudes and values. An important argument is that a focus on incentives and sanctions crowds out attention to values.
2. Deterrence is most likely to be effective when surveillance can be concentrated on a few people or settings and when behavior is difficult to conceal.
3. Of course, from the individual's point of view it may seem most reasonable to adopt a framework of understanding authority that is totally based on self-interest and then evaluate the legitimacy of existing authorities on the basis of whether they reward or punish them.

CHAPTER 2

1. As has been noted, it is important to emphasize that many of the problems with deterrence-based systems reflect resource limits. Given unlimited resources for surveillance, apprehension, and punishment, a system based upon fear can be effective. Hence, this system can be effective when surveillance is difficult to avoid.
2. Kessler notes that "people would not feel free to end their encounters with the police." In fact, "knowledge of one's legal right to end the encounter with the police would not make people feel free to leave" (p. 52).

CHAPTER 3

1. Information about the European Social Survey and its datasets can be obtained from www.europeansocialsurvey.org. Data presented here can be recreated using their online analysis tool: http://nesstar.ess.nsd.uib.no/webview/.

CHAPTER 4

1. Of course, in the studies by Lewin the authority is benevolent, so accepting their directives benefits the members of the group.
2. This reality creates difficulties in societies that are diverse in values or in which there are dominate and subordinate classes of people. Different groups may have different values, and hence the question of whose values define society becomes an important point of contention.

CHAPTER 5

1. For such a review, interested readers can direct their attention to Gibbs (2013), Killen and Smetana (2006), and Turiel (2002).
2. Despite this foreshadowing, there has been very little attention paid to peers within legal reasoning research, except for studies of gangs, a shortcoming of the entire field of legal socialization.
3. While we refrain from giving a complete explanation of the shortcomings of Kohlbergian theory here, interested readers should consult Gibbs (2013), Gilligan (1982), and Lapsley (2006).

CHAPTER 6

1. Our intention is not to provide a full and in-depth discussion of this voluminous and complex literature. Interested readers should direct their attention to Scott and Steinberg's *Rethinking Juvenile Justice* (2010) or Steinberg's *Age of Opportunity: Lessons from the New Science of Adolescence* (2014).
2. It is not our intention to revisit the discussion about innate vs. acquired characteristics. We accept the general view of developmental psychologists that both factors matter (Spencer et al., 2009). However, we suggest that recent studies in neuroscience have contributed important new insights concerning how the neurological and biological elements of development emerge over time.
3. These would primarily include serotonin (Hensler, 2006) and dopamine (Morgane et al., 2005).

CHAPTER 7

1. This data from the World Values Survey can be recreated on their website using their "Online Analysis" tool: http://www.worldvaluessurvey.org/WVSOnline.jsp.
2. This data from the General Social Survey can be recreated on the NORC website using their online data explorer tool: https://gssdataexplorer.norc.org/.
3. Ibid.

CHAPTER 8

1. A separate question is how police authority in schools is understood by teachers and administrators. Wolfe et al. (2015) found that administrators viewed SROs as legitimate and effective and also found that their judgments were primarily based upon whether those officers treated students with procedural justice.

2. These issues matter to everyone. However, adolescence in particular is a period of self-evaluation and self-definition, so while information about one's status and standing is always important, for young people it is crucial. It is for this reason that young people are particularly sensitive to information about respect or disrespect from others (Tyler & Huo, 2002). Adolescents involved in gangs and those who feel socially marginal are especially likely to be attentive to signs of disrespect from others, something widely recognized in discussions of the cycle of gang violence. Disrespect, in other words, is a strong social signal, especially when it comes from a social authority such as a police officer or a teacher.

CHAPTER 9

1. *Scared Straight!* won an Academy Award for Best Documentary Feature and Emmy Awards for Outstanding Individual Achievement-Informational Program and Outstanding Informational Program.
2. Rehabilitation is also effective among adults (MacKenzie, 2006; Lipsey & Cullen, 2007).

PART IV

1. In an era in which parents often argue that they are entitled to exercise total control over their children, even homeschooling them, it is nonetheless the case that other authorities assert legitimate rights to influence how a child is managed. This may come in the form of social welfare agencies looking for signs of child neglect or abuse, in the form of public health officials, or in other ways. At all stages of life the right to be an authority over all spheres of a child's life is a contested concept.

REFERENCES

Adelson, J., & Beall, L. (1970). Adolescent perspectives on law and government. *Law and Society Review, 4*, 495–504.

Adelson, J. G., Green, B., & O'Neil, R. (1969). Growth of the idea of law in adolescence. *Developmental Psychology, 1*, 327–332.

Adelson, J. G., & O'Neil, R. (1966). Growth of political ideas in adolescence. *Journal of Personality and Social Psychology, 4*, 295–306.

Adorno, T. W., Frenkel-Brunswik, E., Levinson, D. J., & Sanford, R. N. (1950). *The authoritarian personality*. New York: Norton.

Aizer, A., & Doyle, J. J., Jr. (2015). Juvenile incarceration, human capital, and future crime: Evidence from randomly assigned judges. *Quarterly Journal of Economics, 130*(2), 759–803.

Almond, G. A., & Verba, S. (1963). *The civic culture: Political attitudes and democracy in five nations*. Princeton, NJ: Princeton University Press.

Alwin, D. F. (2001). Parental values, beliefs, and behavior. *Advances in Life Course Research, 6*, 97–139.

Alwin, D. F., & McCammon, R. J. (2003). Generations, cohorts, and social change. In J. T. Mortimer & M. J. Shanahan (Eds.), *Handbook of the life course* (pp. 23–50). New York: Kluwer Academic Publishers.

Amonini, C., & Donovan, R. J. (2006). The relationship of youth's moral and legal perceptions of alcohol, tobacco and marijuana and use of these substances. *Health Education Research, 21*, 276–286.

Amorso, D. M., & Ware, E. E. (1983). Youth's perception of police as a function of attitudes towards parents, teachers and self. *Canadian Journal of Criminology, 25*, 191–199.

Anderson, E. (1999). *Code of the street: Decency, violence, and the moral life of the inner city*. New York: Newton.

Arsenio, W. F., Preziosi, S., Silberstein, E., & Hamburger, B. (2012). Adolescents' perceptions of institutional fairness: Relations with moral reasoning, emotions and behavior. *New Directions in Youth Development, 136*, 95–110.

Arum, R. (2003). *Judging school discipline*. Cambridge, MA: Harvard University Press.

Ary, D. V., Duncan, T. E., Duncan, S. C., & Hops, H. (1999). Adolescent problem behavior. *Behavioral Research and Therapy, 37*, 217–230.

Augustyn, M. B. (2015). The (ir)relevance of procedural justice in the pathways to crime. *Law and Human Behavior, 39*(4), 388–401.

Axelrod, R. (1984). *The evolution of cooperation*. New York: Basic Books.

Ayres, I., & Braithwaite, J. (1992). *Responsive regulation: Transcending the deregulation debate*. New York: Oxford University Press.

Bandura, A. (1996). Reflections on human agency. In J. Georgas & M. Manthouli (Eds.), *Contemporary psychology in Europe: Theory, research and applications* (pp. 194–210). Seattle, WA: Hogrefe & Huber.

Barker, D. C., Hurwitz, J., & Nelson, T. L. (2008). Of crusades and culture wars: Messianic militarism and political conflict in the United States. *Journal of Politics, 70*(2), 307–322

Baron, R. M., & Kenny, D. A. (1986). The moderator–mediator variable distinction in social psychological research: Conceptual, strategic, and statistical considerations. *Journal of Personality and Social Psychology, 51*(6), 1173–1182.

Bartollas, C., & Schmalleger, F. (2011). *Juvenile delinquency* (8th ed.). New York: Prentice Hall.

Baumeister, R. F., & Leary, M. R. (1995). The need to belong: Desire for interpersonal attachments as a fundamental human motivation. *Psychological Bulletin, 3,* 497–529.

Baumrind, D. (1966). Effects of authoritative parental control on child behavior. *Child Development, 37,* 887–907.

Baumrind, D. (1967). Child care practices anteceding three patterns of preschool behavior. *Genetic Psychology Monographs, 75,* 43–88.

Baumrind, D. (1971). Current patterns of parental authority. *Developmental Psychology, 4,* 1–103.

Baumrind, D. (1978). Parental disciplinary patterns and social competence in children. *Youth and Society, 9,* 238–276.

Baumrind, D. (1991). The influence of parenting style on adolescent competence and substance use. *Journal of Early Adolescence, 11,* 56–95.

Bayraktar, F. (2014). Bullying among adolescents in North Cyprus and Turkey. *Journal of Interpersonal Violence, 27,* 40–65.

Bear, G. G. (1989). Sociomoral reasoning and antisocial behaviors among normal sixth graders. *Merrill-Palmer Quarterly, 35,* 181–196.

Becker, G. 1976. *The economic approach to human behavior.* Chicago: The University of Chicago Press.

Beerthuizen, M. G. C. J. (2013). Oppositional defiance, moral reasoning and moral value evaluation as predictors of self-reported juvenile delinquency. *Journal of Moral Education, 42,* 460–474.

Beetham, D. (1991). *The legitimation of power.* London: Macmillan.

Berti, C., Molinari, L., & Speltini, G. (2010). Classroom justice and psychological engagement. *Social Psychology and Education, 13,* 541–556.

Bethel School District v. Fraser, 478, US 675, p. 683.

Blader, S., & Tyler, T. R. (2003a). What constitutes fairness in work settings? A four-component model of procedural justice. *Human Resource Management Review, 12,* 107–126.

Blader, S., & Tyler, T. R. (2003b). A four component model of procedural justice: Defining the meaning of a "fair" process. *Personality and Social Psychology Bulletin, 29,* 747–758.

Blair, R. J. R. (1995). A cognitive developmental approach to morality? Investigating the psychopath. *Cognition, 57,* 1–29.

Blair, R. J. R. (2005). Responding to the emotions of others: Dissociating forms of empathy through the study of typical and psychiatric populations. *Consciousness and Cognition, 14,* 698–718.

Blakemore, S. J., & Mills, K. L. (2014). Is adolescence a sensitive period for sociocultural processing? *Annual Review of Psychology, 65,* 187–207.

Blasi, A. (1980). Bridging moral cognition and moral action. *Psychological Bulletin,* *88,* 1–45.

Blendon, R. J., Benson, J. M., Morin, R., Altman, D. E., Brodie, M., Brossard, M., & James, M. (1997). Changing attitudes in American. In J. S. Nye, P. D. Bobo, & D. C. King (Eds.), *Why people don't trust government.* Cambridge, MA: Harvard University Press.

Bloom, P. (2013). *Just babies: The origins of good and evil.* New York: Crown.

Bocchiaro, P., & Zimbardo, P. G. (2010). Defying unjust authority: An exploratory study. *Current Psychology, 29,* 155–170.

Bonnie, R. J., Johnson, R. L., Chemers, B. M., & Schuck, J. A. (2013). *Reforming juvenile justice: A developmental approach.* Washington, DC: National Research Council.

Bonnie, R. J., & Scott, E. S. (2013). The teenage brain: Adolescent brain research and the law. *Current Directions in Psychological Science, 22*(2), 158–161.

Borney, N., Snavely, B., & Priddle, A. (2013). Detroit becomes largest U.S. city to enter bankruptcy. *USA Today,* December 3.

Bos, A. L., Williamson, I., Sullivan, J. L., Gonzales, M. H., & Avery, P. G. (2007). The price of rights: High school students' civic values and behaviors. *Journal of Applied Social Psychology, 37,* 1265–1284.

Bowles, S., & Gintis, H. (1976). *Schooling in capitalist America: Educational reform and the contradictions of economic life.* Chicago: Haymarket Books.

Bracy, N. L. (2011). Student perceptions of high-security school environments. *Youth and Society, 43*(1), 365–395.

Bradford, B. (2014). Policing and social identity: Procedural justice, inclusion and cooperation between police and public. *Policing & Society, 24*(1), 22–43.

Bradford, M., Murphy, K., & Jackson, J. (2014). Officers as mirrors: Policing, procedural justice and the (re)production of social identity. *British Journal of Criminology, 54*(4), 527–550.

Bradshaw, W., Roseborough, D., & Umbriet, M. S. (2006). The effects of victim offender mediation on juvenile offender recidcivism. *Journal of Conflict Resolution, 24,* 87–98.

Braga, A., Papachristos, A., & Hureau. (2012). *Hot spots policing effects on crime.* Oslo, Norway: The Campbell Collaboration. doi: 10.4073/csr.2012.8

Braithwaite, J. (1989). *Crime, shame, and reintegration.* New York: Cambridge University Press.

Braithwaite, J. (2002). *Restorative justice and responsive regulation.* Oxford: Oxford University Press.

Brame, R., Turner, M. G., Paternoster, R., & Bushway, S. D. (2012). Cumulative prevalence of arrest from ages 8 to 23 in a National sample. *Pediatrics, 129,* 21–27.

Brank, E. M., Hoetger, L. A., & Hazen, K. P. (2012). Bullying. *Annual Review of Law and Social Science, 8,* 213–230.

Brank, E., Woolard, J. L., Brown, V. E., Fondacaro, M., Leuscher, J. L., Chinn, R. G., & Miller, S. A. (2007). Will they tell?: Weapons reporting by middle-school youth. *Youth Violence and Juvenile Justice, 5*(2), 125–146.

Breyer, S. (2010). *Making our democracy work.* New York: Random House.

Brezina, T. (2002). Assessing the rationality of criminal and delinquent behavior: A focus on actual utility. In A. R. Piquero and S. G. Tibbetts (Eds.), *Rational choice and criminal behavior: Recent research and future challenges* (pp. 241–264). New York: Routledge.

Brickman, P. (1974). *Social conflict.* Lexington, MA: D. C. Heath and Company.

Brower, M. C., & Price, B. H. (2001). Neuropsychiatry of frontal lobe dysfunction in violent and criminal behavior: A critical review. *Journal of Neurology, Neurosurgery, & Psychiatry, 71*, 720–726.

Brown, D. (1974a). Cognitive development and willingness to comply with the law. *American Journal of Political Science, 18*, 583–594.

Brown, D. (1974b). Adolescent attitudes and lawful behavior. *Public Opinion Quarterly, 38*, 98–106.

Brown, C. S., & Bigler, R. S. (2004). Children's perceptions of gender discrimination. *Developmental Psychology, 40*, 714–726.

Bright, C. L., Young, D. W., Bessaha, M. L., & Falls, B. J. (2015). Perceptions and outcomes following teen court involvement. *Social Work Research, 39*(3), 135–146.

Brubacher, M. R., Fondacaro, M. R., Brank, E. M., Brown, V. E., & Miller, S. A. (2009). Procedural justice in resolving family disputes: Implications for childhood bullying. *Psychology, Public Policy, and Law, 15*, 149–167.

Bruch, S. K., & Soss, J. (2016). *Learning where we stand: How school experiences matter for civic marginalization and political inequality.* Unpublished manuscript, Department of Sociology, University of Iowa.

Brunson, R. K., & Weitzer, R. (2009). Police relations with black and white youths in different urban neighborhoods. *Urban Affairs Review, 44*(6), 858–885.

Buss, E. (2011). Failing juvenile courts, and what lawyers and judges can do about it. *Northwestern University School of Law, 6*, 318–333.

Butler, S. M., Leschied, A. W., & Fearon, P. (2007). Antisocial beliefs and attitudes in pre-adolescent and adolescent youth. *Journal of Youth and Adolescence, 36*, 1058–1071.

Campbell, D. E. (2006). What is education's impact on civic and social engagement? In R. Desjardins & T. Schuller (Eds.), *Measuring the effects of education on health and civic/social engagement* (pp. 25–126). Paris: Organisation for Econcomic Co-Operation and Development, Centre for Educational Research and Innovation.

Campbell, D. T. (1975). On the conflicts between biological and social evolution and between psychology and moral tradition. *American Psychologist, 30*(12), 1103–1126.

Carr, P. J., Napolitano, L., & Keating, J. (2007). We never call the cops and here is why. *Criminology, 45*, 445–480.

Carrabine, E. (2005). Prison riots, social order and the problem of legitimacy. *British Journal of Criminology, 45*(6), 896–913.

Casey, B. J. (2015). Beyond simple models of self-control to circuit-based accounts of adolescent behavior. *Annual Review of Psychology, 66*, 295–319.

Center for Civic Education. (2010). *National standard for civics and government.* Calabasas, CA: Center for Civic Education.

Chalfin, A., & McCrary, J. (2014). Criminal deterrence: A review of the literature. *Journal of Economic Literature*, in press.

Chang, F. Y. (1994). School teachers' moral reasoning. In J. R. Rest & D. Narváez (Eds.), *Moral development in the professions* (pp. 71–83). Hillsdale, NJ: Lawrence Erlbaum Associates.

Chein, J., Albert, D., O'Brien, L., Uckert, K., & Steinberg, L. (2011). Peers increase adolescent risk taking by enhancing activity in the brain's reward circuitry. *Developmental Science, 14*(2), F1–F10.

Chory, R. M., Horan, S. M., Carton, S. T., & Houser, M. L. (2014). Toward a further understanding of students' emotional responses to classroom injustice. *Communication Education, 63*, 41–62.

Chory-Assad, R. M. (2002). Classroom justice: Perceptions of fairness as a predictor of student motivation, learning, and aggression. *Communication Quarterly, 50,* 58–77.

Chory-Assad, R. M., & Paulsel, M. L. (2004a). Classroom justice: Student aggression and resistance as reactions to perceived unfairness. *Communication Education, 53*(3), 253–273.

Chory-Assad, R. M., & Paulsel, M. L. (2004b). Antisocial classroom communication. *Communication Quarterly, 52,* 98–114.

Chow, H. P. (2011). Adolescent attitudes toward the police in a western Canadian city. *Policing: An International Journal of Policing Strategies & Management, 34*(4), 638–653.

Claes, E., Hooghe, M., & Marien, S. (2012). A two-year panel study among Belgian late adolescents on the impact of school environment characteristics on political trust. *International Journal of Public Opinion Research, 24,* 208–224.

Clayman, S., & Skinns, L. (2012). To snitch or not to snitch? An exploratory study fo the factors influencing whether young people actively cooperate with police. *Policing and Society, 22*(4), 460–480.

Cohen-Charash, Y., & Spector, P. E. (2001). The role of justice in organizations: A meta-analysis. *Organizational Behavior and Human Decision Processes, 86*(2), 278–321.

Cohn, E. S., Bucolo, D. O, Rebellon, C. J., & Van Gundy, K. (2010). An integrated model of legal and moral reasoning and rule-violating behavior: The role of legal attitudes. *Law and Human Behavior, 34*(4), 295–309.

Cohn, E. S., Trinkner, R. J., Rebellon, C. J., Van Gundy, K. T., & Cole, L. M. (2012). Legal attitudes and legitimacy: Extending the integrated legal socialization model. *Victims and Offenders, 7*(4), 385–406.

Cohn, E., & White, S. (1990). *Legal socialization.* New York: Springer.

Cohn, E. S., & White, S. O. (1992). Taking reasoning seriously. In J. McCord (Ed.), *Advances in Criminological Theory* (Vol. 3, pp. 95–114). New Brunswick, NJ: Transaction Publishers.

Coid, J. W., Yang, M., Ullrich, S., Roberts, A. D. L., & Hare, R. D. (2009). Prevalence and correlates of psychopathic trains in the household population of Great Britain. *International Journal of Law and Psychiatry, 32*(2), 65–73.

Collins, R. (2007). Strolling while poor: How broken-windows policing created a new crime in Baltimore. *Georgetown Journal on Poverty Law & Policy, XIV*(3), 419–440.

Colvin, M., Cullen, F. T., & Vander Ven, T. (2002). Coercion, social support, and crime: An emerging theoretical consensus. *Criminology, 40*(1), 19–42.

Conover, P. J., & Searing, D. D. (2000). A political socialization perspective. In L. M. McDonnell, P. M. Timpane, & R. Benjamin (Eds.), *Rediscovering the democratic purposes of education* (pp. 91–124). Lawrence: University of Kansas Press.

Converse, P. (1972). Change in the American electorate. In A. Campbell & P. E. Converse (Eds.), *The human meaning of social change* (pp. 263–337). New York: Russell Sage Foundation.

Cook, W. K. (2013). Controlling underage drinking: Fear of law enforcement or internalized normative values? *Journal of Addiction Prevention, 1*(3), 1–6.

Cook, C. R., Williams, K. R., Guerra, N. G., Kim, T. E., & Sadek, S. (2010). Predictors of bullying and victimization in childhood and adolescence. *School Psychology Quarterly, 25,* 65–83.

Cordner, G. (2014). Community policing. In M. D. Reisig & R. J. Kane (Eds.), *The Oxford handbook of police and policing* (pp. 148–171). New York: Oxford University Press.

Cornell, D., Shukla, K., & Konold, T. R. (2016). Authoritative school climate and student academic achievement, grades, and aspirations in middle and high schools. *AERA Open, 2*(2), 1–18.

Cox, B., Sughrue, J. A., & Alexander, M. D. (2012). *The challenges to school policing.* Dayton, OH: Education Law Association.

Cumsille, P., Darling, N., Flaherty, B., & Martìnez, M. L. (2006). Chilean adolescents' beliefs about the legitimacy of parental authority: Individual and age-related differences. *International Journal of Child Development, 30*(2), 97–106.

Curran, F. C. (2016). Estimating the effect of state zero tolerance laws on exclusionary discipline, racial discipline gaps, and student misbehavior. *Educational Evaluation and Policy Analysis, 38*(4), 647–668.

Curtis, N. M., Ronan, K. R., & Borduin, C. M. (2004). Multisystemic treatment: A meta-analysis of outcome studies. *Journal of Family Psychology, 18*(3), 411–419.

Dadds, M. R., Maujean, A., & Fraser, J. A. (2003). Parenting and conduct problems in children: Australian data and psychometric properties of the Alabama Parenting Questionnaire. *Australian Psychologist, 38*(3), 238–241.

Dahl, R. E. (2001). Affect regulation, brain development, and behavioral/emotional health in adolescence. *CNS Spectrums, 6*(1), 60–72.

Dalton, R. J. (1994). Communists and democrats: Democratic attitudes in the two Germanies. *British Journal of Political Science, 24*(4), 469–493.

Damon, W., & Killen, M. (1982). Peer interaction and the process of change in children's moral reasoning. *Merril-Palmer Quarterly, 28*(3), 347–367.

Darling, N., Cumsille, P., & Martìnez, M. L. (2007). Adolescents' as active agents in the socialization process: Legitimacy of parental authority and obligation to obey as predictors of obedience. *Journal of Adolescence, 30,* 297–311.

Darling, N., Cumsille, P., & Martìnez, M. L. (2008). Individual differences in adolescents' beliefs about the legitimacy of parental authority and their own obligation to obey. *Child Development, 79,* 1103–1118.

Darling, N., & Steinberg, L. (1993). Parenting style as context. *Psychological Bulletin, 113,* 487–496.

Deigh, J. (1999). Emotion and the authority of law: Variation on themes in Bentham and Austin. In S. A. Bandes (Ed.), *The passions of the law* (pp. 285–308). New York: New York University Press.

Delgado, R. (2008). Law enforcement in subordinated communities: Innovation and response. *Michigan Law Review, 106,* 1193–1212.

Delisi, M. (2005). *Career criminals in society.* Thousand Oaks, CA: Sage.

Denver, D., & Hands, G. 1990. Does studying politics make a difference? *British Journal of Political Science, 20,* 263–279.

Department of Education. (2016). *2013–2014 civil rights data collection: A first look.* Washington, DC: US Department of Education Office of Civil Rights.

Dewey, J. (1916). *Democracy and education.* New York: Free Press.

Dishion, T. J., & Tipsord, J. M. (2011). Peer contagion in child and adolescent social and emotional development. *Annual Review of Psychology, 62,* 189–214.

Dornbusch, S., Erickson, K. G., Laird, J., & Wong, C. A. (2001). The relations of family and school attraction to adolescent deviance in diverse groups and communities. *Journal of Adolescent Research, 16,* 396–422.

Dumontheil, I., Apperly, I. A., & Blakemore, S. J. (2010). Online usage of theory of mind continues to develop in late adolescence. *Developmental Science, 13*(2), 331–338.

Durkheim, E. (1973). *Moral education.* New York: Macmillan.

Durose, M. R., Cooper, A. D., & Snyder, H. N. (2014). Recidivism of prisoners released in 30 states in 2005: Patterns from 2005 to 2010. Washington, DC: US Department of Justice, Bureau of Justice Statistics.

Eagly, A. H., & Chaiken, S. (1998). Attitude structure and function. In D. T. Gilbert, S. T. Fiske, & L. Gardner (Eds.), *The handbook of social psychology* (pp. 269–322). New York: McGraw-Hill.

Earls, F. J. (1994). Violence and today's youth. *The Future of Children, 4*(3), 4–23.

Easton, D. (1965). *A systems analysis of political life.* Chicago: University of Chicago Press.

Easton, D. (1975). A reassessment of the concept of political support. *British Journal of Political Science, 5*, 435–457.

Easton, D. & Dennis, J. (1969). *Children in the political system: Origins of political legitimacy.* New York: McGraw-Hill.

Eccles, J. S., Barber, B. L., Stone, M., & Hunt, J. (2003). Extracurricular activities and adolescent development. *Journal of Social Issues, 59*(4), 865–889.

Eddy, J. M., Whaley, R. B., & Chamberlain, P. (2004). The prevention of violent behavior by chronic and serious male juvenile offenders: A 2-year follow-up of a randomized clinical trial. *Journal of Emotional and Behavioral Disorders, 12*(1), 2–8.

Eller, A., Abrams, D., Viki, G. T., Imara, D. A., & Peerbux, S. (2007). Stay cool, hang loose, admit nothing: Race, intergroup contact and public-police relations. *Basic and Applied Social Psychology, 29*, 213–224.

Emler, N., & Reicher, S. (1995). *Adolescence and delinquency.* Oxford: Blackwell.

Emler, N., & Reicher, S. (2005). Delinquency: Cause of consequence of social exclusion. In D. Abrams, M.A. Hogg, & J.M. Marques (Eds.), *The social psychology of inclusion and exclusion.* New York: Psychology Press.

Eron, L. D. (1987). The development of aggressive behavior from the perspective of a developing behaviorism. *American Psychologist, 42*, 435–442.

Espelage, D. L., Low, S., Rao, M. A., Hong, J. S., & Little, T. (2014). Family violence, bullying, fighting and substance use among adolescents. *Journal of Research on Adolescence, 24*, 337–349.

Estevez, E., Murgui, S., Moreno, D., & Musitu, G. (2007). Family communication styles, attitudes toward institutional authority and adolescents' violent behavior at school. *Psicothema, 19*, 108–112.

Estevez, E., Murgui, S., Musitu, G., & Moreno, D. (2008). Adolescent aggression: Effects of gender and family and school environments. *Journal of Adolescence, 31*, 433–450.

Ewick, P., & Silbey, S. S. (1998). *The common place of law: Stories from everyday life.* Chicago: University of Chicago Press.

Fagan, J., Geller, A., Davies, G., & West, V. (2010). Street stops and *broken windows* revisited: The demography and logic of proactive policing in a safe and changing city. In S. K. Rice and M. D. White (Eds.), *Race, ethnicity, and policing: New and essential readings* (pp. 309–348). New York: New York University Press.

Fagan, J., & Piquero, A. R. (2007). Rational choice and developmental influences on recidivism among adolescent felony offenders. *Journal of Empirical Legal Studies, 4*(4), 715–748.

Fagan, J., & Tyler, T. R. (2005). Legal socialization of children and adolescents. *Social Justice Research, 18*(3), 217–242.

Farrington, D. P. (2005). Childhood origins of antisocial behavior. *Clinical Psychology and Psychotherapy, 12*, 177–190.

Farrington, D. P., & Ttofi, M. M. (2011). Bullying as a predictor of offending, violence and later life outcomes. *Criminal Behavior and Mental Health, 21*, 90–98.

Feeley, M. (1979). *The process is the punishment*. New York: Russell Sage Foundation.

Fehr, E., Bernhard, H., & Rockenbach, B. (2008). Egalitarianism in young children. *Nature, 454*, 1079–1084.

Feldman, S., & Stenner, K. (1997). Perceived threat and authoritarianism. *Political Psychology, 18*(4), 741–770.

Finckenauer, J. O. (1990). Legal socialization theory: A precursor to comparative research in the Soviet Union. In W. S. Laufer and F. Adler (Eds.), *Advances in Criminological Theory* (Vol. 2, pp. 71–85). New Brunswick, NJ: Transaction Publishers.

Finckenauer, J. O. (1995). *Russian youth: Law, deviance, and the pursuit of freedom*. New Brunswick, NJ: Transaction Publishers.

Fine, A., & Cauffman, E. (2015). Race and justice system attitude formation during the transition to adulthood. *Journal of Developmental and Life-Course Criminology, 1*(4), 325–349.

Fine, S. E., Trentacosta, C. J., Izard, C. E., Mastow, A. J., & Campbell, J. L. (2004). Anger perception, caregivers' use of physical discipline, and aggression in children at risk. *Social Development, 13*, 213–228.

Fisher, D. (2010). The global debt bomb. *Forbes*, January 21. Retrieved May 1 from http://www.forbes.com/forbes/2010/0208/debt-recession-worldwide-finances-global-debt-bomb.html.

Fisher, P. A., & Chamberlain, P. (2000). Multidimensional treatment foster care. *Journal of Emotional and Behavioral Disorders, 8*, 155–164.

Flanagan, C. A. (2013). *Teenage citizens: The political theories of the young*. Cambridge, MA: Harvard University Press.

Flanagan, C. A., & Sherrod, L. R. (1998). Youth political development: An introduction. *Journal of Social Issues, 54*(3), 447–456.

Flexon, J. L., Lurigio, A. J., & Greenleaf, R. G. (2009). Exploring the dimensions of trust in the police among Chicago juveniles. *Journal of Criminal Justice, 37*, 180–189.

Fondacaro, M. R., Brank, E. M., Stuart, J., Villanueva-Abraham, S., Luescher, J., & McNatt, P. S. (2006). Identity orientation, voice, and judgments of procedural justice during late adolescence. *Journal of Youth and Adolescence, 35*(6), 987–997.

Fondacaro, M. R., Dunkle, M. E., & Pathak, M. K. (1998). Procedural justice in resolving family disputes: A psychosocial analysis of individual and family functioning in late adolescent. *Journal of Youth and Adolescence, 27*, 101–119.

Fondacaro, M. R., Jackson, S. L., & Luescher, J. (2002). Toward the assessment of procedural and distributive justice in resolving family disputes. *Social Justice Research, 15*, 341–371.

Fraser, M. (1996). Aggressive behavior in childhood and early adolescence. *Social Work, 41*, 347–361.

Fratello, J., Rengifo, A. F., & Trone, J. (2013). *Coming of age with stop and frisk: Experiences, self-perceptions, and public safety implications*. New York: Vera Institute of Justice.

French, J. R. P., Jr., & Raven, B. (1959). The bases of social power. In D. Cartwright (Ed.), *Studies in social power* (pp. 150–167). Ann Arbor: University of Michigan Press.

Freud, S. (1930). *Civilization and its discontents*. New York: Norton.

Frias-Armenta, M., Lopez-Escobar, A. E., & Silveira, G. J. (2016). Procedural and distributive justice and amenability to psychological treatment in juvenile delinquents. *Advances in Applied Sociology, 6*, 57–66.

Furnham, A., & Stacey, B. (1991). *Young people's understanding of society*. London: Routledge.

Galen, B. R., & Underwood, M. K. (1997). A developmental investigation of social aggression among children. *Developmental Psychology, 33*, 589–600.

Gallup. (2015). *Confidence in Institutions.* Retrieved February 4, 2016 from http://www.gallup.com/poll/1597/confidence-institutions.aspx.

Galston, W. A. (2001). Political knowledge, political engagement, and civic education. *Annual Review of Political Science, 4*, 217–234.

Garland, D. (2001). *The culture of control: Crime and social order in contemporary society.* Chicago: University of Chicago Press.

Gau, J. M., & Brunson, R. K. (2010). Procedural justice and order maintenance policing. *Justice Quarterly, 27*, 255–279.

Geller, A., Fagan, J., & Tyler, T. R. (2014). Aggressive policing and the mental health of young urban men. *American Journal of Public Health, 104*, 2321–2327.

Gendron, B. P., Williams, K. R., & Guerra, N. G. (2011). An analysis of bullying among students within schools: Estimating the effects of individual normative beliefs, self-esteem, and school climate. *Journal of School Violence, 10*, 150–164.

Gershoff, E. T. (2002). Corporal punishment by parents and associated child behaviors and experiences. *Psychological Bulletin, 128*, 539–579.

Gershoff, E. T., & Bitensky, S. H. (2007). The case against corporal punishment of children. *Psychology, Public Policy, and Law, 13*, 231–272.

Gerstein, C., & Prescott, J. J. (2015). Process costs and police discretion. *Harvard Law Review Forum, 128*, 268–288.

Gibbs, J. P. (1968). Crime, punishment, and deterrence. *Southwestern Social Science Quarterly, 48*(4), 515–530.

Gibbs, J. P. (1975). *Crime, punishment, and deterrence.* New York: Elsevier.

Gibbs, J. C. (2013). *Moral development and reality* (3rd ed.). New York: Oxford University Press.

Gibson, J. L. (1996). A mile wide but an inch deep(?): The structure of democratic commitments in the former USSR. *American Journal of Political Science, 40*, 396–420.

Gibson, J. L. (2004). *Overcoming apartheid: Can truth reconcile a divided nation?* New York: Russell Sage Foundation.

Gibson, J. L. (2015). Legitimacy is for losers: The interconnections of institutional legitimacy, performance evaluations, and the symbols of judicial authority. In B. H. Bornsteing & A. Tomkins (Eds.), *Motivating cooperation and compliance with authority* (pp. 81–116). New York: Springer.

Gibson, J. L., & Caldeira, G. A. (1995). The legitimacy of transnational legal institutions: Compliance, support, and the European Court of Justice. *American Journal of Political Science, 39*(2), 459–489.

Gibson, J. L., Duch, R. M., & Tedin, K. L. (1992). Democratic values and the transformation of the Soviet Union. *Journal of Politics, 54*, 329–371.

Gifford-Smith, M., Dodge, K. A., Dishion, T. J., & McCord, J. (2005). Peer influence in children and adolescents: Crossing the bridge from developmental to intervention science. *Journal of Abnormal Child Psychology, 33*(3), 255–265.

Gilligan, C. (1982). *In a different voice.* Cambridge, MA: Harvard University Press.

Glueck, S., & Glueck, E. (1950). *Unraveling juvenile delinquency.* New York: Commonwealth Fund.

Goff, P. A., Epstein, L. M., & Reddy, K. S. (2013). Crossing the line of legitimacy: The impact of cross-deputization policy on crime reporting. *Psychology, Public Policy and Law, 19*(2), 250–258.

Gogtay, N., Gied, J. N., Lusk, L., Hayashi, K. M., Greenstein, D., Vaituzis, A. C., Nugent III, T. F., et al. (2004). Dynamic mapping of human cortical development during childhood through early adulthood. *Proceedings of the National Academy of Sciences of the United States of America, 101*(21), 8174–8179.

Gold, L. J., Darley, J. M., Hilton, J. L., & Zanna, M. P. (1984). Children's perceptions of procedural justice. *Child Development, 55,* 1752–1759.

Gonzales, M. H., Riedel, E., Williamson, I., Avery, P. G., Sullivan, J. L., & Bos, A. (2004). Variations of citizenship education: A content analysis of rights, obligations, and participation concepts in high school civic textbooks. *Theory & Research in Social Education, 32*(3), 301–325.

Goode, E. (2012). Stronger hand for judges in the "bazaar" of plea deals. *New York Times,* March 22. Retrieved June 9, 2016 from http://www.nytimes.com/2012/03/23/us/stronger-hand-for-judges-after-rulings-on-plea-deals.html?_r=0.

Gordon, D. A., Graves, K., & Arbuthnot, J. (1995). The effect of functional family therapy for delinquents on adult criminal behavior. *Criminal Justice and Behavior, 22*(1), 60–73.

Gottfredson, G. D., & Gottfredson, D. C. (1985). *Victimization in schools.* New York: Plenum.

Gottfredson, G. D., Gottfredson, D. C., Payne, A. A., & Gottfredson, N.C. (2005). School climate predictors of school disorder. *Journal of Research on Crime and Delinquency, 42,* 412–444.

Gottfredson, M. R., & Hirschi, T. (1990). *A general theory of crime.* Redwood City, CA: Stanford University Press.

Gouveia-Pereira, M., Vala, J., Palmonari, A., & Rubini, M. (2003). School experience, relational justice and legitimation of institutional authority. *European Journal of Psychology of Education, 18,* 309–332.

Grant, H. B. (2006). *Building a culture of lawfulness: Law enforcement, legal reasoning, and delinquency among Mexican Youth.* El Paso, TX: LFB Scholarly Publishing.

Greene, M. B. (2005). Reducing violence and aggression in schools. *Trauma and Violence Abuse, 6,* 236–253.

Greenstein, F. I. (1960). The benevolent leader: Children's images of political authority. *American Political Science Review, 54*(4), 934–943.

Gregory, A., & Ripski, M. B. (2008). Adolescent trust in teachers. *School Psychology Review, 37,* 337–353.

Gregory, A., & Weinstein, R. S. (2004). Connection and regulation at home and in school. *Journal of Adolescent Research, 19,* 405–427.

Gregory, A., & Weinstein, R. S. (2008). The discipline gap and African-Americans: Defiance or cooperation in the high school classroom. *Journal of School Psychology, 46,* 455–475.

Grisso, T. (1997). The competence of adolescents as trial defendants. *Psychology, Public Policy, and Law, 3,* 3–32.

Grisso, T., Steinberg, L., Woolard, J., Cauffman, E., Scott, E., Graham, S., Lexcen, F., et al. (2003). Juveniles' competence to stand trial. *Law and Human Behavior, 27,* 333–363.

Grocke, P., Rossano, F., & Tomasello, M. (2015). Procedural justice in children: Preschoolers accept unequal resource distributions of the procedures provides equal opportunity. *Journal of Experimental Child Psychology, 140,* 197–210.

Grusec, J. E., & Goodnow, J. J. (1994). Impact of parental discipline methods on the child's internalization of values: A reconceptualization of current points of view. *Developmental Psychology, 30*(1), 4–19.

Grusec, J. E., & Hastings, P. D. (Eds.) (2015). *Handbook of socialization* (2nd ed.). New York: Guilford Publications.

Guerra, N. G., Nucci, L., & Huesmann, L.R. (1994). Moral cognition and child-hood aggression. In L. R. Huesmann (Ed.), *Aggressive behavior* (pp. 13–33). New York: Plenum Publishing.

Gummerum, M., Keller, M., Takezawa, M., & Mata, J. (2008). To give or not to give: Children's and adolescents' sharing and negotiations in economic decision situations. *Child Development, 79*, 562–576.

Güroğlu, B., van den Box, W., & Crone, E.A. (2009). Fairness considerations: Increasing understanding of intentionality during adolescence. *Journal of Experimental Child Psychology, 104*(4), 398–409.

Haan, N., Smith, M. B., & Block, J. (1968). Moral reasoning of young adults. *Journal of Personality and Social Psychology, 10*, 183–201.

Haidt, J. (2001). The emotional dog and its rational tail: a social intuitionist approach to moral judgment. *Psychological Review, 108*(4), 814–834.

Harrison, P., Maupin, J. R., & Mays, G. L. (2001). Teen court: An examination of pro-cesses and outcomes. *Crime & Delinquency, 47*(2), 243–264.

Harvell, S. A. S. (2008). *A developmental assessment of procedural justice: Does process matter to juvenile detainees?* Unpublished dissertation, Department of Psychology, Georgetown University.

Harvey, R. J., Fletcher, J., & French, D. J. (2001). Social reasoning: A source of influence on aggression. *Clinical Psychology Review, 21*(3), 447–469.

Helwig, C. C. (1998). Children's conceptions of fair government and freedom of speech. *Child Development, 69*, 518–531.

Helwig, C. C. (2006). Rights, civil liberties, and democracy across cultures. In M. Killen & J. G. Smetana (Eds.), *Handbook of moral development* (pp. 85–210). Mahwah, NJ: Lawrence Erlbaum Associates.

Helwig, C. C., Arnold, M. L., Tan, D., & Boyd, D. (2007). Mainland Chinese and Canadian adolescents' judgments and reasoning about the fairness of democratic and other forms of government. *Cognitive Development, 22*(1), 96–109.

Helwig, C. C., & Jasiobedzka, U. (2001). The relation between law and morality. *Child Development, 72*, 1382–1393.

Henrich, C. C., Brookmeyer, K. A., & Shahar, G. (2005). Weapon violence in adoles-cence. *Journal of Adolescent Health, 37*, 306–312.

Hensler, J. G. (2006). Serotonergic modulation of the limbic system. *Neuroscience and Biobehavioral Reviews, 30*, 203.214.

Herrero, J., Estevez, E., & Musitu, G. (2006). The relationships of adolescent school-related deviant behavior and victimization with psychological distress. *Journal of Adolescence, 29*, 671–690.

Herzon, F. D., Kincaid, J., & Dalton, V. (1978). Personality & public opinion: The case of authoritarianism, prejudice, & support for the Korean & Vietnam wars. *Polity, 11*(1), 92–113.

Hess, R. D., & Torney, J.V. (1967). *The development of political attitudes in children.* Chicago: Aldine.

Hetherington, M. J. (2005). *Why trust matters: Declining political trust and the demise of American liberalism.* Princeton, NJ: Princeton University Press.

Hetherington, M. J., & Weiler, D. J. (2009). *Authoritarianism and polarization in American politics.* Cambridge: Cambridge University Press

Hinds, L. (2007). Building police-youth relationships: The importance of procedural justice. *Youth Justice, 7*(3), 195–209.

Hinds, L. (2009). Youth, police legitimacy and informal contact. *Journal of Police and Criminal Psychology, 24*, 10–21.

Hirschfield, P. J. (2008). Preparing for prison? The criminalization of school discipline in the USA. *Theoretical Criminology, 12,* 79–101.

Hirschi, T. (1969). *Causes of delinquency.* Berkeley: University of California Press.

Hirschi, T. (1983). Crime and the family. In J. Wilson (Ed.), *Crime and public policy* (pp. 53–68). San Francisco: Institute for Contemporary Studies.

Hoeve, M., Blokland, A., Dubas, J. S., Loeber, R., Gerris, J. R. M., & van der Laan, P. H. (2008). Trajectories of delinquency and parenting styles. *Journal of Abnormal Child Psychology, 36,* 223–235.

Hoeve, M., Dubas, J. S., Eichelsheim, V. I., van der Laan, P. H., Smeenk, W., & Gerris, J. R. M. (2009). The relationship between parenting and delinquency: A meta-analysis. *Journal of Abnormal and Child Psychology, 37,* 749–775.

Hoffman, M. L. (1977). Moral internalization. *Advances in Experimental Social Psychology, 10,* 85–133.

Hoffman, M. L. (2000). *Empathy and moral development: Implications for caring and justice.* Cambridge: Cambridge University Press.

Hogan, R., & Mills, C. (1976). Legal socialization. *Human Development, 19,* 261–276.

Hollingsworth, E. J., Luffler, H. S., & Clune, W. H. (1984). *School discipline.* New York: Praeger.

Horan, S. M., & Myers, S.A. (2009). An exploration of college instructors' use of classroom justice, power and behavior alteration techniques. *Communication Education, 58,* 483–496.

Horan, S. M., Chory, R. M., & Goodboy, A. K. (2010). Understanding students' classroom justice experiences and responses. *Communication Education, 59,* 453–474.

Huesmann, L. R., & Guerra, N.G. (1997). Children's normative beliefs about aggression and aggressive behavior. *Journal of Personality and Social Psychology, 72,* 408–419.

Huizinga, D., Schumann, K., Ehret, B., & Elliott, A. (2003). *The effects of juvenile justice processing on subsequent delinquent and criminal behavior.* Washington, DC: Final Report to the National Institute of Justice.

Humes, E. (1997). *No matter how loud I shout.* New York: Simon & Schuster.

Huo, Y. J. (2002). Justice and the regulation of social relations: When and why do group members deny claims to social goods? *British Journal of Social Psychology, 41,* 535–562.

Huq, A. Z., Jackson, J., & Trinkner, R. (2016). Legitimating practices: Revisiting the predicates of police legitimacy. *British Journal of Criminology.* Published online August 31, 2016. doi: 10.1093/bjc/asw037

Hyman, H. H. (1959). *Political socialization.* New York: Free Press.

Hyman, I. A., & Perone, D. C. (1998). The other side of school violence: Educator policies and practices that may contribute to student misbehavior. *Journal of School Psychology, 36,* 7–27.

Jackson, A. (2002). Police-school resource officers' and students' perception of the police and offending. *Policing, 25,* 631–650.

Jackson, J., Bradford, B., Stanko, B., & Hohl, K. (2013). *Just authority? Trust in the police in England and Wales.* New York: Routledge.

Jackson, J., Huq, A. Z., Bradford, B., & Tyler, T. R. (2013). Monopolizing force? Police legitimacy and public attitudes toward the acceptability of violence. *Psychology, Public Policy and Law, 19,* 479–497.

Jackson, S., & Fondacaro, M. (1999). Procedural justice in resolving family conflict: Implications for youth violence prevention. *Law & Policy, 21*(2), 101–127.

James, K., Bunch, J., & Clay-Warner, J. (2015). Perceived injustice and school violence. *Youth Violence and Juvenile Justice, 13*(2), 169–189.

James, N., & McCallion, G. (2013). *School resource officers: Law enforcement officers in schools.* Washington, DC: Congressional Research Service.

Jenkins, P. H. (1997). School delinquency and the school social bond. *Journal of Research in Crime and Delinquency, 34*(3), 337–367.

Jennings, M. K., & Niemi, R.G. (1974). *The political character of adolescence.* Princeton, NJ: Princeton University Press.

Jennings, M. K., & Stoker, L. (2004). Social trust and civic engagement across time and generations. *Acta Politica, 39,* 342–379.

John, P., & Morris, Z. (2004). What are the origins of social capital? *British Elections and Parties Review, 14,* 94–112.

Johnson, S. L. (2009). Improving the school environment to reduce school violence. *Journal of School Health, 79,* 451–465.

Jones, N. (2014). "The regular routine": Proactive policing and adolescent development among young, poor black men. In K. Roy & N. Jones (Eds.), *Pathways to adulthood for disconnected young men in low-income communities: New Directions in Child and Adolescent Development, 143,* 33–54.

Jones, J. M. (2015a). Gallup: Trust in U.S. judicial branch sinks to new low of 53%. Retrieved February 4, 2016 from http://www.gallup.com/poll/185528/trust-judicial-branch-sinks-new-low.aspx.

Jones, J. M. (2015b). Gallup: In U.S., confidence in police lowest in 22 years. Retrieved September 9, 2015 from http://www.gallup.com/poll/183704/confidence-police-lowest-years.aspx.

Jurkovic, G. J. (1980). The juvenile delinquent as a moral philosopher: A structural-developmental perspective. *Psychological Bulletin, 88,* 709–727.

Justice, B., & Meares, T. (2014). How the criminal justice system educates citizens. *Annals of the American Academy of Political and Social Science, 651*(1), 159–177.

Kahan, D. (1999). The secret ambition of deterrence. *Harvard Law Review, 113,* 413–500.

Kam, C. D., & Kinder, D. R. (2007). Terror and ethnocentrism: Foundations of American support for the war on terrorism. *Journal of Politics, 69*(2), 320–338.

Kane, R. J. (2005). Compromised police legitimacy as a predictor of violent crime in structurally disadvantaged communities. *Criminology, 43*(2), 469–498.

Kassa, S. O., Malloy, L. C., & Cauffman, E. (2008). *Procedural justice and the adolescent offender.* Paper presented at the annual meeting of the American Psychology-Law Society. Jacksonville, Fl.

Katz, J. (1988). *Seductions of crime.* New York: Basic Books.

Keijsers, L., & Laird, R. D. (2014). Mother-adolescent monitoring dynamics and the legitimacy of parental authority. *Journal of Adolescence, 37*(5), 515–524.

Kelley, H. H. (1973). The processes of causal attribution. *American Psychologist, 28*(2), 107–128.

Kelman, H. C., & Hamilton, V. L. (1989). *Crimes of obedience.* New Haven, CT: Yale University Press.

Kempf, K. L. (1993). The empirical status of Hirschi's control theory. In F. Adler and W. S. Laufer (Eds.), *New Directions in Criminological Theory* (Vol. 4, 143–185). New Brunswick, NJ: Transaction Publishers.

Kessler, D. K. (2009). Free to leave? An empirical look at the fourth amendment's seizure standard. *Journal of Criminal Law and Criminology, 99*(1), 51–88.

Killen, M., & Smetana, J. G. (Eds.) (2006). *Handbook of moral development*. Mahwah, NJ: Lawrence Erlbaum Associates.

Killen, M., & Smetana, J. G. (2015). Origins and development of morality. In M. E. Lamb (Ed.), *Handbook of child psychology and developmental science* (Vol. 3, 7th ed., pp. 701–749). New York: Wiley-Blackwell.

King, M. L., Jr. (1963). *Letter from a Birmingham jail*. Retrieved from https://kinginstitute.stanford.edu/king-papers/documents/letter-birmingham-jail.

Kirk, D. S., & Matsuda, M. (2011). Legal cynicism, collective efficacy, and the ecology of arrest. *Criminology, 49*(2), 443–472.

Kirk, D. S., & Papachristos, A. (2011). Cultural mechanisms and the persistence of neighborhood violence. *American Journal of Sociology, 116*, 1190–1233.

Kleiman M. (2009). *When brute force fails: Strategic thinking for crime control*. Princeton, NJ: Princeton University Press.

Knafo, A. (2003). Authoritarians, the next generation: Values and bullying among adolescent children of authoritarian fathers. *Analysis of Social Issues and Public Policy, 3*, 199–204.

Kochel, T. R., Parks, R., & Mastrofski, S. D. (2013). Examining police effectiveness as a precursor to legitimacy and cooperation with police. *Justice Quarterly, 30*(5), 895–925.

Kohlberg, L. (1963). The development of children's orientations toward a moral order. *Human Development, 51*, 8–20.

Kohlberg, L. (1980). High school democracy and educating for a just society. In Mosher, R. (Ed.), *Moral education* (pp. 20–57). New York: Praeger.

Kohlberg, L. (1981). *The philosophy of moral development: Essays on moral development* (Vol. 1). New York: Harper & Row.

Kohler-Hausmann, I. (2013). Misdemeanor justice: Control without conviction. *American Journal of Sociology, 119*, 351–393.

Kohler-Hausmann, I. (2014). Managerial justice and mass misdemeanors. *Stanford Law Review, 66*, 611–693.

Kowalski, R. M., Giumetti, G. W., Schroeder, A. N., & Lattanner, M. R. (2014). Bullying in the digital age. *Psychological Bulletin, 140*, 1073–1137.

Kowalski, G. S., & Wilke, A. S. (2001). Juvenile delinquency prediction. *Crime and Juvenile Delinquency, 11*, 352–358.

Kraska, P. B. (Ed.) (2001). *Militarizing the American criminal justice system*. Boston: Northeastern University Press.

Krevans, J., & Gibbs, J. C. (1996). Parents' use of inductive discipline: Relations to children's empathy and prosocial behavior. *Child Development, 67*(6), 3263–3277.

Krislov, S., Boyum, K. O., Clark, J. N., Shaefer, R. C., & White, S. O. (1966). *Compliance and the law: A multi-disciplinary approach*. Thousand Oaks, CA: Sage.

Kroneberg, C., Heintze, I., & Mehlkop, G. (2010). The interplay of moral norms and instrumental incentives in crime causation. *Criminology, 48*(1), 259–294.

Kupchik, A. (2010). *Homeroom security: School discipline in an age of fear*. New York: New York University Press.

Kupchik, A., & Catlaw, T. J. (2014). Discipline and participation: The long-term effects of suspension and school security on the political and civic engagement of youth. *Youth & Society, 47*(1), 95–124.

Kupchik, A., & Ward, G. (2014). Race, poverty and exclusionary school security. *Youth Violence and Juvenile Justice, 12*, 332–354.

Laible, D. J., Carlo, G., & Roesch, S. (2004). Pathways to self-esteem in late adolescence: The role of parent and peer attachment, empathy, and social behaviours. *Journal of Adolesence*, 27(6), 703–716.

Laible, D., Eye, J., & Carlo, G. (2008). Dimensions of conscience in mid-adolescence: Links with social behavior, parenting, and temperament. *Journal of Youth and Adolescence*, 37, 875–887.

Landenberger, N. A., & Lipsey, M. W. (2005). The positive effects of cognitive-behavioral programs for offenders. *Journal of Experimental Criminology*, 1, 451–476.

Langton, K. P., & Jennings, M. K. (1968). Political socialization and the high school civics curriculum in the United States. *American Political Science Review*, 62, 852–867.

Lansford, J. E., Chang, L., Dodge, K. A., Malone, P. S., Oburu, P., Bombi, A. S., et al. (2005). Physical discipline and children's adjustment: Cultural normativeness as a moderator. *Child Development*, 76, 1234–1246.

Lapsley, D. K. (2006). Moral stage theory. In M. Killen & J. G. Smetana (Eds.), *Handbook of moral development* (pp. 37–66). Mahwah, NJ: Lawrence Erlbaum Associates.

Larzelere, R. E., Klein, M., Schumm, W. R., & Alibrando, S. A. Jr. (1989). Relations of spanking and other parenting characteristics to self-esteem and perceived fairness of parental discipline. *Psychological Reports*, 64, 1140–1142.

Latimer, J., Dowden, C., & Muise, D. (2005). The effectiveness of restorative justice practices. *Prison Journal*, 85, 127–144.

Laub, J. H., & Sampson, R. J. (2003). *Shared beginnings, divergent lives: Delinquent boys to age 70*. Cambridge, MA: Harvard University Press.

Laub, J. H., Sampson, R. J., & Sweeten, G. A. (2008). Assessing Sampson and Laub's life-course theory of crime. In. F. T. Cullen, J. P. Wright, & K. R. Blevins (Eds.), *Taking stock: The status of criminological theory* (pp. 313–333). New Brunswick, NJ: Transaction Publishers.

Laupa, M. (1991). Children's reasoning about three authority attributes: Adult status, knowledge, and social position. *Developmental Psychology*, 27, 321–329.

Laupa, M., & Turiel, E. (1986). Children's conceptions of adult and peer authority. *Child Development*, 57, 405–412.

Laupa, M., & Turiel, E. (1993). Children's concepts of authority and social contexts. *Journal of Educational Psychology*, 85, 191–197.

Leisering, L. (2003). Government and the life course. In J. T. Mortimer & M. J. Shanahan (Eds.), *Handbook of the life course* (pp. 205–228). New York: Kluwer Academic Publishers.

Leve, L. D., Chamberlain, P., & Reid, J. B. (2005). Intervention outcomes for girls referred from juvenile justice. *Journal of Consulting and Clinical Psychology, 73*, 1181–1185.

Leventhal, G. S. (1980). What should be done with equity theory? New approaches to the study of fairness in social relationships. In K. Gergen, M. Greenberg, & R. Willis (Eds.), *Social exchange* (pp. 27–55). New York: Plenum Press.

Levine, F. J., & Tapp, J. L. (1977). The dialectic of legal socialization in community. In J. L. Tapp & F. J. Levine (Eds.), *Law, justice, and the individual in society* (pp. 163–182). New York: Holt, Rinehart, & Winston.

Levy, K. S. (2001). The relationship between adolescent attitudes toward authority, self-concept and delinquency. *Adolescence*, 36(142), 333–346.

Lewin, K., Lippitt, R., & White, R.K. (1939). Patterns of aggressive behavior in experimentally created social hierarchies. *Journal of Social Psychology*, 10(2), 269–299.

Limber, S. P., & Small, M. A. (2003). State laws and policies to address bullying in schools. *School Psychology Review, 32*, 445–455.

Lind, E. A., & Tyler, T. R. (1988). *The social psychology of procedural justice.* New York: Plenum.

Lipset, S. M. (1959). Some social requisites of democracy: Economic development and political legitimacy. *American Political Science Review, 53*(1), 69–105.

Lipsey, M. (1999). Can rehabilitative programs reduce the recidivism of young offenders? *Virginia Journal of Social Policy and Law, 6*, 611–641.

Lipsey, M. W., & Cullen, F. T. (2007). The effectiveness of correctional rehabilitation: A review of systematic reviews. *Annual Review of Law and Social Science, 3*, 297–320.

Liska, A. E., & Reed, M. D. (1985). Ties to conventional institutions and delinquency. *American Sociological Review, 50*, 547–560.

Loeber, R., & Stouthamer-Loeber, M. (1986). Family factors as correlates and predictors of juvenile conduct problems and delinquency. *Crime and Justice, 7*, 29–149.

Long, R., & Chase, J. (2003). Schools to target "bad" kids for prison: But law to scare youths has critics. *Chicago Tribune*, August 19. Retrieved June 11, 2016 from http://articles.chicagotribune.com/2003-08-19/news/0308190228_1_state-prison-prison-tour-chicago-public-schools.

Losen, D. (2011). *Discipline policies, successful schools, and racial justice.* Boulder, CO: National Education Policy Center.

Luong, G., Rauers, A., & Fingerman, K. L. (2015). The multifaceted nature of late-life socialization: Older adults as agents and targets of socialization. In J. E. Grusec & P. D. Hastings (Eds.), *Handbook of Socialization* (pp. 109–134). New York: Guilford Publishers.

Maccoby, E. E., & Martin, J. A. (1983). Socialization in the context of the family: Parent-child interaction. In P. H. Mussen (Series Ed.) & E.M. Hetherington (Vol. Ed.), *Handbook of child psychology: Vol. 4. Socialization, personality, and social development* (4th ed., pp. 1–101). New York: Wiley.

MacCoun, R. (1993). Drugs and the law: A psychological analysis of drug prohibition. *Psychological Bulletin, 113*, 497–512.

MacKenzie, D. L. (2006). *What works in corrections.* New York: Cambridge University Press.

Mahoney, J. L., Larson, R. W., & Eccles, J. S. (Eds.). (2005). *Organized activities as contexts of development: Extracurricular activities, after school and community programs.* New York: Psychology Press.

Maltais, M. (2014). Raising a black son. *Los Angeles Times*, August 15. Available online at http://www.latimes.com/opinion/opinion-la/la-ol-raising-black-brown-boys-ferguson-20140815-story.html.

Mansbridge, J. (2014). What is political science for? *Perspectives on Politics, 12*(10), 8–17.

Marsh, A., & Kaase, M. (1979). Background of political action. In S. H. Barnes & M. Kaase (Eds.), *Political action: Mass participation in five western democracies* (pp. 57–96). Thousand Oaks, CA: Sage.

Mayer, M. J., & Leone, P. E. (1999). A structural analysis of school violence and disruption: Implications for creating safer schools. *Education and Treatment of Children, 22*, 333–356.

May, T., Gyateng, T., & Hough, M. (2010). *Differential treatment in the youth justice system.* London: Institute for Criminal Policy Research, King's College London.

Mazerolle, L., Bennett, S., Davis, J., Sargeant, E., & Manning, M. (2013). Procedural justice and police legitimacy: A systematic review of the research evidence. *Journal of Experimental Criminology, 9*, 245–274.

McAra, L., & McVie, S. (2007). Youth justice? The impact of system contact on patterns of desistance from offending. *European Journal of Criminology, 4*, 315–345.

McCord, J. (1979). Some child-rearing antecedents of criminal behavior in adult men. *Journal of Personality and Social Psychology, 37*(9), 1477–1486.

McCord, J. (1991). Family relationships, juvenile delinquency, and adult criminality. *Criminology, 29*(3), 397–417.

McCord, J., Widom, C. S., & Crowell, N. A. (2001). *Juvenile Crime, Juvenile Justice.* Wasghington, DC: National Academy Press.

McMahan, J. (2004). The ethics of killing in war. *Ethics, 114*(4), 693–733.

Meares, T. L. (2000). Norms, legitimacy and law enforcement. *Oregon Law Review, 79*, 391–416.

Meares, T. L. (2009). The legitimacy of police among young African-American men. *Marquette Law Review, 92*(4), 651–666.

Meares, T. L., & Tyler, T. R. (2014). Justice Sotomayor and jurisprudence of procedural justice. *Yale Law Journal Forum.*

Meares, T. L., Tyler, T., & Gardener, J. (2016. Lawful or fair? How cops and laypeople view good policing. *Journal of Criminal Law and Criminology, 105*(2), 297–344.

Melton, G. B. (Ed.). (1985). The law as a behavioral instrument. *Nebraska Symposium on Motivation* (Vol. 33). Lincoln: University of Nebraska Press.

Miklikowska, M. (2012). Psychological underpinnings of democracy: Empathy, authoritarianism, self-esteem, interpersonal trust, normative identity style, and openness to experience as predictors of support for democratic values. *Personality and Individual Differences, 53*, 603–608.

Milnitsky-Sapiro, C., Turiel, E., & Nucci, L. (2006). Brazilian adolescents' conceptions of autonomy and parental authority. *Cognitive Development, 21*, 317–331.

Miller, E. K., Freedman, D. J., & Wallis, J. D. (2002). The prefrontal cortex: Categories, concepts, and cognition. *Philosophical Transactions of the Royal Society of London. Series B: Biological Sciences, 357*(1424), 1123–1136.

Mills, K. L., Lalonde, F., Clasen, L. S., Giedd, J. N., & Blakemore, S. J. (2014). Developmental changes in the structure of the social brain in late childhood and adolescence. *Social Cognitive Neuroscience, 9*(1), 123–131.

Moffitt, T. E. (1993). Adolescent-limited and life-course-persistent antisocial behavior. *Psychological Review, 100*, 674–701.

Moffitt, T. E. (2007). A review of research on the taxonomy of life-course persistent versus adolescence-limited antisocial behavior. In D. J. Flannery, A. T. Vazsonyi, & I. D. Waldman (Eds.), *The Cambridge handbook of violent behavior and aggression* (pp. 49–74). New York: Cambridge University Press.

Moffitt, T. E., & Caspi, A. (2001). Childhood predictors differentiate life-course persistent and adolescent-limited pathways, among males and females. *Development and Psychopathology, 13*, 355–375.

Moore, C. (2009). Fairness in children's resource allocation depends on the recipient. *Psychological Science, 20*(8), 944–948.

Morash, M. A. (1978). *Implications of the theory of legal socialization for understanding the effect of juvenile justice procedures on youth.* Unpublished dissertation, Department of Criminology and Criminal Justice, University of Maryland.

Morash, M. A. (1981). Cognitive developmental theory: A basis for juvenile correctional reform? *Criminology, 19*, 360–371.

Morash, M. A. (1982). Relationships of legal reasoning to social class, closeness to parents and exposure to a high level of reasoning among adolescents varying in seriousness of delinquency. *Psychological Reports, 50*, 755–760.

Morell, M. E. (2010). *Empathy and democracy: Feeling, thinking, and deliberation.* University Park: Penn State University Press.

Morgan, A. B., & Lilienfeld, S. O. (2000). A meta-analytic review of the relation between antisocial behavior and neuropsychological measures of executive function. *Clinical Psychology Review, 20*(1), 113–136.

Morgane, P. J., Galler, J. R., & Mokler, D. J. (2005). A review of systems and networks of the limbic forebrain/limbic midbrain. *Progress in Neurobiology, 75,* 143–160.

Morrill, C., Tyson, K., Edelman, L. B., & Arum, R. (2010). Legal mobilization in schools: The paradox of rights and race among youth. *Law & Society Review, 44*(3–4), 651–694.

Morris, M. W. (2012). *Race, gender, and the school-to-prison pipeline.* New York: African American Policy Forum.

Morris, S. Z., & Gibson, C. L. (2011). Corporal punishment's influence on children's aggressive and delinquent behavior. *Criminal Justice and Behavior, 38,* 818–839.

Mowen, T. J. (2010). Shifting parenting styles and the effect of juvenile delinquency. Unpublished thesis, Department of Sociology, University of Louisville.

Mukherjee, E. (2007). *Criminalizing the classroom: The over-policing of New York City schools.* New York: American Civil Liberties Union.

Murphy, K. (2015). Does procedural justice matter to youth? Comparing adults' and youths' willingness to collaborate with police. *Policing and Society, 25*(1), 53–76.'

Musitu, G., Estevez, E., & Emler, P. (2007). Adjustment problems in the family and school contexts, attitudes toward authority, and violent behavior at school in adolescence. *Adolescence, 42,* 779–794.

Myrdal, G. (1995). *An American dilemma: The Negro problem and modern democracy.* New Brunswick, NJ: Transaction Publishers.

Nagin, D. S. (1998). Criminal deterrence research at the outset of the twenty-first century. In M. Tonry's (Ed.), *Crime and justice: An annual review of research* (Vol. 23, pp. 1–42). Chicago: University of Chicago Press.

Nance, J. P. (2014). School surveillance and the fourth amendment. *Wisconsin Law Review, 2014,* 79–137.

National Center for Mental Health and Juvenile Justice. (2013). *Improving diversion policies and programs for justice-involved youth with co-occurring mental and substance use disorders.* Retrieved from http://www.ncmhjj.com/wp-content/uploads/2013/10/improvingdiversionstrategies.pdf.

Niemi, R. G., & Junn, J. (1998). *Civic education: What makes students learn.* New Haven, CT: Yale University Press.

Nessel, P. A. (1998). Teen court: A national movement. *Technical Assistance Bulletin No. 17.* Chicago: American Bar Association. Available online at http://files.eric.ed.gov/fulltext/ED431671.pdf

Neuman, C. S., & Hare, R. D. (2008). Psychopathic trains in a large community sample: Links to violence, alcohol use, and intelligence. *Journal of Consulting and Clinical Psychology, 76*(5), 893–899.

New Jersey v. T.L.O. 469 US 325, 1985, p. 384.

Newman, K., Harrison, L., Dashiff, C., & Davies, S. (2008). Relationships between parenting styles and risk behaviors in adolescent health: An integrative literature review. *Revista Latino-Americana de Enformagem, 16*(1), 142–150.

Nie, N. H., Junn, J., & Stehlik-Barry, K. (1996). *Education and democratic citizenship in America.* Chicago: University of Chicago Press.

Norman, J. (2009). Seen and not heard: Young people's perceptions of the police. *Policing, 3,* 364–372.

Nucci, L. P., & Nucci, M. (1982a). Children's social interactions in the context of moral and conventional transgressions. *Child Development, 53*(2), 403–412.

Nucci, L. P., & Nucci, M. (1982b). Children's responses to moral and social conventional transgressions in free-play settings. *Child Development, 53*(5), 1337–1342.

Nucci, L. P., & Turiel, E. (1978). Social interactions and the development of social concepts in preschool children. *Child Development, 49*, 400–407.

Nucci, L. P., & Weber, E. K. (1995). Social interactions in the home and the development of young children's conceptions of the personal. *Child Development, 66*, 1438–1452.

Nugent, W. R., Williams, M., & Umbreit, M. S. (2003). Participation in victim-offender mediation and the prevalence and severity of subsequent delinquent behavior. *Utah Law Review, 2003*, 137–166.

Nye, J. S., Zelikow, P., & King, D. C. (Eds.). (1997). *Why people don't trust government.* Cambridge, MA: Harvard University Press.

Olson, K. R., & Spelke, E. S. (2008). Foundations of cooperation in young children. *Cognition, 108*, 222–231.

Paine, T. (1997). *Common sense.* Mineola, NY: Dover Publications.

Paoline, E. A. (2004). Shedding light on police culture: An examination of officers' occupational attitudes. *Police Quarterly, 7*(2), 205–236.

Parker, J. S., & Benson, M. J. (2004). Parent-adolescent relations and adolescent functioning: Self-esteem, substance abuse, and delinquency. *Adolescence, 39*(155), 519–530.

Parker, A. L., & Sarre, R. (2008). Policing young offenders: What role discretion? *International Journal of Police Science and Management, 10*, 474–485.

Parsons, T. (1937). *The structure of social action.* New York: Free Press.

Paternoster, R. (2006). How much do we really know about criminal deterrence? *Journal of Criminal Law and Criminology, 100*(3), 765–824.

Paternoster, R., & Iovanni, L. (1989). The labeling perspective and delinquency: An elaboration of the theory and an assessment of the evidence. *Justice Quarterly, 6*(3), 359–394.

Paternoster, R., & Pogarsky, G. (2009). Rational choice, agency, and thoughtfully reflective decision making: The short and long-term consequences of making good choices. *Journal of Quantitative Criminology, 25*, 103–127.

Patterson, G., & Yoerger, K. (1993). Developmental models for delinquent behavior. In S. Hodgins (Ed.), *Mental Disorders and Crime.* Thousand Oaks, CA: Sage.

Paulsel, M. L. (2005). The relationship between student perceptions of instructor power and classroom justice. *Communication Research Reports, 22*, 207–215.

Payne, A. A. (2008). A multilevel analysis of the relationships among communal school organization, student bonding, and delinquency. *Journal of Research on Crime and Delinquency, 45*(4), 429–455.

Pellerin, L. A. (2005). Applying Baumrind's parenting typology to high schools. *Social Science Research, 34*, 283–303.

Perry, B. L., & Morris, E. W. (2014). Suspending progress. *American Sociological Review, 79*, 1067–1087.

Perry, D. G., Perry, C., & Kennedy, E. (1992). Conflict and the development of antisocial behavior. In C. U. Shantz & W. W. Hartup (Eds.), *Conflict in child and adolescent development* (pp. 301–329). New York: Cambridge University Press.

Peterson, P. L., Hawkins, D. J., Abbott, R. D., & Catalano, R. F. (1994). Disentangling the effects of parental drinking, family management, and parental alcohol norms on current drinking by black and white adolescents. *Journal of Research on Adolescence, 4*, 203–227.

Petrosino, A., Turpin-Petrosino, C. T., & Buehler, J. (2004). "Scared straight" and other juvenile awareness programs for preventing juvenile delinquency. Oslo, Norway: The Campbell Collaboration. doi: 10.4073/csr.2010.1

Petrosino, A., Turpin-Petrosino, C. & Guckenburg, S. (2010). *Formal system processing of juveniles: Effects on delinquency*. Oslo, Norway: The Campbell Collaboration. doi: 10.4073/csr.2013.5

Pew Center on the States. (2008). *One in 100: Behind bars in American 2008*. Washington, DC: Pew Charitable Trusts.

Pew Research Center. (2013). Trust in government nears record low, but most federal agencies are viewed favorably. October 18. Washington, DC: Pew Research Center for the People & the Press. Retreived from http://www.people-press.org/2013/10/18/trust-in-government-nears-record-low-but-most-federal-agencies-are-viewed-favorably/.

Pew Research Center. (2014). Few people say police forces nationally do well in treating races equally: Most have at least "fair amount" of confidence in local police. Retrieved from http://www.people-press.org/files/2014/08/8-25-14-Police-and-Race-Release.pdf.

Pew Research Center. (2014b). Millennials in adulthood: Detached from institutions, networked with friends. March 7. Washington, DC: Pew Research Center. Retrieved from http://www.pewsocialtrends.org/2014/03/07/millennials-in-adulthood/.

Pharr, S. J., Putnam, R. D., & Dalton, R. J. (2000). Trouble in the advanced democracies? A quarter-century of declining confidence. *Journal of Democracy, 11*(2), 5–25.

Piaget, J. (1932). *The moral judgment of the child*. New York: Hartcourt, Brace & World.

Piko, B. F., & Balazs, M. A. (2012). Authoritative parenting style and adolescent smoking and drinking. *Addictive Behaviors, 37*, 353–356.

Piquero, A. R., Gomez-Smith, Z., & Langton, L. (2004). Discerning unfairness where others may not: Low self-control and unfair sanction perceptions, *Criminology, 42*, 699–733.

Piquero, A. R., Fagan, J., Mulvey, E. P., Steinberg, L., & Odgers, C. (2005). Developmental trajectories of legal socialization among serious adolescent offenders. *Journal of Criminal Law and Criminology, 96*(1), 267–298.

Poulson, B. (2003). A third voice: A review of empirical research on the psychological outcomes of restorative justice. *Utah Law Review, 2003*, 167–204.

Pratt, T. C., Cullen, F. T., Blevins, K. R., Daigle, L. E., & Madensen, T. D. (2006). The empirical status of deterrence theory: A meta-analysis. In F. T. Cullen, J. P. Wright, & K. R. Blevins (Eds.), *Taking stock: The status of criminological theory— Advances in criminological theory* (Vol. 15, pp. 367–395). New Brunswick, NJ: Transaction Publishers.

President's Task Force on 21st Century Policing. (2015). *Final report of the President's task force on 21st century policing*. Washington, DC: Office of Community Oriented Policing Services.

Public Policy Polling. (2013). Congress less popular than cockroaches, traffic jams. Raleigh, NC: Public Policy Polling. Retrieved from http://www.publicpolicypolling.com/pdf/2011/PPP_Release_Natl_010813_.pdf.

Raaijmakers, Q. A. W., Engels, R. C. M. E., & van hoof, A. (2005). Delinquency and moral reasoning in adolescence and young adulthood. *International Journal of Behavioral Development, 29*, 247–258.

Rahr, S., & Rice, S. K. (2015). From warriors to guardians: Recommitting American police culture to democratic ideals. Washington, DC: National Institute of Justice Executive Session on Policing and Public Safety.

Redding, R.E. (2010). Juvenile transfer laws. An effective deterrent to delinquency? Washington, DC: Department of Justice.

Regalado, M., Sareen, H., Inkelas, M., Wissow, L. S., & Halfon, N. (2004). Parents' discipline of young children: Results from the National Survey of Early Childhood Health. *Pediatrics, 113*(6), 1952–1958.

Reicher, S., & Emler, N. (1985). Delinquent behavior and attitudes toward formal authority. *British Journal of Social Psychology, 24*, 161–168.

Reiner, R. (2010). *The Politics of the Police* (4th ed.). Oxford: Oxford University Press.

Reisig, M. D., & Lloyd, C. (2009). Procedural justice, police legitimacy, and helping the police fight crime. *Police Quarterly, 12*(1), 42–62.

Reisig, M. D., Tankebe, J., & Mesko, G. (2013). Compliance with the law in Slovenia: The role of procedural justice and police legitimacy. *European Journal of Criminal Policy Research, 20*(2), 259–276.

Reiter, D., & Stam, A.C. (2002). *Democracies at war*. Princeton, NJ: Princeton University Press.

Renshon, S. A. (Ed.). (1977). *Handbook of political socialization*. New York: Free Press.

Resh, N., & Sabbagh, C. (2014a). Justice, belonging and trust among Israeli middle school students. *British Educational Research Journal, 40*(6), 1036–1056.

Resh, N., & Sabbagh, C. (2014b). Sense of justice in school and civic attitudes. *Social Psychology and Education, 17*(1), 51–72.

Riesman, D., Glazer, N., & Denney, R. (2001). *The lonely crowd*. New Haven, CT: Yale University Press.

Rigby, K., Mak, A. S., & Slee, P. T. (1989). Notes and short communications: Impulsiveness, orientations to institutional authority, and gender as factors in self-reported delinquency among Australian adolescents. *Personality and Individual Differences, 6*, 689–692.

Rigby, K., & Rump, E. E. (1981). Attitudes toward parents and institutional authorities during adolescence. *Journal of Psychology, 109*, 109–118.

Rigby, K., Schofield, P, & Slee, P. T. (1987). The similarity of attitudes towards personal and impersonal types of authority among adolescent schoolchildren. *Journal of Adolescence, 10*, 241–253.

Rios, V. M. (2011). *Punished: Policing the lives of Black and Latino boys*. New York: New York University Press.

Roberts, J. V., & Stalans, L. J. (2004). Restorative sentencing: Exploring the views of the public. *Social Justice Research, 17*, 315–334.

Robins, L. N., & Ratcliff, K. S. (1978). Risk factors in the continuation of childhood antisocial behavior into adulthood. *International Journal of Mental Health, 7*, 96–116.

Rodgers, D. T. (2011). *Age of fracture*. Cambridge, MA: Harvard University Press.

Rosen, H. (2014). The overprotected kid. *The Atlantic*. April. Retrieved from http://www.theatlantic.com/magazine/archive/2014/04/hey-parents-leave-those-kids-alone/358631.

Rothbaum, F., & Weisz, J. R. (1994). Parental caregiving and child externalizing behavior in nonclinical samples: A meta-analysis. *Psychological Bulletin, 116*(1), 55–74.

Ruderman, W. (2012a). Rude or polite, city's officers leave raw feelings in stops. *New York Times*, June 26. Retrieved from http://www.nytimes.com/2012/06/27/nyregion/new-york-police-leave-raw-feelings-in-stops.html.

Ruderman, W. (2012b). For women in street stops, deeper humiliation. *New York Times*, August 6. Retrieved from http://www.nytimes.com/2012/08/07/nyregion/for-women-in-street-stops-deeper-humiliation.html.

Rusinko, W. T., Johnson, K. W., & Hornung, C. A. (1978). The importance of police contact in the formulation of youths' attitudes toward police. *Journal of Criminal Justice, 6*(1), 53–67.

Saad, L. (2015). Gallup: Americans faith in honesty, ethics of police rebounds. Retrieved February 4, 2016 from http://www.gallup.com/poll/187874/americans-faith-honesty-ethics-police-rebounds.aspx.

Samet, D. D. (2004). *Willing obedience*. Redwood City, CA: Stanford University Press.

Sampson, R. J., & Bartusch, D. J. (1998). Legal cynicism and (subcultural?) tolerance of deviance: The neighborhood context of racial differences. *Law & Society Review, 32*(4), 777–804.

Sampson, R. J., & Laub, J. H. (1993). *Crime in the making: Pathways and turning points through life*. Cambridge, MA: Harvard University Press.

Sampson, R. J., Raudenbush, S. W., & Earls, F. (1997). Neighborhoods and violent crime: A multilevel study of collective efficacy. *Science, 277*(5328), 918–924.

Schmidt, M. F. H., & Tomasello, M. (2012). Young children enforce moral rules. *Psychological Science, 21*, 232–236.

Scott, E. S. (1992). Judgment and reasoning in adolescent decision making. *Villanova Law Review, 37*, 1607–1669.

Scott, E. S., & Grisso, T. (2005). Developmental incompetence, due process, and juvenile justice policy. *North Carolina Law Review, 83*, 793–846.

Scott, E. S. & Steinberg, L. (2008). Adolescent development and the regulation of youth crime. *The Future of Children, 18*(2), 18–33.

Scott, E. S., & Steinberg, L. (2010). *Rethinking juvenile justice*. Cambridge, MA: Harvard University Press.

Schulhofer, S. J., & Tyler, T. R., & Huq, A. Z. (2011). American policing at a crossroads: Unsustainable policies and the procedural justice alternative. *Journal of Criminal Law & Criminology, 101*(2), 335–374.

Sears, D. O. (1975). Political socialization. In F. I. Greenstein and N. W. Polsby (Eds.), *Handbook of political science* (Vol. 2, pp. 93–153). Reading, MA: Addison-Wesley.

Sears, D. O., & Brown, C. (2013). Childhood and adult political development. In L. Huddy, D. O. Sears, & J. S., Levy (Eds.), *The Oxford handbook of political psychology* (2nd ed.). Oxford: Oxford University Press.

Shackleton, R. (1961). *Montesquieu: A critical biography*. New York: Oxford University Press.

Shaw, A., & Olson, K. (2014). Fairness as partiality aversion: The development of procedural justice. *Journal of Experimental Child Psychology, 119*, 40–53.

Shaw, J. M., & Scott, W. A. (1991). Influence of parent discipline style on delinquent behaviour: the mediating role of control orientation. *Australian Journal of Psychology, 43*(2), 61–67.

Sherer, Y. C., & Nickerson, A. B., (2010). Anti-bullying practices in American schools: Perspectives of school psychologists. *Psychology in the Schools, 47*(3), 217–229.

Sherman, L. (1993). Defiance, deterrence, and irrelevance. *Journal of Research in Crime and Delinquency, 30*, 445–473.

Sherman, L. (1999). *Consent of the governed*. Presentation at Hebrew University, Jerusalem. January.

Sherman, L. & Rogan, D. P. (1995). The effects of gun seizures on gun violence: "Hot spots" patrol in Kansas City. *Justice Quarterly, 12*, 673–693.

Sherrod, L. R. (2008). Adolescents' perceptions of rights as reflected in their views of citizenship. *Journal of Social Issues, 64*(4), 771–790.

Shore, N. (2011). Millennials are playing with you. *Harvard Business Review*, December 12. Retrieved from https://hbr.org/2011/12/millennials-are-playing-with-y.

Silbey, S. S. (1991). *Child's play: The origins of hegemony, acquiescence, and obligation in adolescents' studies of law*. A Colloquium in Honor of Egon Bittner, Brandeis University, Waltham, MA. May.

Silbey, S. S. (2005). After legal consciousness. *Annual Review of Law and Social Science*, *1*, 323–368.

Silbey, S. S. (2010). Invocations of law on snowy streets. *Journal of Comparative Law*, *5*, 66–91.

Simons, R. L., Johnson, C., Conger, R. D., & Elder, G. (1998). A test of latent trait versus lifecourse perspectives on the stability of adolescent antisocial behavior. *Criminology, 36*(2), 217–244.

Simons, R. L., Simons, L. G., Burt, C. H., Brody, G. H., & Cutrona, C. (2005). Collective efficacy, authoritative parenting and delinquency. *Criminology, 43*(4), 989–1029.

Skiba, R. J. (2000). *Zero tolerance, zero evidence*. Bloomington, IN: Education Policy Center.

Sklansky, D. A. (2005). Police and democracy. *Michigan Law Review*, *103*(7), 1699–1830.

Sklansky, D. A. (2006). Not your father's police department: Making sense of the new demographics of law enforcement. *Journal of Criminal Law & Criminology*, *96*(3), 1209–1244.

Skogan, W., & Frydl, K. (2004). *Fairness and effectiveness in policing*. Washington, D.C.: National Research Council.

Slobogin, C., & Fondacaro, M. R. (2011). *Juveniles at risk: A plea for preventative justice*. Oxford: Oxford University Press.

Slocum, L. A., Tayler, T. J., Brick, B. T., & Esbensen, F. A. (2010). Neighborhood structural characteristics, individual-level attitudes, and youths' crime reporting intentions. *Criminology, 48*(4), 1063–1100.

Slocum, L. A., Wiley, S. A., & Esbensen, F. (2013). The unintended consequences of being stopped or arrested. *Criminology, 51*, 927–966.

Smetana, J. G. (1988). Adolescents' and parents conceptions of parental authority. *Child Development, 59*, 321–335.

Smetana, J. G. (1995a). Parenting styles and conceptions of parental authority during adolescence. *Child Development, 66*, 299–316.

Smetana, J. G. (1995b). Morality in context: Abstractions, ambiguities and applications. In V. Ross (Ed.), *Annals of child development* (Vo. 10, p. 83–130). London: Jessica Kingsley Publishers.

Smetana, J. G. (2002). Culture, autonomy, and personal jurisdiction in adolescent-parent relationships. *Advances in Child Development, 29*, 51–87.

Smetana, J. G., & Asquith, P. (1994). Adolescents' and parents' conceptions of parental authority and personal autonomy. *Child Development, 65*, 1147–1162.

Smetana, J. G., & Bitz, B. (1996). Adolescents' conceptions of teachers' authority and their relations to rule violations in school. *Child Development, 67*(3), 1153–1172.

Smetana, J. G., Campione-Barr, N., & Yell, N. (2003). Children's moral and affective judgments regarding provocation and retaliation. *Merrill-Palmer Quarterly, 49*, 209–236.

Smetana, J. G., & Daddis, C. (2002). Domain-specific antecedents of parental psychological control and monitoring. *Child Development, 73*, 563–580.

Smith, T. W., & Son, J. (2013). *General social survey 2012 final report: Trends in public attitudes about confidence in institutions*. Chicago: NORC at the University of Chicago.

Snyder, H. N. (2012). *Arrest in the United States, 1990–2010*. Washington, DC: US Department of Justice, Bureau of Justice Statistics.

Spear, L. P. (2000). The adolescent brain and age-related behavioral manifestations. *Neuroscience and Biobehavioral Reviews, 24*, 417–463.

Spencer, J. P., Blumberg, M. S., McMurray, B., Robinson, S. R., Samuelson, L. K., & Tomblin, J. B. (2009). Short arms and talking eggs: Why we should no longer abide the nativist-empiricist debate. *Child Development Perspectives, 3*, 79–87.

Srole, L. (1956). Social integration and certain corollaries: An explanatory study. *American Sociological Review, 21*, 709–716.

Stams, G. J., Brugman, D., Dekovic, M., van Rosmalen, L., van der Lann, P., & Gibbs, J. C. (2006). The moral judgment of juvenile delinquents. *Journal of Abnormal and Child Psychology, 34*, 697–713.

Starks, B., & Robinson, R. V. (2005). Who values the obedient child now? The religious factor in adult values for children, 1986–2002. *Social Forces, 84*(1), 343–359.

Steffensmeier, D., & Ulmer, J. (2002). Age and the patterning of crime. In S. Kadish (Ed.), *Encyclopedia of crime and justice* (pp. 22–28). New York: Macmillan.

Steinberg, L. (2008). A social neuroscience perspective on adolescent risk-taking. *Developmental Review, 28*, 78–106.

Steinberg, L. (2009). Adolescent development and juvenile justice. *Annual Review of Clinical Psychology, 5*, 459–485.

Steinberg, L. (2014). *Age of opportunity: Lessons from the new science of adolescence*. Boston: Houghton Mifflin Harcourt

Steinberg, J., & Cauffman, E. (1996). Maturity of judgment in adolescence. *Law and Human Behavior, 20*, 249–272.

Stenner, K. (2005). *The authoritarian dynamic*. Cambridge: Cambridge University Press

Stickle, W. P., Connell, N. M., Wilson, D. M., & Gottfredson, D. (2008). An experimental evaluation of teen courts. *Journal of Experimental Criminology,4*(2), 137–163.

Stoudt, B. G., Fine, M., & Fox, M. (2011–2012). Growing up policed in the age of aggressive policing policies. *New York Law School Law Review, 56*, 1331–1372.

Straus, M. A. (1991). Discipline and deviance: Physical punishment of children and violence and other crime in adulthood. *Social Problems, 38*(2), 133–154.

Straus, M. A., & Donnelly, D. A. (2001). *Beating the devil out of them: Corporal punishment in American families and its effects on children*. New Brunswick, NJ: Transaction Publishers.

Stuart, J., Fondacaro, M., Miller, S. A., Brown, V., & Brank, E. M. (2008). Procedural justice in family conflict resolution and deviant peer group involvement among adolescents. *Journal of Youth and Adolescence, 37*, 674–684.

Stuart-Cassel, V., Bell, A., & Springer, J. F. (2011). *Analysis of state bullying laws and policies*. Washington, DC: US Department of Education, Office of Planning, Evaluation and Policy Development.

Stuss, D. T., & Knight, R. T. (2002). *Principles of frontal lobe function*. New York: Oxford University Press.

Sullivan, C. J. (2008). Childhood emotional and behavioral problems and predictions of delinquency. *Applied Psychology in Criminal Justice, 4*(1), 45–80.

Sullivan, J. L., & Transue, J. E. (1999). The psychological underpinnings of democracy. *Annual Review of Psychology, 50*, 625–650.

Sunshine, J., & Tyler, T. R. (2003a). The role of procedural justice and legitimacy in shaping public support for policing. *Law and Society Review, 37*, 513–548.

Sunshine, J., & Tyler, T. R. (2003b). Moral solidarity, identification with the community, and the importance of procedural justice: The police as prototypical representatives of a group's moral values. *Social Psychology Quarterly, 66*(2), 153–165.

Tangney, J. P., & Dearing, R. L. (2002). *Shame and guilt.* New York: Guilford.

Tapp, J. L. (1966). Persuasion to virtue. In Krislov, S., Boyum, K. O., Clark, H. N., Shaefer, R. C., & White, S. O (Eds.), *Compliance with the law.* Thousand Oaks, CA: Sage.

Tapp, J. L. (1976). Psychology and the law: An overture. *Annual Review of Psychology, 27,* 359–404.

Tapp, J. L. (1987). The jury as a socialization experience: A socio-cognitive view. In R.W. Rieber (Ed.), *Advances in forensic psychology and psychiatry* (Vol. 2, pp. 1–32). Norwood, NJ: Ablex Publishing Corporation.

Tapp, J. L. (1991). The geography of legal socialization: Scientific and social markers. *Droit et Sociètè, 19,* 331–358

Tapp, J. L, & Kohlberg, L. (1971). Developing sense of law and legal justice. *Journal of Social Issues, 27*(2), 65–91.

Tapp, J. L., & Levine, F. J. (1970). Persuasion to virtue: A preliminary statement. *Law & Society Review, 4,* 565–582.

Tapp, J. L., & Levine, F. J. (1972). Compliance from kindergarten to college: A speculative research note. *Journal of Youth and Adolescence, 1,* 233–249.

Tapp, J. L., & Levine, F. J. (1974). Legal socialization: Strategies for an ethical legality. *Stanford Law Review, 27,* 1–72.

Tapp, J. L., & Levine, F. J. (1977). *Law, justice, and the individual in society.* New York: Holt.

Tapp, J. L., & Melton, G. B. (1983). Preparing children for decision making: Implications of legal socialization research. In. G. B. Melton, G. P. Koocher, & M. J. Saks (Eds.), *Children's competence to consent* (pp. 215–233). New York: Plenum.

Tarry, H., & Emler, N. (2007). Attitudes, values and moral reasoning as predictors of delinquency. *British Journal of Developmental Psychology, 25,* 169–183.

Thomas, R. M. (2005). *Comparing theories of child development* (6th ed.). Belmont, CA: Thomason Wadsworth.

Thompson, R. A. (2008). Early attachment and later development: Familiar questions, new answers. In J. Cassidy & P. R. Shaver (Eds.), *Handbook of attachment* (pp. 348–365). New York: Guilford Press.

Thibaut, J., & Walker, L. (1975). *Procedural justice: A psychological analysis.* Mahwah, NJ: Lawrence Erlbaum Associates.

Thoreau, H. D. (1993). *Civil disobedience and other essays.* Mineola, NY: Dover Publications.

Thorkildsen, T. A., & White-McNulty, L. (2002). Developing conceptions of fair context procedures and the understanding of luck and skill. *Journal of Educational Psychology, 94,* 316–326.

Tillman, J. (2010). Illinois is broke. September. Retrieved from https://www.illinoispolicy.org/illinois-is-broke.

Tisak, M. S. (1986). Children's conceptions of parental authority. *Child Development, 57,* 166–176.

Tisak, M. S., Crane-Ross, D., Tisak, J., & Maynard, A. M. (2000). Mothers' and teachers' home and school rules. *Merrill-Palmer Quarterly, 46,* 168–187.

Tisak, M. S., Tisak, J., & Goldstein, S. E. (2006). Aggression, delinquency, and morality: A social-cognitive perspective. In M. Killen & J. G. Smetana (Eds.), *Handbook of moral development* (pp. 611–629). Mahwah, NJ: Lawrence Erlbaum Associates.

Torney, J. V. (1971). Socialization of attitudes toward the legal system. *Journal of Social Issues, 27*(2), 137–154.

Torney-Purta, J. (2002). The school's role in developing civic engagement: A study of adolescents in twenty-eight countries. *Applied Developmental Science, 6*(4), 203–212.

Torney-Purta, J., & Wilkenfeld, B. (2008). How adolescents in 27 countries understand, support and practice human rights. *Journal of Social Issues, 64,* 857–880.

Travis, J., Western, B., & Redburn, S. (Eds.) (2014). *The growth of incarceration in the United States.* Washington, DC: National Academies Press.

Trinkner, R. (2012). *Testing the procedural justice model of legal socialization: Expanding beyond the legal world.* Unpublished dissertation, Department of Psychology, University of New Hampshire.

Trinkner, R. (2015). *The ubiquity of legal socialization: Parental influences on legal attitudes and values in adulthood.* Paper presented at the annual meetings of the American Psychology-Law Society in San Diego, CA.

Trinkner, R., & Cohn, E. S. (2014). Putting the "social" back in legal socialization: Procedural justice, legitimacy, and cynicism in legal and nonlegal authorities. *Law and Human Behavior, 38*(6), 602–617.

Trinkner, R., Cohn, E.S., Rebellon, C. J., & Van Gundy, K. (2012). Don't trust anyone over 30: Parental legitimacy as a mediator between parenting style and changes in delinquent behavior over time. *Journal of Adolescence, 35,* 119–132.

Trinkner, R., & Goff, P. A. (2016. The color of safety: The psychology of race & policing. In B. Bradford, B. Jauregui, I. Loader, & J. Steinberg (Eds.), *The SAGE handbook of global policing* (pp. 61–81). London: Sage.

Trinkner, R., Jackson, J. P., & Tyler, T. R. (2016). Expanding 'appropriate' police behavior beyond procedural justice: Bounded authority & the legitimation of the law. Unpublished manuscript. Available online at https://papers.ssrn.com/sol3/papers.cfm?abstract_id=2846659.

Trinkner, R., & Tyler, T. R. (2016). Legal socialization: Coercion vs. consent in an era of mistrust. *Annual Review of Law and Social Science, 12,* 417–439.

Turiel, E. (1987). Potential relations between the development of social reasoning and childhood aggression. In D. Crowell, I. Evans, & C. R. O'Connell (Eds.), *Childhood aggression and violence* (pp. 95–114). New York: Plenum.

Turiel, E. (2002). *The culture of morality.* New York: Cambridge University Press.

Twenge, J. M. (2006). *Generation me.* New York: Free Press.

Tyler, T. R. (1988). What is procedural justice?: Criteria used by citizens to assess the fairness of legal procedures. *Law and Society Review, 22,* 103–135.

Tyler, T. R. (1997). The psychology of legitimacy: A relational perspective on voluntary deference to authorities. *Personality and Social Psychology Review, 1,* 323–345.

Tyler, T. R. (2000). Social justice: Outcome and procedure. *International Journal of Psychology, 35,* 117–125.

Tyler, T. R. (2004). Enhancing police legitimacy. *Annals of the American Academy of Political and Social Science, 593*(1), 84–99.

Tyler, T. R. (2006a). *Why people obey the law.* Princeton, NJ: Princeton University Press.

Tyler, T. R. (2006b). Legitimacy and legitimation. *Annual Review of Psychology, 57,* 375–400.

Tyler, T. R. (2009). Legitimacy and criminal justice: The benefits of self-regulation. *Ohio State Journal of Criminal Law, 7,* 307–359.

Tyler, T. R. (2011). *Why people cooperate.* Princeton, NJ: Princeton University Press.

Tyler, T. R., & Blader, S.L. (2000). *Cooperation in groups: Procedural justice, social identity, and behavioral engagement.* Philadelphia: Psychology Press.

Tyler, T. R., & Blader, S. L. (2003). The group engagement model: Procedural justice, social identity, and cooperative behavior. *Personality and Social Psychology Review*, 7, 349–361.

Tyler, T. R., & Boeckmann, R. J. (1997). Three strikes and you are out, but why? The psychology of public support for punishing rule breakers. *Law & Society Review*, 31(2), 237–265.

Tyler, T. R., Casper, J. D., & Fisher, B. (1989). Maintaining allegiance toward political authorities: The role of prior attitudes and the use of fair procedures. *American Journal of Political Science*, 33, 629–652.

Tyler, T. R., & Fagan, J. (2008). Why do people cooperate with the police? *Ohio State Journal of Criminal Law*, 6, 231–275.

Tyler, T. R., Fagan, J., & Geller, A. (2014). Street stops and police legitimacy: Teachable moments in young urban men's legal socialization. *Journal of Empirical Legal Studies*, 11, 751–785.

Tyler, T. R., Goff, P. A., & MacCoun, R. J. (2015). The impact of psychological science on policing in the United States: Procedural justice, legitimacy, and effective law enforcement. *Psychological Science in the Public Interest*, 16(3), 75–109.

Tyler, T. R., & Huo, Y. J. (2002). *Trust in the law*. New York: Russell Sage Foundation.

Tyler, T. R., & Jackson, J. (2013). Future challenges in the study of legitimacy and criminal justice. In J. Tankebe and A. Liebling (Eds.), *Legitimacy and criminal justice: An international exploration*. Oxford: Oxford University Press.

Tyler, T. R., & Jackson, J. (2014). Popular legitimacy and the exercise of legal authority: Motivating compliance, cooperation and engagement. *Psychology, Public Policy and Law*, 20, 78–95.

Tyler, T. R., Jackson, J., & Mentovich, T. (2014). *The consequence of being an object of suspicion: Potential pitfalls of proactive policing*. Paper presented at the annual meetings of the Society for Empirical Studies, Berkeley, CA.

Tyler, T. R., & Lind, E. A. (1992). A relational model of authority in groups. *Advances in Experimental Social Psychology*, 25, 115–191.

Tyler, T. R., Lind, E. A., & Huo, Y. J. (2000). Cultural values and authority relations. *Psychology, Public Policy, and Law*, 6(4), 1138–1163.

Tyler, T. R., & Rankin, L. (2012). The mystique of instrumentalism. In J. Hanson (Vol. Ed.) & J. Jost (Series Ed.), *Ideology, psychology, and law* (pp. 537–573). New York: Oxford University Press.

Tyler, T. R., Schulhofer, S. J., & Huq, A. Z. (2010). Legitimacy and deterrence effects in counter-terrorism policing. *Law and Society Review*, 44(2), 365–402.

Tyler, T. R., & Sevier, J. (2013/2014). How do the courts create popular legitimacy? The role of establishing the truth, punishing justly, and/or acting through just procedures. *Albany Law Review*, 77(3), 1095–1137.

Tyler, T. R., Sherman, L. W., Strang, H., Barnes, G. C., & Woods, D. J. (2007). Reintegrative shaming, procedural justice, and recidivism: The engagement of offenders' psychological mechanisms in the Canberra RISE drinking-and-driving experiment. *Law and Society Review*, 41(3), 553–586.

Ufer, U. (2012). Criminalizing the classroom: The rise of aggressive policing and zero tolerance discipline in New York City public schools. *New York Law School Law Review*, 56, 1373–1411.

Unnever, J. D., Colvin, M., & Cullen, F. T. (2004). Crime and coercion: A test of core theoretical propositions. *Journal of Research in Crime and Delinquency*, 41(3), 244–268.

van Prooigen, J., Gallucci, M. & Toeset, G. (2008). Procedural justice in punishment systems: Inconsistent punishment procedures have detrimental effects on cooperation. *British Journal of Social Psychology*, 47, 311–324.

Vandeleur, C. L., Perrez, M., & Schoebi, D. (2007). Associations between measures of emotion and familial dynamics in normative families with adolescents. *Swiss Journal of Psychology*, 66, 5–16.

Vignati, J. (2011). "Beyond Scared Straight" is beyond common sense. January. Retrieved November 6 from http://jjie.org/joe-vignatibeyond-scared-straight-beyond-common-sense.

Viki, G. T., Culmer, M. J., Eller, A., & Abrams, D. (2006). Race and willingness to cooperate with the police. *British Journal of Social Psychology*, 45, 285–302.

Wang, J., Iannotti, R.J., & Nansel, T.R. (2009). School bullying among adolescents in the United States: Physical, verbal, relational, and cyber. *Journal of Adolescence Health*, 45, 368–75.

Ward, J. T., Nobles, M. R., Lanza-Kaduce, L., Levett, L. M., & Tillyer, R. (2011). Caught in their own speed trap: The intersection of speed enforcement policy, police legitimacy, and decision acceptance. *Police Quarterly*, 14(3), 251–276.

Wasserman, G. A., Keenan, K., Tremblay, R. E., Cole, J. D., Herrenkohl, T. I., Loeber, R., & Petechuk, D. (2003). *Risk and protective factors of child delinquency*. Washington, DC: Office of Juvenile Justice and Delinquency Prevention.

Way, S. M. (2011). School discipline and disruptive classroom behavior. *Sociological Quarterly*, 52, 346–375.

Weber, M. (1968). *Economy and society*. (G. Roth & C. Wittich, Eds.). Berkeley: University of California Press.

Weisz, V., Wingrove, T., & Faith-Slaker, A. (2007/2008). Children and procedural justice. *Court Review*, 44, 36–43.

Welsh, W. N. (2001). Effects of student and school factors on five measures of school disorder. *Justice Quarterly*, 18, 911–947.

Welsh, W. N. (2003). Individual and institutional predictors of school disorder. *Youth Violence and Juvenile Justice*, 1, 346–368.

West, D. J., & Farrington, D. P. (1973). *Who becomes delinquent?* London: Heinemann.

Westholm, A., Lindquist, A., & Niemi, R. G. 1990. Education and the making of the informed citizen. In O. Ichilov (Ed.), *Political socialization, citizenship education, and democracy* (pp. 177–204). New York: Teachers College Press.

White, S. O. (2001). Reasoning and justice. In S. O. White (Ed.), *Handbook of Youth and Justice* (pp. 307–327). New York: Plenum Publishers.

Whitman, J. Q. (2003). *Harsh justice: Criminal punishment and the widening divide between America and Europe*. New York: Oxford University Press.

Wilson, D. (2004). The interface of school climate and school connectedness and relationships with aggression and victimization. *Journal of School Health*, 74, 293–299.

Wilson, J. Q., & Kelling, G. L. (1982). Broken windows. *The Atlantic*. March. Retrieved from http://www.theatlantic.com/magazine/archive/1982/03/broken-windows/304465/.

Wolfe, S. E., Chrusciel, M. M., Rojek, J., Hansen, J. A., & Kaminski, R. J. (2015). Procedural justice, legitimacy and school principals' evaluations of school resource officers. Available online at *Criminal Justice Policy Review*. doi: 10.1177/0887403415573565

Woolard, J. L., Fried, C. S., & Reppucci, N. D. (2001). Toward an expanded definition of adolescent competence in legal situations. In R. Roesch, R. R. Corrado, & R. Dempster (Eds.), *Psychology in the courts* (pp. 21–40). New York: Routledge.

Wu, S.C., Pink, W., Crain, R., & Moles, O. (1982). Student suspension: A critical reappraisal. *Urban Review, 14,* 245–303.

Yariv, E. (2009). Students' attitudes on the boundaries of teachers' authority. *School Psychology International, 30*(1), 92–111.

Yau, J., & Smetana, J.G. (2003). Conceptions of moral, social-conventional, and personal events among Chinese preschoolers in Hong Kong. *Child Development, 74*(3), 647–658.

Younts, C. W. (2008). Status, endorsement and the legitimacy of deviance. *Social Forces, 87*(1), 561–590.

INDEX

Page references for tables are indicated by *t*.

CPSIA information can be obtained
at www.ICGtesting.com
Printed in the USA
JSHW020237240220
4358JS00004B/21

9 780197 520697